SYMBOLIC COMPUTATION

Computer Graphics – Systems and Applications

Springer-Series
SYMBOLIC COMPUTATION
Computer Graphics – Systems and Applications

J. L. Encarnação, R. Schuster, E. Vöge (eds.):
Product Data Interfaces in CAD/CAM Applications. Design, Implementation and Experiences. IX, 270 pages, 147 figs., 1986

U. Rembold, R. Dillmann (eds.):
Computer-Aided Design and Manufacturing. Methods and Tools. Second, revised and enlarged edition. XIV, 458 pages, 304 figs., 1986

G. Enderle, K. Kansy, G. Pfaff:
Computer Graphics Programming. GKS – The Graphics Standard. Second, revised and enlarged edition. XXIII, 651 pages, 100 figs., 1987

Y. Shirai:
Three-Dimensional Computer Vision. XII, 297 pages, 313 figs., 1987

D. B. Arnold, P. R. Bono:
CGM and CGI. Metafile and Interface Standards for Computer Graphics. XXIII, 279 pages, 103 figs., 1988

J. L. Encarnação, P. C. Lockemann (eds.):
Engineering Databases. XII, 229 pages, 152 figs., 1990

J. L. Encarnação, R. Lindner, E. G. Schlechtendahl:
Computer Aided Design. Fundamentals and System Architectures. Second, revised and extended edition, 240 pages, 240 figs., 1990

P. Wisskirchen:
Object-Oriented Graphics. From GKS and PHIGS to Object-Oriented Systems. XIII, 236 pages, 83 figs., 1990

Peter Wisskirchen

Object-Oriented Graphics

From GKS and PHIGS to Object-Oriented Systems

With 83 Figures

Springer-Verlag Berlin Heidelberg New York
London Paris Tokyo Hong Kong Barcelona

Dr. Peter Wisskirchen

Institute for Applied Information Technology
National Research Center for Computer Science (GMD)
Schloss Birlinghoven, D-5205 Sankt Augustin 1, FRG

ISBN-13:978-3-642-84249-8 e-ISBN-13:978-3-642-84247-4
DOI: 10.1007/978-3-642-84247-4

Softcover reprint of the hardcover 1st edition 1990

2145/3140-543210 – Printed on acid-free paper

Foreword

At present, object-oriented programming is emerging from the research laboratories and invading into the field of industrial applications. More and more products have been implemented with the aid of object-oriented programming techniques and tools, usually as extensions of traditional languages in hybrid development systems. Some of the better known examples are OSF-Motif, News, Objective-C on the NeXT computer, the C extension C++, and CLOS an object-oriented extension of LISP. All of these developments incorporate interactive graphics.

Effective object-oriented systems in combination with a graphics kernel—does it mean that the field of computer graphics has now become merely an aspect of the object-oriented world? We do not think so. In spite of interesting individual developments, there are still no sound object-oriented graphics *systems* available. If it is desired to develop a complex graphics application embedded in a window-oriented system then it is still necessary to work with elementary tools. What is to be displayed and interactively modified inside a window must be specified with a set of graphics primitives at a low level, or has to be written with a standardized graphics kernel system such as GKS or PHIGS, i.e., by kernels specified and implemented in a non-object-oriented style.

With the terms GKS and PHIGS we enter the world of international graphics standards. GKS and PHIGS constitute systems, not mere collections of graphics primitives. The definitions of these systems incorporate the results of a long tradition in the field of computer graphics and put them into a systematic order.

After involvement in the design of GKS a long time ago and after a study and review of PHIGS followed by an analysis of the possibilities of graphics in object-oriented systems, the author came to a surprising and disturbing conclusion: there are at present two completely separate communities working in the field of computer graphics, they have no knowledge of each other, and they are working on similar problems in two terrains divided by a broad river.

Without question, the motivation for writing a book about object-oriented graphics was strengthened by this shock or, to phrase it positively, by the insight that communication between the two different groups of researchers should be encouraged. To encourage communication, one has to assure that both sides have something positive to offer each other. To build a bridge and to establish linkages combining traditional approaches such as GKS and PHIGS with object-oriented systems is the goal of our book. Not as a highway over a wide bridge, but as a path over a footbridge that connects the two shores and may help to explore the terrain on the other side, the system GEO++ is introduced, which attempts to combine object-oriented philosophy and tools with traditional functionality.

The book is aimed at researchers and practitioners bound by tradition, especially those who take part in the specification of larger graphics programming systems, for instance in connection with standardization. It is meant to help them in incorporating object-oriented concepts in their work. Perhaps it will be recognized that the object-oriented paradigm of thinking leads to the correct programming model for interface design and programming in computer graphics—that object-orientation leads to the "right" perspective on the functionality stemming from traditional graphics.

Nevertheless, the book is also aimed at researchers and developers of object-oriented graphics systems. What can it offer to this community? Perhaps it can motivate contemplation about the functionality of graphics kernel systems as grown from tradition and specified by standardization. Maybe it can also motivate work on new graphics standards.

In standardization, the idea of a "prefabricated" kernel plays a dominant role: a kernel whose functionality is standardized, whose internal implementation is hidden, and which is then put in the hands of the applications programmer. Next to the basic advantages of this idea—systematic incorporation of functionality, portability of software, device independence, and the chance to optimize the performance by special hardware or software developments—the concept of a predefined kernel has a substantial weak point. It is manifested in the low degree of flexibility often remarked upon by developers and programmers. But flexibility is exactly the point where the potential of object-oriented systems can help most: inheritance is an elegant concept for modification and extension of predefined functionality. So there are strong reasons for the next graphics standard to be defined as an object-oriented system.

In order to extend the footbridge to a broad highway, we would have to add high performance graphics with rendering and lighting models and object-oriented computer animation. I hope that, even with these aspects left out, the potential of the object-oriented perspective is demonstrated, especially by the comparisons and programming examples. Understanding the programming examples requires only basic knowledge of computer graphics, ideally of the functionality of a graphics kernel system such as GKS. Knowledge of an object-oriented programming language would help but is not necessary, as the introduction to Smalltalk-80 should suffice for understanding the examples and basic principles of object orientation.

The managing editor of this series, J. Encarnação, led me to the field of standardization of graphics systems many years ago and made participation in the appropriate committees possible. I owe him thanks in several regards. The journey to this book began when Paul ten Hagen invited me to give a tutorial on object-oriented graphics at the Eurographics conference in 1987. A second tutorial was held together with my colleague Erich Rome, whom I thank for his help, at SIGGRAPH '88 in Atlanta. In 1989, the Eurographics conference in Hamburg saw a third tutorial, held together with Edwin Blake of CWI in Amsterdam. Edwin Blake has made many suggestions for my work, and several passages in the book surely stem from his pen in their original form.

Special thanks are due to all my colleagues at our Institute for Applied Information Technology of the German National Research Center for Computer Science (GMD). Dieter Bolz and Rüdiger Kolb answered many questions, and they designed and implemented many examples—already for the tutorials. I also thank Klaus Kansy—detailed discussions were always possible with him, especially as he always had an answer to specific questions on existing standards and was constantly up to date on the pros and cons, being hotly discussed in the various committees. Klaus also made many constructive suggestions for the overall concept of the book. Special thanks go also to Mike Spenke and his team for their support in formulating the section on object-oriented application frameworks.

Many people had a hand in the preparation of the final version of this book. Edgar Sommer translated the manuscript, and I appreciate it that he managed the translation in a very short time—despite being freshly in love. Günther Schrack of the University of British Columbia, Vancouver, who is currently working as guest researcher in our institute, deserves recognition for his valuable editorial suggestions concerning the complexities and delicate aspects of English style. I thank Springer-Verlag executive editor Hans Wössner for his support in realizing this book project and copy editor J. Andrew Ross for making the final touches to the language, and thank Springer-Verlag for publishing the book so speedily.

St. Augustin, May 1990 *Peter Wisskirchen*

Table of Contents

1 Introduction

In recent years the term *object-oriented* has become one of the most heavily used slogans in computer science. In fact, it is used in two different contexts: in describing user interfaces and in connection with object-oriented programming languages and environments.

By an *object-oriented user interfaces* we mean interfaces, which allow, as the Apple Macintosh does, the direct manipulation of objects using icons and a mouse at the user interface. The concept *object* is meant in a intuitive sense here and refers to the representation of components of the entire on-screen information. The user views these components as a unit; they may be manipulated as such by user actions. They could, for instance, be mouse-clicked, moved, erased or have their representation changed. Examples of such objects are graphically visualized file folders, which may be opened by mouse clicks, *pop-up menus* which may be positioned and activated as desired, and *windows* which may be opened, enlarged, reduced, shifted, or closed. The design of object-oriented interfaces does not require object-oriented programming languages.

If we consider the object-oriented user interfaces, mentioned above, from the perspective of interactive computer graphics, we find nothing essentially new. Interactive graphics as a field of research has always been concerned with the design of object-oriented interfaces. What is new is the broad breakthrough of that type of interface that has always been central to concerns in computer graphics. Interactive object-oriented interfaces are no longer confined to those applications where they are essential, for instance Computer Aided Design (CAD) or cartography. They have replaced command-oriented interfaces almost everywhere as the medium of choice, as the success of more recent systems shows.

By *object-oriented programming* we understand an object-oriented programming language or, in more general terms, the use of an object-oriented programming environment in order to program. Object-oriented programming languages are general purpose programming languages, and so are suited to all kinds of tasks. Nevertheless, we believe the object-oriented paradigm offers new capabilities specifically for interactive computer graphics. To say more, the philosophy which underlies object-oriented programming is the major guideline for the design of programming tools for interactive computer graphics.

1.1 Object-Oriented Languages and Tools

"Object-orientation", as mentioned before, has sometimes been used rather loosely in a more intuitive sense. This is not what is meant by the term here.

Following Cardelli & Wegner (1985), Rentsch (1982), and Stefik & Bobrow (1985) object-orientation is some combination of:

- *Data abstraction* (named interfaces and hidden local state) plus *object types* (or classes) plus *type inheritance* (attributes inherited from superclasses).
- Processing is achieved by objects sending and replying to *messages*.

Languages need not conform to all these characteristics to be called "object-oriented". Object-oriented languages descend from Simula (Dahl & Hoare, 1973) and are exemplified by Smalltalk-80 (Goldberg & Robson, 1983). In Hewitt's actor formalism (Agha, 1986, Agha & Hewitt, 1987) greater emphasis is placed on concurrency and message passing. The NeWS windowing system (NeWS, 1987) has shown how naturally PostScript supports object-oriented programming for user interfaces (Adobe Systems, 1985, Densmore & Rosenthal, 1987). Meyer discusses general features of object-oriented programming as well as the language Eiffel (Meyer, 1988).

Tools that support object-oriented programming are available "almost everywhere". The spectrum reaches from *hybrid* approaches, where object-oriented concepts have been appended to existing programming languages, to complete object-oriented languages embedded in comfortable programming environments:

- In the field of Artificial Intelligence, object-oriented enhancements of the language Lisp have been available for some time, notably on Lisp machines. Object-oriented language formalisms are combined with other programming paradigms (rule or logic-based formalisms) here, and embedded in shells for the development of knowledge-based systems. Many years of experience with object-oriented extensions of Lisp, e.g., the Flavor system or LOOPS, have sparked standardization activities whose goal is the definition of a standardized object-oriented Common Lisp (CLOS) (Keene, 1989; Bobrow et al., 1988).
- The Smalltalk-80 language, together with an elegant programming environment, is available on almost all computers and operating systems. It is widely recognized as the most stringent implementation of the object-oriented paradigm, simply because it is an absolutely object-oriented language. We have chosen Smalltalk-80 with Xerox Park's program development environment as the reference system and basis for the description of the examples for a variety of reasons. As mentioned, Smalltalk-80 is absolutely object-oriented. It is well known and excellently documented in the famous Xerox Park books (Goldberg & Robson 1983, Goldberg 1984) and it is widely available. Primarily performance problems with the Smalltalk-80 system have hitherto barred it from being accepted widely in the commercial software development sector.
- Object Pascal and recent versions of Turbo Pascal are object-oriented extensions of the Pascal language. Object Pascal is available for the Apple Macintosh. It is used mainly in conjunction with MacApp, an object-oriented Application Framework (Schmucker, 1986).

- Objective C (Cox, 1984 and Cox, 1986) and C++ (Stroustrup, 1986) are object-oriented extensions of C. They were motivated foremost by the goal to combine the elegance of object-oriented programming with the speed of C.

As above list already shows, a diversity of realizations for the object-oriented paradigm exists combining a variety of concepts (Stefik & Bobrow, 1985). Our book is focussed on graphics programming, and it is not a survey of object-oriented systems. Such a survey would discuss existing approaches to object-oriented programming stressing their differences. We follow an almost diametrically opposed path. We will be hiding some of the differences and concentrating instead on the common denominator and its relevance and utility to computer graphics. Computer graphics will be in the foreground throughout this book, and most of it—even when expressed in Smalltalk-80 syntax—can be transferred easily to other object-oriented languages.

1.1.1 Support of Graphics

Many of the object-oriented systems available today offer tools for graphics programming. In this book, we will discuss the Smalltalk-80 graphics kernel in some detail.

Generally, in the conception of an object-oriented graphics system, we can draw interesting ideas from the tools for graphics programming made available in existing object-oriented systems. We will touch on the elements which seem most important to us. The tools we will come across in this context are, however, not as comprehensive and systematized as the *traditional* graphics systems.

Often we will be citing *traditional graphics systems* by which we mean procedurally defined interactive graphics systems, so-called graphics kernel systems with a long tradition. This is manifested in the standardizations of GKS and PHIGS (ISO 1985, ISO 1989a).

In our opinion, the graphics tools in existing object-oriented systems, e.g., on the Lisp machine, do not intend to compete with full scale graphics systems such as PHIGS. They can be more readily compared to the tools made available on modern workstations. These are essentially libraries of predefined graphics objects intended to support the user/system dialogue. Among them are window systems, graphics menus, dialogue boxes, etc.

Activities and results in the research sector, on the other hand, seem to us to be more interesting than what is currently being offered in the form of products. Here we would like to mention specifically the modeling of part hierarchies in object-oriented systems and the work on graphics constraints (Borning, 1979; Blake & Cook, 1987; Borning et al., 1987; Freeman-Benson et al., 1990; Leler, 1988; Pineda, 1988). The earliest work in this context is Ivan Sutherland's Sketchpad (Sutherland, 1963).

The idea of *object-oriented application frameworks* is particularly relevant to developments in the design of user interfaces. This idea, first currently available realizations of which are the MVC-model in Smalltalk-80 (Krasner & Pope 1988) and MacApp (Schmucker, 1986), harbors much potential for further work (Coutaz, 1987).

Object-oriented *user interface management systems*, esp. *interface builders*, take us yet another step ahead. Their goal is to allow the end user himself to exert a maximum of influence on the design of the interface by providing a graphics user interface (Myers, 1989; Myers, 1987; Foley et al. 1990; Sibert et al., 1986). As an object-oriented approach to support graphical interfaces we mention the work of Barth (Barth, 1989). Object-oriented approaches have also been applied in the field of computer animation, with great promise of success (Badler, 1987; Breen et al., 1987; Blake, 1989; Duisberg, 1987; Fiume et al., 1987; Kahn, 1986; Magnenat-Thalmann & Thalmann, 1985; Reynolds, 1982; Zeltzer, 1985; Blake & Wisskirchen, 1989).

1.1.1.1 Perspectives for Standardization

In the context of the standardization of graphics systems, little or no attention has been given to the possibilities of the object-oriented paradigm and object-oriented programming. Thus, an important sector of graphics data processing has been left virtually untouched by interesting developments in the field of object-oriented programming. We hope the examples discussed and suggestions made in this book stimulate further activities in the field of standardization.

1.1.1.2 Computer Graphics is "Object-Oriented"

As we have said before, from the point of view of computer graphics, the object-oriented user interfaces favored so strongly today are nothing new. Interactive graphics has always been object-oriented in the sense that what we intuitively consider to be objects were indeed the central subject of treatment. That is what it was all about: the representation of objects and their manipulation, including representation, construction, editing, geometric transformation, and identification with a graphics input device. An intuitive feeling for the concept of an object is provided by the use of an interactive graphics editor, e.g., MacDraw, as is illustrated by Fig. 1.1 which will infer statements such as:

- Objects are things with their own specific data.
- Objects may have different display attributes.
- Objects may contain other objects as components.
- Objects may be regarded as single entities. They may be selected and manipulated (deleted, modified, shifted, rotated).
- Some objects are similar in such a way that we may regard them as representatives of a common description.

1.1.1.3 Where is the Problem?

If a discipline is so naturally "object-oriented", we may ask if there remains a problem to be solved. Perhaps such a field offers completely satisfactory possibilities for the treatment of its objects with the help of programming languages, on the basis of its history and tradition alone? Unfortunately this is not the case.

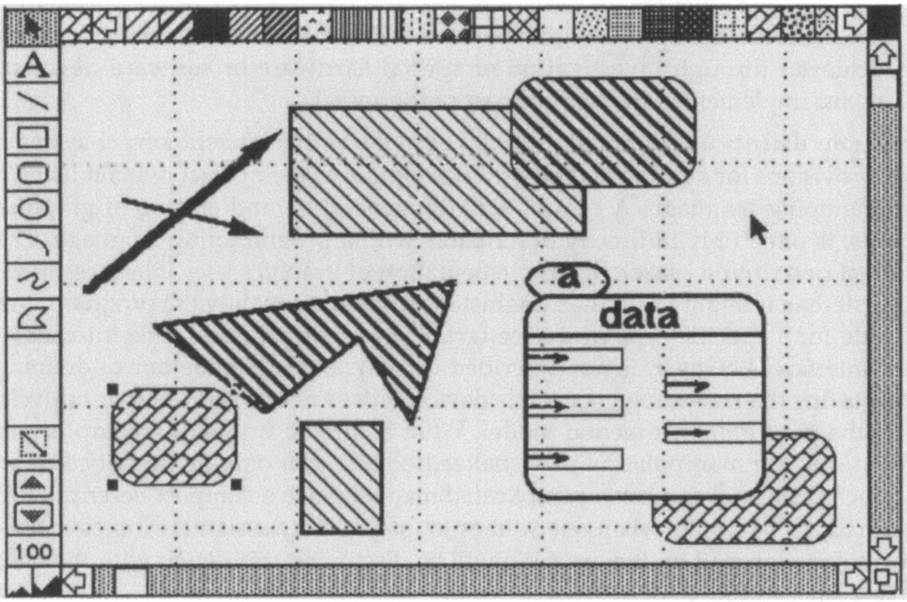

Fig. 1.1. The "object-oriented" user interface of MacDraw. A typical application of computer graphics is a graphics editor. The entities which will be created and edited will be intuitively interpreted as objects.

1.1.1.4 Traditional Kernel Systems

The strength of existing standards lies in their comprehensive functionality. A model is described of how a graphics data structure (object structure) can and must be constructed and edited. The entire model behind a graphics standard becomes more than the sum of its graphics functions. In this fashion, graphics primitives, for example, may not be used arbitrarily, but must be fitted into the model in some prescribed context; in PHIGS, for instance, primitives must be inserted into an existing structure. Structures can be connected to form structure networks, and *multi-level networks* are supported. This strict model concept forces a certain discipline upon the graphics programmer. However, the extensive services offered by the kernel are adequately compensated: by hardware independence, well-defined attribute and transformation concepts, inquiry functions, automatic coupling of input and output functions (the pick operation), and administration of graphics information in an archive. In this sense, the traditional graphics kernel extends beyond a toolbox; it is truly a *system*. In standardization, the idea of a "prefabricated" kernel plays an dominant role: a kernel whose functionality is standardized, whose internal implementation is hidden and which is then placed in the hands of the applications programmer. We call this idea the *principle of the hidden kernel*. The basic advantages of this idea are:

- systematic incorporation of the functionality,
- portability of application software using the kernel,

- device independence,
- the freedom to optimize the performance of the kernel, which can be achieved through investigation of special hardware or software developments implemented by the producer of the kernel.

The main deficit of traditional graphics systems is that current kernel systems lack provisions for a fitting and elegant description of their object domain using a programming language. A central activity, generation and editing of graphics objects, is often only indirectly describable with a programming language. The indirect description makes the implementation of graphics user interfaces more difficult than it might be. PHIGS, for instance, describes mainly the programming of code for a specific type of device (graph traversing device). The interactive user interface, however, is not described directly, but by the detour of defining and posting the traversing list for this device. It does not coincide very intuitively with the programmer's mental model. What he or she wants to accomplish on screen, i.e., the manipulation of visualized objects, can only be described in an indirect, unnatural and often complicated manner. Such a complex description is required, for example, when one wishes to interactively assign attributes to specific objects selected by the user. We will be discussing this deficit with the help of several examples in Sect. 9.4.

1.1.1.5 Evaluation of Existing Object-Oriented Kernel Systems

Parallel to the world of traditional graphics data processing, the emergence of object-oriented languages and systems sparked the birth of a second branch of development. The *object-oriented branch* is concerned with the conception of object-oriented languages and the development of object-oriented programming environments which were implemented as *graphics* programming environments. Graphics programming environments called for graphics tools. As a result, many tools stemming from object-oriented environments were made available as support to the general software developer. Thus, graphics-oriented editors, window systems allowing concurrent work with several texts, and graphics supported debugging tools were developed. The effectiveness of these developments has greatly influenced the entire field of computer technology, in particular the area of modern workstations. Due to differences in motivation, they have not, however, produced what could be termed a graphics kernel, capable of succeeding GKS or PHIGS.

In comparison with a traditional graphics kernel system, object-oriented development systems do not offer extensive, contained sets of kernel functions for hardware-independent graphics programming. With the exception of the Smalltalk-80 environment, which we will be discussing in more detail later, object-oriented development environments, as for instance MacApp, OSF-Motif (Berlage, 1990) or those on the Lisp machine, are far from being completely object-oriented. They do offer certain complex, predefined graphics classes similar to those in traditional graphics kernels, e.g., for the creation of graphics menus and dialogue boxes. On the other hand, they do not integrate these into a model for the construction and maintenance of graphics object hierarchies, or any comparable type of universally usable *graphics semantics*. The control of more standard input devices is made available with the prerequisite, minimal programming support, but the concept of a higher-level input device such as the pick device in GKS or PHIGS is missing. Such a concept is important in so far as it generally represents the connection between input and graphics object structures.

The lack of good graphics support often has curious consequences. In the development of knowledge-based systems, for example expert systems, modern, hybrid software development shells integrate object-oriented (frame-oriented), rule-, logic- and constraint-oriented programming support in a sophisticated manner. In contrast, the design of graphics user interfaces is usually confined to a rather unsystematic addition of so-called *attached procedures*, i.e., it is purely procedural.

1.1.1.6 A Synthesis is Necessary

All in all, a synthesis is necessary between the new ideas arising from object-oriented programming and the practical experiences from traditional computer graphics. For the specification of a handy graphics kernel system, tradition could provide the overall functionality, while the object-oriented paradigm could add quality, such as *flexibility*, offered by inheritance, *transparency*, provided by the object-oriented naming concept, and *modularity*, supported by a new system architecture.

1.2 Guidelines for the Design of a Graphics System

The following thoughts offer some guidelines for the design of an interactive graphics system.

1.2.1 Transforming the Mental Model into Programming Code

The applications programmer using an interactive graphics system must employ its functionality to implement an interactive and graphics application. Therefore interactive graphics systems are sometimes called the *application programmer's interface* for computer graphics. An interactive graphics application is generally devised first in a process of discussion on a rather informal level: one speaks with colleagues, end-users or the customer to determine the desired scope of performance. In which manner is this carried out? By our observations, it occurs often—and especially during the first phase—in an intuitively object-oriented manner. The discussion involves agreeing on which objects exist at what state of dialogue, how and when they are visualized, and to what extent they can be augmented, modified, or deleted with interactive tools. In the course of this, the applications programmer forms a *mental model* of the functionality to be implemented in the system. For achieving a real interactive application the mental model must be translated into constructs of the interactive graphics system as the schematic illustration Fig. 1.2 shows.

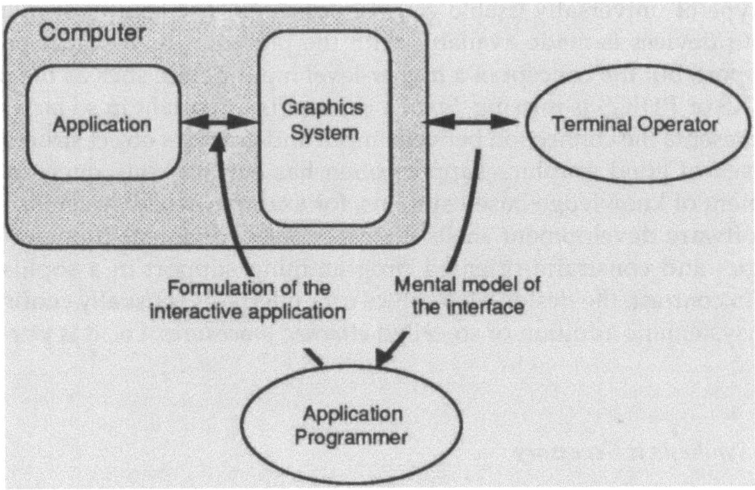

Fig. 1.2. Translation of the mental model. An application programmer forms a mental model of how the user will be working with the interactive graphics system. The model must be translated into the language constructs offered by a graphics system. Which graphics systems allow a natural formulation of the model? Is the object-oriented approach superior to others? Such issues are central to this book.

An essential aspect for the quality of an interactive graphics system will be its property to translate the mental model smoothly and naturally into the language constructs (data structures and operations) of the graphics system. The fewer structure clashes arise in the process of translating the mental model, the more appropriate an interactive graphics system is. Therefore an attempt will be made to verify whether the object-oriented programming paradigm provides a natural expression of the intuitive concept of graphics objects. Already at this stage, however, the hypothesis is stated that the object-oriented approach offers very good potential in the following sense:

- Object-oriented approaches motivate one to think in terms of objects, that is, higher-level structures and methods associated with them. Such objects as constructs of a programming system may be defined in close accordance with the items seen as intrinsic graphics objects.
- Object-oriented approaches allow one to construct systems that greatly outdo existing ones, at least as far as elegance in translation of the mental model to the program code is concerned. Conceptual breaks between the functionality of an interactive graphics interface and its description in code can be avoided much more consistently than by other approaches.

Being forced to think in terms of objects lead to a natural description of the functionality of graphics systems. It entails:

- direct naming of items that can be visualized,
- the treatment—description, assignment, and modification—of objects' attributes as inherent information about these objects,

- an easy grasp on the concurrent existence of graphics objects that the user may freely select and modify,
- viewing different objects with equal behavior as instances of a common class.

Beyond easy translation of the mental model into a program language description, that is to say, beyond a natural model, there are other marks of quality to be aspired to. We proceed with some comments on information hiding.

1.2.1.1 Information Hiding

Information hiding is also a mark of quality in software technology. For an interactive graphics system, it means:

- No over-specification when formulating graphics functionality! If at all possible, each transition of the interface should be expressed one-to-one by a corresponding operation of the graphics system—no more and no less.
- The internal implementation of the kernel provided by the system should remain hidden. For traditional systems it means that all additions to and changes in functionality of the kernel are implemented by software in a layer above the kernel, not by modification of the kernel's internal implementation itself. In object-oriented systems, the rule not to modify the functionality of the kernel should still be obeyed, but the layer model may be extended by allowing programming by definition of subclasses as well.

1.2.1.2 Limitations of Traditional Systems

What was said so far seems at first glance to be so self-evident that one must ask if this view has not perhaps always underlain the design of interactive graphics systems. Terms such as simplicity and naturalness can be found in the guidelines to GKS and PHIGS. But as already mentioned in the introduction there are still deficits.

Several of these deficits can be understood from historical reasons:

- The low level of performance of interactive graphics devices over long years must be mentioned here. Poor hardware performance called for non-object-oriented encoding of graphics object structures.
- Poor performance also demanded a programming interface-oriented strongly towards the capabilities of the device. Thus the functions available to the application programmer could not differ significantly from what the hardware demanded as device driver interface.
- Object-oriented programming languages were simply not available. In terms of practical usability, they are only now finding widespread use. The functionality of graphics programming systems therefore had to be expressed in conventional languages. In addition, the field of graphics was long held captive in a world ruled by Fortran.

Problems arising from historical limitations, the unavailability of the proper programming languages, even the lack of familiarity with modern programming concepts all resulted in the consequence that the actual functionality of systems could be achieved only in a round about way. An example is the traversing model of PHIGS—where linear ordered structures produce an artificial over-specification—which fulfills neither the principle of object orientation, nor the principle of information hiding. The sequential arrangement makes it difficult to use parallel methods for displaying internal structures, or to assign attributes to visible objects in a part hierarchy. The consequences and solution will be discussed in greater detail below. A second example is the unsatisfactory functionality of GKS. Because GKS supports only single-level object structures, remarkably complicated programs must be written to handle multi-level object hierarchies. Such programs are often required to bridge a structure clash between application and graphics kernel.

The weaknesses of existing approaches may be analyzed in two ways by the implementation of typical applications and by analysis of the differences that occur in their treatment when object-oriented methods are employed.

1.2.2 Using the Advantages of the Object-Oriented Approach

Even though the potential of the object-oriented approach will be illustrated more precisely in the chapters to come, let us here summarize some of the characteristics of this praradigm that are useful specifically for graphics modeling and programming:

- The general advantage already pointed out is the intuitiveness of applying object-oriented concepts to graphics. The idea of objects with associated methods allows a much more direct description of the items relevant to graphics, both in their visual appearance (geometric data, attributes) and in their behavior (reaction to graphics input). The principle of *locality* is supported. Once an object has been named, its own inherent information, e.g., attributes, can be assigned and inquired by name. Direct naming avoids the problem that important characteristics are only derivable after further steps are taken (collecting in lists, introducing additional names, search procedures). This concept considerably simplifies the applications programmer's task of assigning and inquiring graphics information to multi-level part hierarchies, as is shown for instance by the examples in Chap. 9.
- In object-oriented systems, the use of *multiple references* is trivial and customary. Multiple references to rather complex structures have always been necessary in computer graphics for accessing predefined geometric description.
- The *consistent* modification of a geometrical description, that is, a new version of a description that takes effect immediately wherever it is used, can easily be attained by the object-oriented reference mechanism. On the other hand, should inconsistent, individual changes be desirable, object-oriented systems offer effective copying mechanisms.
- The object-oriented *naming* concept offers further advantages. There is practically no difference between names, instantiated by corresponding methods as symbolic identifiers, and the actual objects referred by them. In traditional systems, segments and structures must be identified by additional, usually integer, variables. The equivalence of name and object is not established here;

there is just a two-sided relation between different entities, arranged by the application programmer.

- Objects in the object-oriented approach, viewed as abstract data types with associated methods, represent simultaneously existing, "smart" entities, capable of communicating flexibly with one another. Objects may exchange data and demand services of one another. Coexisting objects with functional capabilities correspond exactly with what was always required for modeling in graphics: concurrently instantiated primitives and collections of these primitives (segments, structures) managed by a graphics kernel, and, in addition, application objects that can communicate in a flexible manner with the graphics entities of the system.
- When a graphics object is constructed using the primitives of a kernel system in a traditional programming environment, construction is performed by a corresponding subroutine. Such a subroutine provides no internal memory and thus cannot keep non-graphics application data. These data must therefore be ferried between program and sub-program by means of parameter lists. (Graphics data storage is provided by the graphics program, e.g., a structure in PHIGS). In contrast, object-oriented systems offer the possibility to construct *virtual graphics objects*. They can be constructed through subclassing of a predefined kernel class. From the point of view of the applications programmer, it is integrated into the system as a normal graphics object. Internally, however, a virtual object stores its own data and it may use its own methods for displaying.
- Object-oriented systems offer *flexible communication mechanisms*. In the traditional layered model, the components of the graphics kernel are always invoked—they never themselves activate procedures written by the applications programmer. But in object-oriented systems, objects of the graphics kernel may send messages to application objects. By instantiating special messages, named *call-back messages*, communication from kernel objects to application objects can be established, without any modification of the kernel's implementation which would violate the principle of the hidden, non-modifiable kernel. With the call-back mechanism, reactions of an interactive system to user actions can be modeled in a much more natural style than in traditional systems. The user activates an input tool to send information to a graphics object; the graphics object as a receiver evaluates this messages for its own purposes and then may inform an application object about the user's interaction. In contrast, traditional systems demand a more centralized control of the dialogue: a central dialogue evaluator implemented by the applications programmer, queries input tools, interprets them, and branches to the individual sections of the application program or the graphics kernel system.
- *Inheritance* can be employed in a graphics system in a multitude of applications. It is frequently used as a programming technique to customize a graphics kernel for specific needs—much more easily than is possible in a traditional system. Furthermore, the possibility to employ the predefined kernel's classes to form specialized subclasses with modified (either augmented or restricted) functionality is in many cases a much more natural structuring aid

than yet another layer above the kernel. Inheritance allows the integration of application-specific knowledge (geometric modeling, product data) into graphics objects without loss of functionality. Moreover, new graphics functionality such as new attributes or special primitives can be integrated as instances of subclasses for the predefined kernel's classes. Note that the idea of constructing higher levels above a kernel system can of course be implemented as well as in traditional systems by introducing new classes and methods that use the kernel's functionality by message passing.

With the combination of a predefined kernel with hidden implementation, flexible communication between concurrently existing graphics and application objects, and inheritance of predefined kernel classes (resulting in mixed objects, representing graphics and application-oriented knowledge) a new system architecture will be achieved, which we name *the extended layer model.*

1.2.2.1 Elegance, Not Just Power

When graphics systems are compared in this book, we are not primarily interested in high performance. Elegance, that is, the ease with which the applications programmer can create an interface, is more important to us. Thus we have restricted ourselves to the field of two-dimensional graphics as two-dimensional graphics are sufficient to demonstrate the potential of the object-oriented approach.

Object-oriented systems are not superior to traditional systems in the power of their predetermined functional capabilities. Both approaches allow the implementation of complex graphics algorithms. Reduction of expenditures is significant for us: the resources that must be spent for the encoding of a model, and especially the intellectual resources that must be spent in designing an interactive graphics interface. Further criteria are: flexibility in customizing a graphics system to the needs of certain types of application and the possibility of modifying an existing first version of an interactive graphics interface with a reasonable amount of effort. The restriction to elegance does not mean, however, that efforts in designing modern graphics system should disregard powerful new algorithms, e.g., for the representation of three-dimensional objects.

1.2.2.2 Which Classes and Objects?

The object-oriented approach is not a miracle cure that automatically delivers the ideal specification of an interactive graphics system. Although it forms a guideline, it still leaves a large degree of freedom to specify what should be made available to the applications programmer in the form of objects, methods, and class hierarchy. The specification of the application is not a formalized process that can be automated.

To define the classes of a graphics system we try to proceed as follows. At first, through corresponding classes and methods, displayable entities which are intuitively felt to be objects of the same class are defined. These objects will include *individual* graphics objects, which we call *parts,* and geometric descriptions on which parts are based on, which we call *building patterns*—in short, everything that can be manipulated, modified, assigned attributes. Then we find that attributes should not only be assignable to a visual object by means of parameter lists, but that it makes sense to make attributes available to the applications programmer as objects of a class—and beyond that, to offer whole sets of attributes consisting of attributes of different types. Many such ideas are derived from existing object-oriented graphics systems, such as the Smalltalk-80 graphics kernel. The essential specifications of the functionality will be derived from the tradition of the field of computer graphics, which is manifested in graphics standards.

1.2.2.3 Extending the Semantics of a Part Hierarchy

The tradition of graphics systems is strongly influenced by the support of graphics concepts that correspond to the semantics of a part hierarchy. Even GKS allows graphics primitives to be collected in segments and treat them as units: attributes may be assigned to them and they can be inserted into other segments. PHIGS steps even further in the direction of modeling part hierarchies: a multi-level system with fully editable structures is provided.

Multi-level systems support the concept of building conglomerates from smaller units, and handling conglomerates as new entities that may be treated as higher-level graphics primitives. The structuring facilities of multi-level systems mean no less than supporting the semantic concept of a part hierarchy.

Inheritance in object-oriented systems introduces another semantic concept into graphics: transferring properties from classes to subclasses. With composition of parts and inheritance, the two most important general semantic concepts can be modelled, the concepts that are primarily known from by knowledge-based systems in the field of artificial intelligence.

It is important to realize that the field of computer graphics encompasses applications that employ part hierarchies, but in which these play a rather subordinate role. Other semantics dominate, such as rules for geometric relations *between* individual objects, as for example positions relative to each other, and not their order in a hierarchy. Additional semantic relations are usually tailored to the needs of individual applications or types of applications, hence supporting them directly in a general purpose graphics system makes little sense. To support application-specific semantics, a graphics kernel system that can easily be combined with tools such as constraint evaluators or rule interpreters would be ideal. Rules or constraints are well suited to formulate complex relationships between graphics data, or between graphics data and the application. For a graphics system to truly assist the realization of such relationships, some additional considerations are necessary. Elegant access and modification mechanisms for part hierarchies no longer suffice. Also needed is easy access to information that is orthogonal to the graphics part hierarchy. Prerequisites for this are effective query mechanisms for graphics information and the possibility of applying operations to sets which can be orthogonal to the part hierarchy. The object-oriented approach offers support for the realization of such operations, too.

1.3 Overview

A short overview will now be presented in order to give the reader a better understanding of the organization of this book.

1.3.1 What Does the Book Concentrate on?

We concentrate on the issues of *interactive* graphics. The area traditionally termed *construction and editing of graphics data structures* is in the foreground. We will always stay close to graphics kernel systems and we will not discuss questions of geometric modeling, rendering, lighting models, or problems of computer animation.

1.3.1.1 Programming in Smalltalk-80

The basic principles of object-oriented programming are explained, tied with a minimal introduction to Smalltalk-80. It should then be possible to understand the functionality of GEO++, expressed in Smalltalk-80 syntax, and to follow the programming examples.

1.3.1.2 Principles of Interface Design in Object-Oriented Systems

One of the interesting topics in the context of object-oriented systems is the design of (not necessarily graphics) interactive user interfaces and its support by means of predefined objects and methods. We will be discussing some of the basic principles of such systems by two examples: the Model-View-Controller concept in Smalltalk-80 and GINA (acronym for generic interactive application, developed at the author's institute, Institute for Applied Information Technology of GMD). In systems like these, it is possible to offer the applications programmer a predefined, executable generic application; the applications programmer is then able to tailor his own application from the generic one, using object-oriented mechanisms.

1.3.1.3 Graphics in Smalltalk-80

Graphics in Smalltalk-80 is then discussed in aspects which are important to the following chapters. We will be paying special attention to the differences between graphics in Smalltalk-80 and in GKS and PHIGS.

The Smalltalk-80 graphics kernel differs quite extensively from GKS and PHIGS in functionality. An important characteristic is that it supports no object hierarchy, not even a single-level hierarchy. As a consequence, there is no predefined model for a graphics picture structure, and no pick-operation. Essentially, the system provides only individual objects. All types of graphics objects hierarchies must therefore be implemented with available programming tools, which are, however, very comfortable.

Many of the object-oriented principles we have mentioned before are implemented in the Smalltalk-80 graphics kernel. Therefore—although the functionality of the kernel is rather low-level—it sparks useful suggestions for graphics systems with augmented functionality.

All graphics primitives in Smalltalk-80 are objects, therefore they can be called by name and referred to repeatedly. They can be directly assigned attributes whose values can also be inquired directly. A very important characteristic of the kernel is that primitives can be edited. So it is possible, for example, to append new coordinates to an existing polyline. Editable primitives are especially useful for the implementation of graphics input. Next to editing graphics primitives, the variety of possibilities for setting and querying geometric parameters is remarkable. The principle of minimization, which was a guideline in the development of GKS and PHIGS, has been abandoned, a very rich set of methods is provided.

1.3.1.4 GKS Seen Through the Object-Oriented Lens

The functionality of GKS and PHIGS is described independently of a specific programming language. For a specific language an additional specification according to the general functional specification and to the specific capabilities of the language is described as an additional standard document. We indicate that such a language binding could also be defined without any problems for Smalltalk-80. Because everything in Smalltalk-80 is object-oriented, this would result, from a purely formalistic point of view, in an object-oriented system. It is somewhat degenerate, however, and we show the direction in which a truly object-oriented modification would have to be pursued.

1.3.1.5 Modeling Part Hierarchies

The organization of objects in a part hierarchy is one of the most frequently used methods of modeling and describing phenomena of the real world. Behind modeling part hierarchies stands the basic idea of constructing and describing complex objects through composition of simpler ones. Part hierarchies play an important role in many areas of science and technology.

In computer graphics, part hierarchies are of interest wherever complex graphics representations can be interpreted as conglomerations of simpler parts—which is the case in most applications. An interactive graphics editor, such as MacDraw, is a typical application program based on the concept of composition: simple graphics primitives can be selected from a menu and grouped to form higher aggregates. Copy operations serve to replicate parts and support the idea of the repeated use of objects having the same building pattern.

The basic demands of modeling part hierarchies in an interactive graphics system are described in Chap. 6, in preparation for discussing their functional support by graphics systems such as PHIGS and our own concept, GEO++, a specification for a kernel, described in Chap. 8.

1.3.1.6 PHIGS and Part Hierarchies

The standard Programmer's Hierarchical Interactive Graphics System (PHIGS) is a programming system that supports the construction and editing of hierarchical graphics data structures much more directly that GKS does. PHIGS supports a multi-level data structure which allows the implementation of part hierarchies. These hierarchies are organized as networks of structures, i.e., as directed, acyclical graphs.

The editing mechanism of PHIGS aid arbitrary editing of the elements of a structure. Nearly all operations provided by PHIGS essentially serve the purpose of constructing and editing part hierarchies. Typical operations for part hierarchies, however, may only be performed by skillful combination of the elementary operations offered by PHIGS. PHIGS cannot verify whether a combination of elementary editing operations is correct, i.e., is a valid operation on a graphics object hierarchy. PHIGS has only very limited knowledge, so to speak, of the semantics of part hierarchies modeled by a structure network.

1.3.1.7 The Object-Oriented System GEO++

The system GEO++ (Graphics System with Editable Objects, version 2) is a design proposal for an object-oriented multi-level graphics system. In it the thoughts and recommendations discussed in this book will be concretized. In its description and in the use of its functionality, GEO++ is influenced by object-oriented programming. The functionality follows the tradition of GKS and PHIGS and may be considered as an extension of them. GEO++ is a typical graphics kernel system—application-independent, rich, and sufficiently general in its functionality to be used in a wide variety of application areas.

Accepted principles of object-oriented programming are applied in GEO++. Graphics primitives, grouping of primitives, building pattern, attribute, etc., can be addressed by a name and referred to by its name, which is specified by the applications programmer as object identifier as it is common in object-oriented systems.

Another aspect in the specification of GEO++'s functionality is the implementation of generally accepted elementary operations for the manipulation of part hierarchies. In this regard, GEO++ exceeds the very low-level editing operations offered by PHIGS. Operations requiring a whole series of PHIGS commands are replaced by a single atomic action in GEO++. Such atomic actions include operations for navigating through the part-of hierarchy, for editing the hierarchy, and for rebuilding the hierarchy, for example, group and ungroup.

1.3.1.8 Programming Examples

Unfortunately, hardly any detailed descriptions of PHIGS with well-commented programming examples are available. We have therefore given PHIGS a little more room than might be expected in a book about object-oriented graphics. There is another reason for an extended treatment of PHIGS, however. We will compare PHIGS as a typical representative of the traditional approach with GEO++, to show how much can be won by an object-oriented design of a graphics system.

Several typical programming examples will demonstrate the applicability of object-oriented concepts. The examples in Chap. 9 do not yet make use of inheritance. They are therefore solely influenced by thinking in terms of objects (without the use of inheritance). As a consequence, the overall principles which will be demonstrated by GEO++ will also apply to programming languages which are in not (strictly) object-oriented. Examples are ADA, that uses only abstract data types, or even Pascal and Fortran.

1.3.1.9 Inheritance in a Predefined Kernel System

In Chap. 10 several examples illustrating inheritance are presented. It will be assumed that a kernel with hidden implementation is used. A few general examples will show that it is quite easy to modify and extend substantially the functionality of GEO++ by using inheritance:

- The first example demonstrates an alternative naming concept for GEO++, where the names of the edges in the GEO++-tree are instantiated from the outside as input parameters.
- The second example demonstrates how frame-like part hierarchies can be constructed. Each graphics object supplies a fixed number of slots, into which parts can be inserted.
- The third example shows how reaction to call-back messages can be implemented by subclassing.

1.3.1.10 Prototypes and Delegation

An alternative to the class-instance concept is the *prototype-delegation* model where an instance's protocol may change during the execution of a program. Instance variables and methods may be added to or deleted from an already existing instance. An instance may also benefit from the functionality of another instance on which it depends by a dependency relation.

The relevance of a prototype model for computer graphics is stressed by several authors, for example by Borning (Borning, 1986). In computer graphics objects have often to be created dynamically by interactive editing procedures, and their behavior must be changed dynamically. For modeling and implementing such a flexibility, the prototype-delegation concept seems to be very natural and powerful. This is illustrated by defining a modification of GEO++ based on prototypes.

1.3.1.11 Implementation Aspects

In Chap. 12 an efficient implementation of GEO++ will be described. GEO++ allows an internal implementation that is completely different from the model as seen from the outside. Even though GEO++ is based on a tree-oriented part-hierarchy, a compact implementation as an acyclical graph is feasible. This implementation is at least as compact as a PHIGS implementation.

In addition, some thought are given about posting PHIGS structures and GEO++ groups by use of parallel architectures.

1.3.1.12 Additional Concepts and Tools

So far, the support of part hierarchies in graphics systems have played a dominant role. But of course plenty of other semantics may be required for different fields of applications of computer graphics. Some such applications will be discussed with the help of a few examples in Chap. 13. The semantic concept of *connectivity* is introduced, and it is shown how it can be supported by subclassing of the predefined GEO++ classes. In general additional semantic aspects are application-dependent and therefore they need to be programmed for every special type of application, requiring much programming effort. Constraints are discussed which aim at reducing this task of higher programming by introducing concepts that describe complex geometrical relations between objects in a declarative style and that provide mechanisms for evaluating these relations. The discussion focuses on the question of how constraints may be smoothly added to a predefined object-oriented kernel.

New mechanisms for knowledge representation are motivated by the desire to map phenomena of the real world as "naturally" as possible onto computer systems. Connecting the functionality of computer graphics quite naturally with hybrid representation mechanisms is discussed as a subject for future research.

1.3.1.13 An Object-Oriented Standard?

In Chap. 14 the question as to whether there should be an object-oriented graphics standard is considered. The "political" situation for the definition of an object-oriented standard is quite favorable at present. Work towards the second-generation graphics standard under the heading *New Application Programmer's Interface* (New API) has just started. But standardization requires more than the merely specification and implementation of *one* useful kernel system for a *given* object-oriented environment. Definitions must be language independent and different aspects of portability have to be studied so that work is still to be done in this field.

2 Object-Oriented Concepts

The principles of object-oriented programming are introduced in this chapter using Smalltalk-80. Only concepts which are essential to understand this book, and especially to follow the programming examples, are presented.

2.1 Objects and Messages

The basic constructs, i.e., all entities, in an object-oriented system are objects. Examples of objects are numbers, text strings or graphics objects, such as lines and rectangles. An object may be regarded as a collection of the internal data which represent its current state. A typical example is the rectangle, aligned with the axes (ithotetic), defined by the diagonal vertices (40,100) and (120,200).

An object is addressed by a variable name, used as *identifier* for sending *messages* to it. Messages may be sent from any existing object, called the *sender*, to the addressed object, the *receiver*; information to a receiver is "transported" by the *arguments* of a message. An object's *protocol* defines what type of messages may be received by it. The internal state of an object is hidden and only accessible by messages defined for this object.

An object offers different choices of reacting to a message. It may change its internal state or, while processing a message, it may send messages to other objects or even to itself. After processing a message, a *result* is generated and it is returned to the sender.

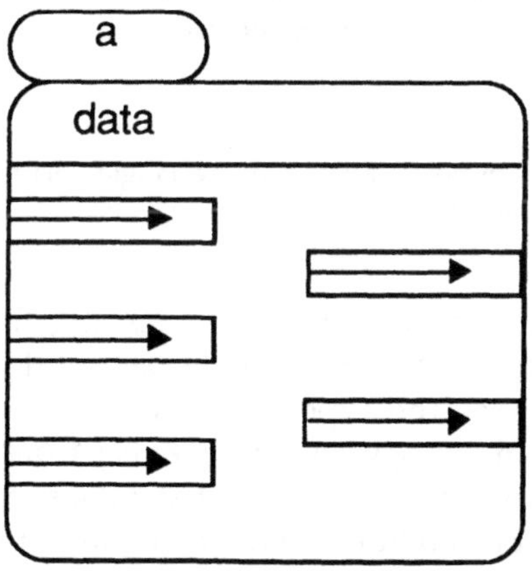

Fig. 2.1. Illustration of an object. Here an object can receive three different types of messages. The object itself may send messages to other objects while evaluating a received message.

We symbolize objects by squares with rounded edges and attach on top a variable name used as identifier, as shown in Fig. 2.1. This style of graphics representation serves for illustration only and has no formal meaning. The inserts on the left indicate that the object may receive three different types of messages. The inserts on the right show that the object may communicate with other objects while processing a message. The internal data (not visible from outside) are displayed by the sub-section "data".

A rectangle a may receive coordinates by the following message:

(1) a origin: p1 corner: p2 .

In (1) p1 and p2 are two existing point objects used as arguments; they are sent to a and modify the internal state of the rectangle: the upper left-hand vertex is set to p1 and the lower left-hand one to p2. Figure 2.2, adopted from the "blue book" (Goldberg & Robson, 1983), clarifies what names are used for the relevant locations of a rectangle (note that the y-coordinate increases from top to bottom).

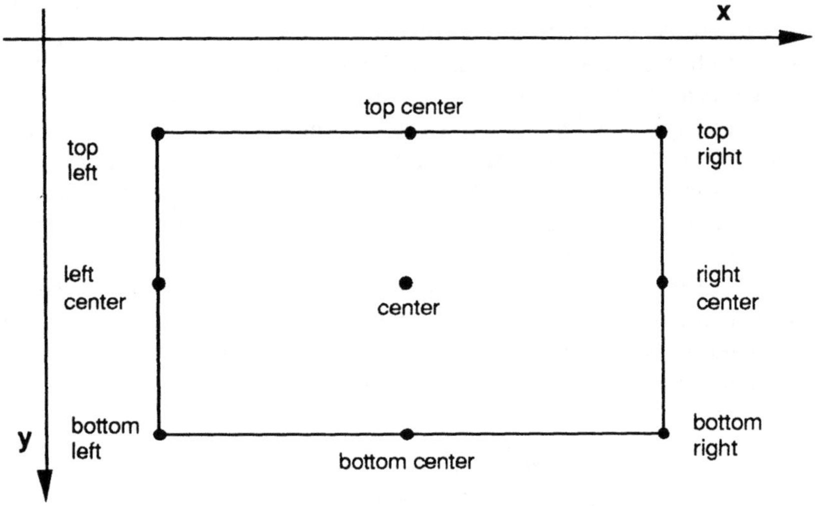

Fig. 2.2. Notations for the main points related to a rectangle, relative to the axes. Note that the y-axis increases from top to bottom.

There are two components of a in the above message, the name of the message, the *message selector* origin:corner:, and the *arguments* of the message, p1 and p2. A message selector describes the type of message a receiver can respond to. Following traditional terminology, the arguments p1 and p2 could be viewed as input data. With the above message (1), we have the simple case where only the internal state of an object is modified (and where the result is irrelevant).

The next example, illustrated in Fig. 2.3, shows how a message to the rectangle a returns another object as a result of message passing:

(2) topLeftPoint ← a topLeft .

When we look at the expression we first observe that a message of another type, without any parameter, was sent to a, a *unary* message. This unary message used in (2) consists only of the selector topLeft. The result of the message topLeft returns the top left corner of the rectangle a; topLeftPoint represents a two-dimensional point. The arrow ← is the *assignment* operator. It is used to assign a variable to the result of a message. The assignment therefore may be seen as analogous to an output parameter of a procedure in conventional systems. If a variable name used for an assignment was used previously, the old reference is destroyed. It is possible, as shown in (1), to omit referencing by the assignment operator if one refrains from accepting the result and only wishes to change the internal state of an object.

It may be surprising that all information which may be represented by different output parameters in traditional languages are concentrated in only one object, the result object. The components of the result may, however, may be inquired by sending different types of messages to the result. In the last example, this may be done by sending messages which are defined for points, such as:

```
xCoordinate ← topLeftPoint x
yCoordinate ← topLeftPoint y .
```

delivering the x- and y- coordinate of the point topLeftPoint.

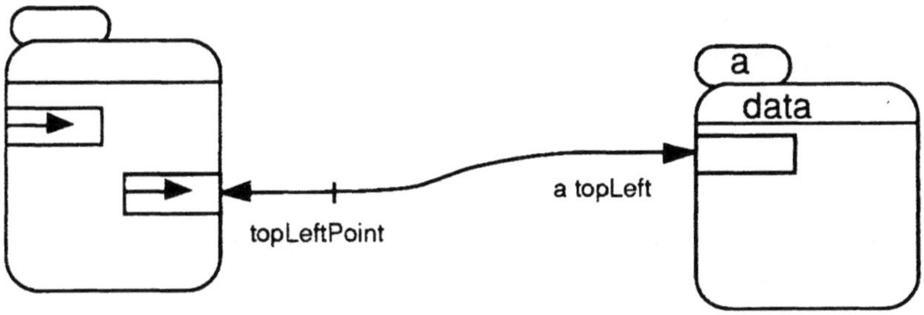

Fig. 2.3. Message passing to a with topLeftPoint as result. In Smalltalk-80, message passing is always two-way communication: the receiver delivers as an effect of a message a result back to the sender.

In addition to the message types introduced already there exist also *binary messages*. A binary message selector consists of one or two non-alphanumeric characters. Examples are:

```
a + b        "message selector: +"
a <= 5       "message selector: <="
a , b        "message selector: , "
30@40        "message selector: @"
```

By introducing this type of message it is possible to define even arithmetic operations as messages. In the example the receivers are a, a, a, 30 and the arguments are b, 5, b, 40. The last message is defined for the elementary object type Number for representing numbers and it delivers a two-dimensional point. In this manner, for an existing rectangle a (defined by a message new to its class Rectangle, see next paragraph) a complete instantiation of a with top left corner (40,100) and bottom right corner (120,200) will be achieved by:

```
p1 ← 40@100
p2 ← 120@200
a origin: p1 corner: p2 .
```

A less trivial message to a rectangle may be its intersection with a second one. At first, two rectangles a and b are instantiated:

```
a origin: 100@200 corner: 300@400
b origin: 150@190 corner: 400@300 .
```

Then the following message creates as a result the intersection:

```
myRectangle ← a intersect: b .
```

The top left and bottom right vertices of myRectangle are (150,200) and (300,300).

It should be noted that message passing to an object is similar to calling a procedure. There are, however, two important differences:

- Objects may store their own data.
- Many objects may exist in parallel.

2.2 The Class

So far it was not mentioned how and where to program the *methods* which evaluate the different types of messages (characterized by different message selectors) that an object may receive. For describing groups of objects with similar behavior the concept of the *class* is used. Every object is an instance of exactly one class and behaves as specified by the class definition. A class describes the form of the private memory of its instances, and it defines which types of messages an object may receive and how they are carried out.

The *protocol description* of a class list's the messages understood by instances of a particular class. An *implementation description* of a class consists of a class name, a declaration of the variables available to the instances, and a set of methods used by instances to respond to messages. If *all* methods are listed one speaks about a *complete* implementation description.

A method has access to *instance variables* and *class variables*. Instance variables are used for representing the current state of each individual object. Class variables represent states common to all instances of a class; they are shared by all instances of a class. Instance and class variables exist for the entire lifetime of an object. In addition there are *global variables* which may be addressed system-wide, and *temporary variables* available only for the duration of an activity as the execution of a method.

The definition of the different types of variables is supported by the interactive system browser, providing an elegant user interface for programming. In the implementation descriptions, used below, cf. Sect. 2.2.1, temporary variable declarations are delimited by vertical bars, as shown in the method intersect: for class Rectangle. Instance and class variables are grouped in a specific section under the labels "instance variable names" and "class variable names". The only global variables explicitly used in the examples are variables as identifiers for classes, such as Rectangle, Point, Group, Part.

Communication with objects can only be performed by message passing; direct access to the internal state of an object, e.g., to the instance or class variables, is not possible. Information hiding established in this manner has the advantage that the programmer is free in how to code methods and change them later if it would be required.

Each class provides a unique identifier which begins with an upper case character—in the examples below: Point and Rectangle. The class Rectangle owns the instance variables origin and corner (class variables are not defined for the class Rectangle).

The code of a message starts with a *message pattern*—a message selector and a set of argument names, one for each argument—followed by a sequence of expressions. For defining the object delivered back to the sender as a result of a message, a special notation, an uparrow (↑) is used. It indicates that the result of the expression preceded by the arrow is returned. In the default case the result of a method is the receiver itself. The default result is delivered for many of the following examples for the class Rectangle , where no new object is generated and only the internal state of the receiver is changed by the method.

In addition to instance methods evaluating messages sent to instances of a class, messages may be sent directly to a class. These messages are defined by means of *class methods*, which are often used to generate new instances of a class. A predefined standard message, the unary message new, is frequently used for this purpose. The effect of the message new is usually the generation of a new object with non-instantiated instance variables. Thus with

```
aRectangle new
```

a new rectangle which is not yet provided with coordinates (i.e., the value of the instance variables is nil) is created.

The class Rectangle provides a class method with selector origin:corner:. It does not matter that the identical selector is defined for an instance method of the same class. The last message may be used as follows:

```
aRectangle ← Rectangle origin: 200@200 corner: 300@300 .
```

As result, a new rectangle is created and coincidentally instantiated with the coordinates described by the arguments. The following figure illustrates the structure of a class. (The concept of a superclass which is part of the illustration and the implementation descriptions will be introduced below).

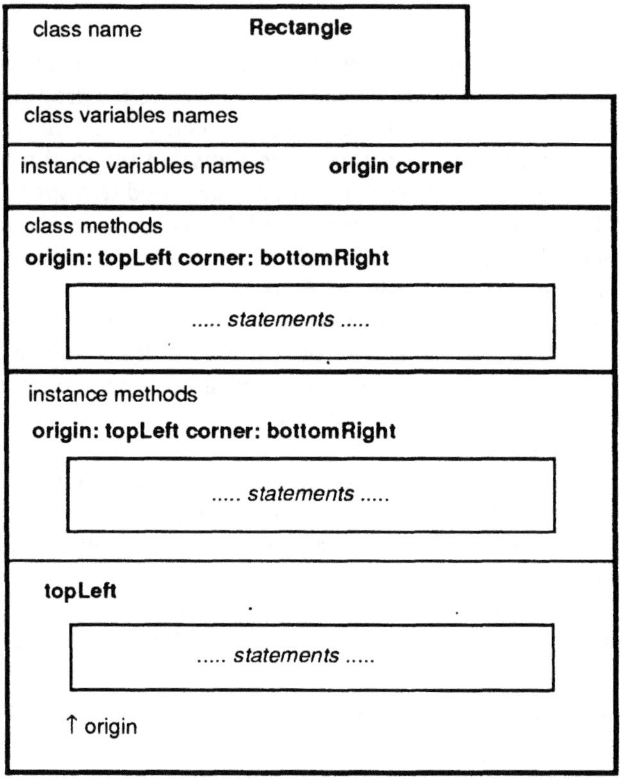

Fig. 2.4. Components of a class. The structural components of a class are shown here. In a class the internal variables for instances of the class are defined. The methods determine which types of messages can be sent to an instance of the class or the class itself. The example shows one class method and two instance methods. The first two methods do not use the uparrow so that the receiver itself (the class or the addressed instance) is delivered as result; the last message delivers the instance variable origin back to the sender.

By repeatedly sending messages such as new or origin:corner: to a class, many concurrently existing instances may be created. New instances may, however, also be created by sending messages—such as intersect:—to an instance. As can be seen by the implementation of intersect: (see implementation description of Rectangle below), the new instance is created internally by a class method. Note that in Smalltalk-80 classes (such as the class Rectangle) are itself defined as objects (classes are instances of their metaclass).

2.2.1 Implementation Descriptions

The following implementation descriptions for Point and Rectangle should give a feeling of how methods are implemented. The descriptions represent a subset of the complete implementation of these classes as provided by the Smalltalk-80 environment. It is not assumed that all details can be understood right now, because some concepts are introduced only later on. The examples (see, for instance, intersect:) show nicely, how a method uses methods of other objects (Point) while evaluating a message. Note that methods may be grouped into categories, e.g., *Accessing*. Categories do not affect the operation of a class; they are only intended to make the description more readable.

Point *Implementation Description*

"Adopted and slightly modified from Smalltalk-80, Version 2.3 of 13 June 1988 on 11 April 1990 at 7:21:03 am "

class name	**Point**
superclass	**Object**
instance variable names	x y
class variable names	
instance methods	

"Class Point represents an x-y pair of numbers usually designating a location on the screen."

Accessing

x "Answer the x coordinate."

```
↑ x
```

x: xInteger "Set the x coordinate."

```
x ← xInteger
```

y "Answer the y coordinate."

```
↑ y
```

y: yInteger "Set the y coordinate."

```
y ← yInteger
```

Point methods for.: 'comparing'

< aPoint "Answer whether the receiver is 'above and to the left' of the argument, aPoint."

```
↑ x < aPoint x and: [y < aPoint y]
```

<= aPoint

"Answer whether the receiver is 'neither below nor to the right' of aPoint."

```
↑ x <= aPoint x and: [y <= aPoint y]
```

= aPoint

"Answer whether the receiver's class and coordinates match those of the argument, aPoint."

```
self class = aPoint class
  ifTrue: [↑ x = aPoint x and: [y = aPoint y]]
  ifFalse: [↑ false]
```

> aPoint

"Answer whether the receiver is 'below and to the right' of aPoint."

```
↑ x > aPoint x and: [y > aPoint y]
```

max: aPoint

"Answer the lower right corner of the rectangle uniquely defined by the receiver and aPoint."

```
↑ Point x: (x max: (aPoint x)) y: (y max: (aPoint y))
```

Arithmetic

*** scale**

"Answer a new Point that is the product of the receiver and scale (which is a Point or Number)."

```
| scalePoint |

scalePoint ← scale asPoint. .
↑ x * scalePoint x @ (y * scalePoint y)
```

+ delta

"Answer a new Point that is the sum of the receiver and delta (which is a Point or Number)."

```
| deltaPoint |

deltaPoint ← delta asPoint. .
↑ x + deltaPoint x @ (y + deltaPoint y)
```

abs

"Answer a new Point whose x and y are the absolute values of the receiver's x and y."

↑ Point x: x abs y: y abs

corner: aPoint

"Answer a new Rectangle whose origin is the receiver and whose corner is aPoint. This is one of the infix ways of expressing the creation of a rectangle."

↑ Rectangle origin: self corner: aPoint

---

class methods

Instance creation

x: xInteger y: yInteger

"Answer a new instance of a Point with coordinates xInteger and yInteger."

↑ self new setX: xInteger setY: yInteger

Rectangle *Implementation Description*

"Adopted and slightly modified from Smalltalk-80, Version 2.3 of 13 June 1988 on 16 March 1990 at 7:21:03 am "

class name	**Rectangle**
instance variable names	origin corner
class variable names	
instance methods	

"Class Rectangle usually represents a rectangular area on the screen. Arithmetic functions take points as arguments and carry out scaling and translating operations to create new Rectangles. Rectangle functions create new Rectangles by determining intersections of rectangles with rectangles."

Accessing

area

"Answer the receiver's area, the product of width and height."

```
    ↑ (self width) * (self height)
```

bottom "Answer the position of the receiver's bottom horizontal line."

```
    ↑ corner y
```

bottom: anInteger "Set the position of the bottom horizontal line of the receiver."

```
    corner y: anInteger
```

bottomCenter "Answer the point at the center of the bottom horizontal line of the receiver."

```
    ↑ self center x @ self bottom
```

bottomLeft "Answer the point at the left edge of the bottom horizontal line of the receiver."

```
    ↑ origin x @ corner y
```

bottomRight "Answer the point at the right edge of the bottom horizontal line of the receiver."

```
    ↑ corner
```

bottomRight: bottomRightPoint "Set the position of the right corner of the bottom horizontal line of the receiver."

```
    corner ← bottomRightPoint
```

center "Answer the point at the center of the receiver."

```
    ↑ self topLeft + self bottomRight // 2
```

corner "Answer the point at the bottom right corner of the receiver."

```
    ↑ corner
```

corner: cornerPoint "Set the point at the bottom right corner of the receiver."

```
    corner ← cornerPoint
```

extent "Answer a Point representing the extent of the receiver, that is one whose x coordinate is the width and whose y coordinate is the height."

```
    ↑ corner - origin
```

extent: extentPoint "Set the extent (width and height) of the receiver to be the argument extentPoint."

```
    corner ← origin + extentPoint
```

height "Answer the height of the receiver."

```
    ↑ corner y - origin y
```

height: heightInteger "Change the receiver's bottom y to make its height the argument heightInteger."

```
    corner y: origin y + heightInteger
```

left "Answer the position of the receiver's left vertical line."

```
    ↑ origin x
```

left: anInteger "Set the position of the receiver's left vertical line."

```
    origin x: anInteger
```

leftCenter "Answer the point at the center of the receiver's left vertical line."

```
    ↑ self left @ self center y
```

origin "Answer the point at the top left corner of the receiver."

```
    ↑ origin
```

origin: originPoint "Set the point at the top left corner of the receiver."

```
    origin ← originPoint
```

origin: originPoint corner: cornerPoint "Set the points at the top left corner and the bottom right corner of the receiver."

```
    origin ← originPoint .
    corner ← cornerPoint
```

origin: originPoint extent: extentPoint "Set the point at the top left corner of the receiver to be originPoint and set the width and height of the receiver to be extentPoint."

```
    origin ← originPoint.
    corner ← origin + extentPoint
```

right "Answer the position of the receiver's right vertical line."

```
    ↑ corner x
```

right: anInteger "Set the position of the receiver's right vertical line."

    corner x: anInteger

rightCenter "Answer the point at the center of the receiver's right vertical line."

    ↑ self right @ self center y

top "Answer the position of the receiver's top horizontal line."

    ↑ origin y

top: anInteger "Set the position of the receiver's top horizontal line."

    origin y: anInteger

topCenter "Answer the point at the center of the receiver's top horizontal line."

    ↑ self center x @ self top

topLeft "Answer the point at the top left corner of the receiver's top horizontal line."

    ↑ origin

topLeft: topLeftPoint "Set the point at the top left corner of the receiver's top horizontal line."

    origin ← topLeftPoint

topRight "Answer the point at the top right corner of the receiver's top horizontal line."

    ↑ corner x @ origin y

width "Answer the width of the receiver."

    ↑ corner x - origin x

width: widthInteger "Change the receiver's right vertical line to make its width widthInteger."

    corner x: origin x + widthInteger

intersect: aRectangle "Answer a Rectangle that is the area in which the receiver overlaps with aRectangle."

| intersection |

```
intersection ← (self class)
                    origin: (origin max: aRectangle origin)
                    corner: (corner min: aRectangle corner)

↑ intersection
```

moveBy: aPoint

"Change the corner positions of the receiver so that its area translates by the amount defined by the argument, aPoint."

```
origin ← origin + aPoint.
corner ← corner + aPoint
```

---

class methods

instance creation

origin: originPoint corner: cornerPoint

"Answer an instance of the receiver whose corners (top left and bottom right) are determined by the arguments."

```
↑ (self new) origin: originPoint corner: cornerPoint
```

2.3 Message Passing

It was already indicated that objects support very flexible communication mechanisms. Following is another example, in which some additional mechanisms in the context of message passing will be introduced.

2.3.1 How Can an Object Call Itself?

First, with a small example we will illustrate how an object can call itself. Again we take the example Rectangle. We assume the object aRectangle should receive a message with the selector area for the calculation of the area and, while doing so, should send the message width and height to itself.

At the time the method area is defined, i.e., coded, the receiver aRectangle is of course as yet unknown. Therefore another identifier, the so-called pseudo variable self, for self-addressing of the receiver, is provided. As can be seen from the implementation description above, the area is calculated by:

```
↑(self width) * (self height) .
```

Figure 2.5 shows the information flow for the method calculating the area.

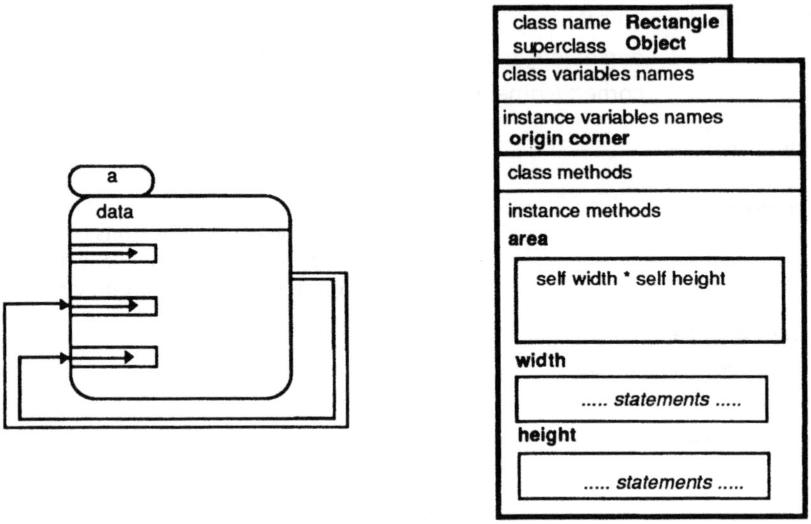

Fig. 2.5. Message to self. A method may use methods that are defined for its own class. Because at method generation time the receiver is unknown a pseudovariable called self is used for defining the receiver.

2.3.2 Additional Mechanisms for Message Passing

Now that we have discussed the basic model of message passing, let us continue with some further forms for handling messages.

2.3.2.1 Combination of Messages

In Smalltalk-80, it is possible to combine messages, as can be seen from the previous implementation descriptions. In this, one can send a message to the result of another, without first assigning its result to a variable. To achieve this, parentheses are used. For example, the expression

```
b ← (a at:1) value .
```

has the same effect as the two expressions

```
c ← a at: 1
b ← c value .
```

Parentheses can frequently be omitted. Parsing then occurs according to certain priority rules (see Goldberg & Robson, 1983).

2.3.2.2 Cascading

Several messages can be sent to one object in a single expression by *cascading* them. Cascading is performed by separating messages by semicolons:

```
aSequencableCollection addFirst: a; addFirst: b; addLast: c .
```

The last expression is identical to:

```
aSequencableCollection addFirst: a
aSequencableCollection addFirst: b
aSequencableCollection addLast: c .
```

2.3.2.3 Perform

There are sometimes situations where it is desirable to leave the type of message, used inside a method, undefined at definition time, and instantiate and change its pattern (selector, arguments) dynamically at execution time. For implementing this, a perform method with the selector perform:withArguments: is provided, defined for all objects. If, for example, the following expression is used within a method:

```
(1) anObject perform: aSelector withArguments: myArray .
```

and the receiver and the arguments are instantiated as

```
anObject ← myRectangle
aSelector ← #origin:corner:
myArray ← #( (50@50) (100@100)) .
```

then the expression (1) evaluates exactly as

```
myRectangle origin: (50@50) corner: (100@100) .
```

Note that the # sign is used for *symbols* —a special object class, used for names in the systems—for handling the message pattern origin:corner:. The same sign, followed by a sequence, is used for the *literal* representation of arrays—for handling the arguments of the above message.

The perform message allows us to leave open in a predefined method what actual message will be sent at the execution time of the method. Consequently, a flexible style of programming is made possible. We need this mechanism to realize *call-backs* in the graphics system GEO++ (cf. 8.3.9). Through call-backs an individual graphics object may be told what message it has to send back to an application as a reaction to a specific input-event. In the Smalltalk-80 environment, this technique is also used for reacting to an input event, but here for controlling menu events (cf. 3.2.5.2).

2.3.2.4 Triggering Messages By Dependency Relations

In the options for message passing discussed so far, the receiver of a message was always addressed—together with the message itself—by the sender. Smalltalk-80 supports mechanisms in which addressing the receiver and passing a message to it is handled by different components.

One component can establish a *dependency* between a sender a and receiver b by:

```
a addDependent: b .
```

In this case b is called *dependent* of a. The class of the receiver has to define a method with the pattern

```
update: aSymbol .
```

If, after these prearrangements, the object a receives a message with the selector changed: in the following manner:

```
a changed: aSymbol.
```

then this event automatically triggers

```
b update: aSymbol .
```

Thus the method update: aParameter is selected and executed. The procedure described here is used very frequently in the special case, where the changed message is sent to a by a itself. For example

```
self changed: #delete .
```

would cause triggering of a message update: #delete sent to its dependent. This mechanism is used in the Model-View-Controller triad for an indirect addressing scheme between an application object and its visual representation on a display medium, cf. 3.2.2.

2.3.3 Polymorphism

The ability to define messages with the same selector for different types of objects has already been mentioned above. In addition, it is allowed to instantiate an argument of a message with instances of different classes. An example for this can be found in our implementation description for Point, for instance in the method + delta where delta is allowed to be a point or a number. Inheritance, introduced in the next paragraph, is almost based on the principle of passing identical messages to instances of different classes. The feature allowing different classes to define message with identical selectors is called *polymorphism* (Ingalls, 1986; Cardelli & Wegner, 1985).

Polymorphism is used for flexible programming, making it very simple to code expressions that assign messages to instances of classes that are unknown at method generation time. The only requirement for applying this practice successfully is that the receiver understands these messages at method execution time.

In computer graphics, polymorphism may be used, for example, to realize an interactive graphics editor in the following manner: operations—such as attribute assignment, deletion, or transformations—to be applied to a picked object may be coded without prior knowledge of the exact class of the receiver, as long as the detected object (line, polyline, group) can understand it. The same principle of coding expressions for "unknown" object types is also used in object-oriented application frameworks (cf. Chap. 3) where "pre-manufactured products" must be extended by a customer. Similar techniques can be used for predefined kernels with hidden implementation, to be extended by subclassing (cf. Chap. 10).

Note that this flexibility also has disadvantages: a compiler cannot find as many programming errors as is possible in programming environments based on languages with strong typing, such as Pascal.

2.4 Inheritance

Classes in object-oriented languages form a hierarchy. A subclass is a specialization of their superclasses, and it inherits all their characteristics. Simple classes with rather general behavior characterize the higher levels of the hierarchy while more specific behavior is modeled in the lower levels of the class hierarchy.

The strict hierarchy of inheritance relationships can be extended to a graph of relationships. This is referred to as multiple inheritance.

2.4.1 Hierarchical Inheritance

A programming environment supporting (only) hierarchical inheritance requires that classes must be organized in a tree structure, i.e., for each class (except for the root) of the tree, exactly one directly super-ordinated class, the *direct superclass*, is defined, as it is illustrated in Fig. 2.6.

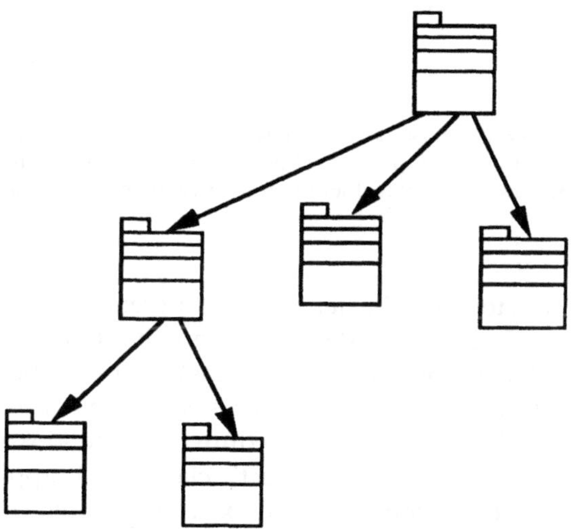

Fig. 2.6. Inheritance tree. In the case of hierarchical inheritance, as supported in Smalltalk-80, the classes are organized as a tree. Although hierarchical inheritance is not the most flexible concept supporting inheritance, it is very transparent because the rules for inheriting behavior from "parents" to "children" is very easy to understand.

Smalltalk-80 (in its basic concept) supports only hierarchical inheritance; the root of the hierarchy is the class Object.

2.4.1.1 *What are the Semantics of Inheritance?*

The semantics of inheritance mean that methods and variables of the superclass (including characteristics which the superclass itself has inherited from above) are valid for the subclass. In particular, all messages for which inherited methods exist can be sent to an object of a class, i.e., inheritance is a principle for organizing behavior.

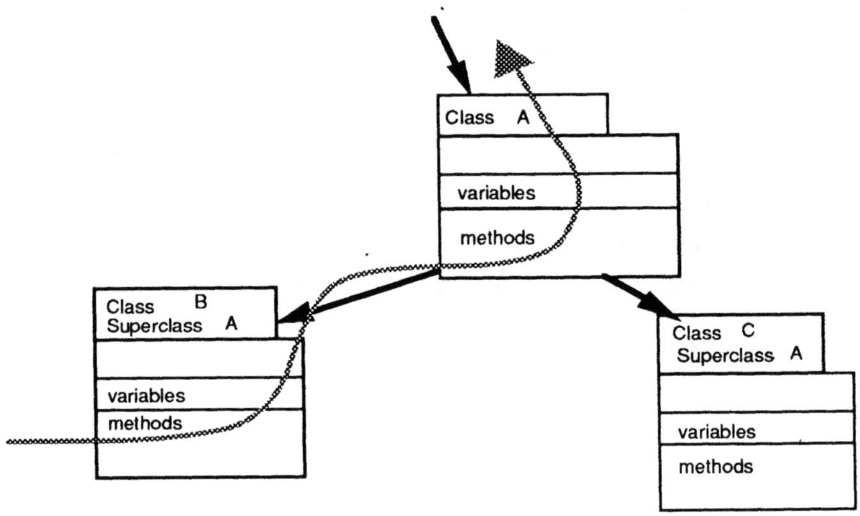

Fig. 2.7. Searching for inherited messages. If a message is sent to an object whose class owns no method for evaluating it, the search process follows the path defined by the inheritance tree. If several methods for the message exist further up in the tree, then the first one encountered along this path is evaluated.

Identical message selectors may be defined for different classes even if they occur in a class-superclass relation defined by the inheritance tree. To solve ambiguities a rule must be established for defining what method has to be applied to an object. This rule is defined for the Smalltalk-80 environment as follows: when a message is sent to an object, a search procedure is started looking for a matching selector. The procedure starts at the object's class and it applies the matching method if it exists. If no matching method exists, the search continues along the uniquely defined superclass chain until the first matching method is found. The search for a matching method is illustrated by Fig. 2.7.

The figure illustrates that several classes, in this example B and C, can inherit methods and variables from a common superclass. Inheritance provides a concept for sharing code. When the application programmer has to decide how to organize two different classes and integrate them in the existing inheritance tree, an analysis of their intended behavior is useful. The following questions should be answered:

- what functionality already provided by the existing environment can be used?
- what type of behavior common to both classes can be factored in one direct superclass common to both new classes?

The result of this consideration may lead to *three* new classes A, B, and C: a class A factorizing out common behavior and two different classes with "empty" common behavior, specific respectively to B and C. This type of system design is called *factorization*. The resulting classes B and C may be characterized against A by saying they add only special behavior to the functionality of A. Therefore, the generation of subclasses is often called *specialization*.

2.4.1.2 Overriding Inherited Methods

As mentioned already, the search for methods matching the selector of a message begins bottom-up. The special case, illustrated in Fig. 2.8, shows that the message myMessage: is implemented both for A and its subclass B. Therefore, when it is sent to an instance of B the method of B is responsible for evaluating it. In this case, the method for myMessage: in A which would be normally inherited from A to B was *overridden*.

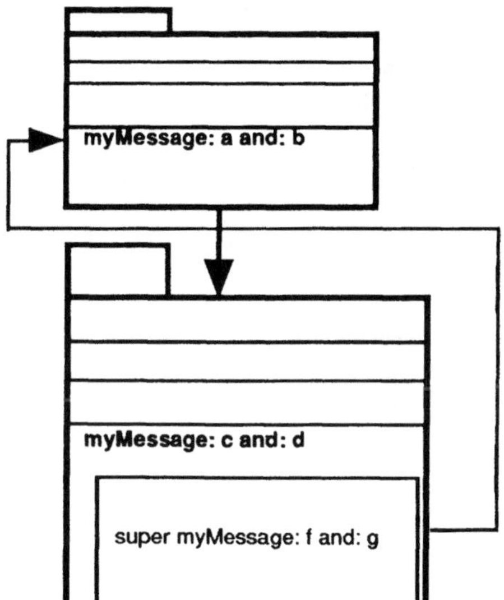

Fig. 2.8. A typical case of the use of super is shown. Here a subclass uses an inherited method in its own method with the same selector. One can therefore interpret the subclass' method as a kind of augmented—and not completely overridden—method.

2.4.1.3 The Pseudo-Variable super

The usual way of searching for methods along the superclass chain can be modified through the introduction of the pseudo-variable super. This refers to the receiver of the message, just as self does. In contrast to self, however, the search strategy for methods is different. When super is used in a method of a class the search begins *in the superclass of this class*. The search procedure is independent of the possible case that the receiver may be an instance of one of the subclasses of the class where super was used. The search rule is static in the sense that it is known at compile time what method will be evaluated if a message is sent to super. This is very different from the normal search procedure for self. Here the decision for method searching can be made only at execution time: only at this time is the exact class of self known, and this information is needed for defining the starting point of the normal search procedure as it was defined above ("start at the receiver's class!").

2.4.1.4 Examples for Method Search

If the pseudo-variables self and super are employed in more complex situations, then some careful thought must be given to the correct interpretation of the above definitions. Therefore the search rules through use of self and super are explained through more complex examples. Let A, B, and C be three classes, A the superclass of B and B the superclass of C, with the following methods.

---

class name	**A**
superclass	AClass
instance methods	

message1: arg1

statements A

...

---

class name	**B**
superclass	A
instance methods	

message1: arg1

statements

...

message2: arg2

statements

super message1: test .

```
self message1: test .
statements
...
```

---

class name	**C**
superclass	B
instance methods	

message1: arg1

statements for message1: in C

...

In the first example, we create

```
objectOfC ← C new .
```

and perform

```
objectOfC message2: arg .
```

In this case, the method defined in class B will be executed. In message2: of B the expression super message1: test will be reached and the super controls search in the sense that message1: in A is executed.

Now to the next expression in B. The expression self message1: test evaluates method message1: in C, because the receiver is instance of C and the normal search rule is valid.

In the second example, if we create

```
objectOfB ← B new .
```

and then execute

```
objectOfB message2: arg .
```

then super message1: test is handled as in the first case, that is, A is responsible. For the next expression, self message1: test, however, message1: in B is evaluated.

The example shows the difference of the two different search strategies quite clearly. The pseudovariables self and super are often used in the following context. Usually the classes higher in the hierarchy are predefined classes of the environment. In a growing system more and more subclasses are defined by the application programmer and added to the environment as subclasses of the predefined classes. In a growing system super should be preferable used for evaluating methods of classes which already exist at method generation time. The variable self, however, should be preferable used, when the result of the message sent to self is required for the final system, but when its method is as yet unknown or non-existent at code generation time. To complete the final system the missing method must be implemented by the application programmer in an application-dependent subclass. The last case happens often in predefined generic application frameworks, where, for example, messages for printing or displaying are applied to objects with unknown class membership, and the customer has to add methods to evaluate these messages.

2.4.1.5 Skipping a Method

The following question is posed on the basis of the constellation described above:

- How can a method in class C make use of a method message1: in a class AClass which is superclass of A?

If super message1: is used in a method of C, one always ends up in B. So one has to look for a procedure for skipping over the methods in B and in A and reaching the version defined in AClass.

Smalltalk-80 offers no mechanisms for method search beyond the ones we have mentioned. The advantage of the search strategy in Smalltalk-80 is that the inheritance strategy is easily defined, requiring few mechanisms and program constructs. However, it does at times cause problems that can only be solved with certain tricks. In our case, the jump can be forced by defining an additional method in A, which we name addMessage1: in the example.

We then define the expression super addMessage1: in C. This fulfills our purpose, but we have also to ensure that the selector addMessage1: is not used for a method of a class lying between C and A. We could also have accomplished the jump by using self in C. But using super in C has the advantage of "stability", i.e., we are free to use the selector addMessage1: in C or its subclasses. The principle is shown in the following implementation description.

---

class name	**A**
superclass	AClass
instance methods	

addMessage1: arg1

"message1: of AClass"

↑ super message1: arg1

---

class name	**C**
superclass	B
instance methods	

aMessage:...

"jump to method of C"

super addMessage1: anArgument

Why are we dependent on such tricks in the context of this book on computer graphics? The above mechanisms become necessary when the highest class, in this case AClass, is a class of a predefined graphics kernel system, with a hidden implementation. Then the counterpart of message1: could be a typical graphics method. If such a method was overridden in intermediate classes between a class in question and the kernel's class then skipping may be desired, and may be achieved by adding the counterpart of addMessage1: to the method protocol *of the direct user defined subclass* (i.e., the counterpart of A) of the predefined kernel class.

2.4.2 Multiple Inheritance

The strategy of multiple inheritance is not directly supported by Smalltalk-80. But there are some augmented versions of Smalltalk-80 with multiple inheritance based on the extension described by Borning & Ingalls, 1982.

In case of hierarchical inheritance described in the last section, behavior is inherited from an uniquely defined inheritance chain. More flexibility is provided by *multiple inheritance* where a subclass may inherit from several superclasses as illustrated in Fig. 2.9. Limitations of hierarchical inheritance—also arising in graphics applications (cf. 5.6.1.2)—may be solved almost completely by means of multiple inheritance.

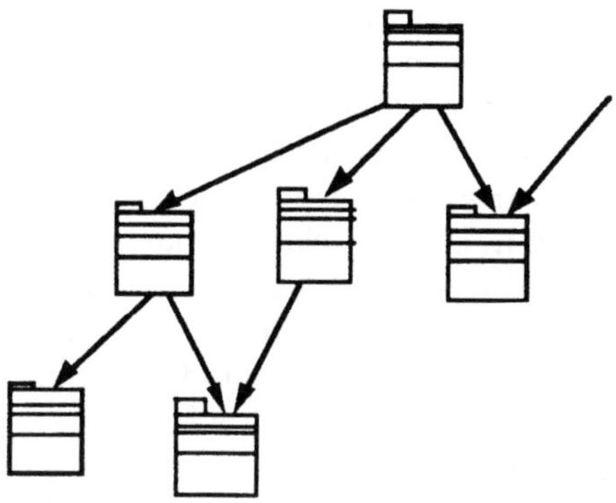

Fig. 2.9. Inheritance graph. With multiple inheritance, data and methods can be inherited from more than one superclass. Inheritance relations are then organized by an inheritance graph. Because of possible naming conflicts, additional concepts to guide inheritance must be introduced.

2.5 The Smalltalk-80 Programming Environment

In this section, selected components of the Smalltalk-80 environment are described for a better understanding of the programming code used in the examples.

With multiple inheritance, however, a new problem arises. Which search strategy for methods should be applied in the inheritance graph? There is no longer a unique path in the inheritance chain. Problems arise when methods of identical message patterns are available in both parents. Therefore, it is required to specify explicit rules for method adoption in order to avoid search conflicts in the case of identical message selectors. Thus no messages can be sent to super, for example, since there is more than one superclass as a rule. The concept of multiple inheritance therefore implies an additional complexity leading to the result that the available systems differ with respect to the facilities they provide for controlling method search. The Flavor system on the Lisp machines even permit the definition of cyclic inheritance paths (Weinreb, Moon et. al., 1987). Nevertheless, it is important to state that the combination of methods from different superclasses is quite reasonable and desirable in system construction.

2.5.1 Programmers' Support in Smalltalk-80

Application programmers are supported by two important components of the Smalltalk-80 environment: a user-friendly interface for creation and testing of programs, and a rich and elaborated set of predefined classes and methods.

2.5.1.1 The User Interface

The basis of the Smalltalk-80 user interface is a window-oriented raster graphics system with a mouse as the primary graphics input device. Programming is supported by a comfortable editor, diverse tools for testing and a browser. Essentially all tools in the Smalltalk-80 system are object-oriented. Even elementary editing operations are implemented as messages, passed to objects.

Object-oriented programming consists of naming new classes, inserting them into an existing class-hierarchy by specifying their superclasses, and defining instance variables, class variables and methods (that is, producing the corresponding code). In addition, existing classes may be modified by changing or deleting parts of their methods, or by adding new methods. Programming in Smalltalk-80 is usually an incremental process. It can be viewed as a series of modifications of an existing world of classes and methods.

The process of changing a class definition by using the editor is also implemented as message passing to the describing object of the class, the class's *metaclass*. A class's metaclass is automatically generated by the environment. Usually this creation is visible from the outside. There exists, however, the possibility of sending messages directly to a metaclass in cases of deep intervention into the Smalltalk-80 system. It is a way of circumventing the usual manner of defining a method through editing. Such uncommon operations are necessary, for example, if a class definition, i.e., its variables and methods, is to be modified dynamically during the execution of a program. With similar deep interventions into the Smalltalk-80 system, important components of the system's behavior can be modified, e.g., the inheritance strategy. New programming concepts such as the introduction of prototypes could also be realized in this way, as Borning has shown (Borning, 1986). It should be pointed out, however, that normally the definition of a class is not dynamically modified: a class definition remains stable during runtime. In contrast, the generation of instances is a highly dynamic process.

The usual practice of programming in Smalltalk-80 consists of the well-known steps: code-writing, test, and execution of the completed program. The process of programming, however, differs from the use of a conventional system because of the great number of predefined classes and methods, the comfortable editor and especially the possibilities provided by inheritance: taking over predefined functionality and modifying it to fit current needs. Object-oriented programming is characterized by a high degree of re-use and modification of existing code. This style of programming—described in its cognitive aspects in Fischer, 1987—is a new experience for the programmer accustomed to working in a conventional environment.

2.5.1.2 Predefined Classes and Methods

The Smalltalk-80 environment provides an abundant hierarchy of predefined classes and methods, organized by a tree with the class Object at its root. All classes are subclasses of Object, including the metaclasses mentioned above. Object is supplied with a large number of methods that are useful for almost all classes, as for example the method copy for copying an object. The Smalltalk-80 environment contains over 200 classes with nearly 5000 methods, including the graphics kernel.

2.5.2 Frequently Used Classes and Methods

Let us first discuss several collection classes and some of the control structures made available by them.

2.5.2.1 Collection Classes

Collection classes are subclasses of the class Collection that are made available by the environment. Collection and its subclasses describe all techniques to collect any objects—sets, arrays, etc.—twenty in all. The variety to provide so many different options is due to the programmers' requirement to be able to specify exactly—in the sense of not to few and not too many—that class required by the problem at hand. So if the nature of an application is based on the existence of a set (without any ordering relation) of graphics objects, Smalltalk-80 provides the class Set for mapping the application structure to a structure of the programming environment. Using the class OrderedCollection would be an over-specification. On the other hand, the class Bag, which models a multi-set, would not be specific enough, because it does not check whether an element to be added is already contained in the collection. In later examples, the classes Array, Dictionary, OrderedCollection, Set will be used, so we proceed with some examples of these.

```
aSet ← Set new .                    "Generate a new set"
```

```
aSet add: 'hi'; 'hallo' .                "Add the strings 'hi' and 'hallo' "

isItIn ← aSet includes: 'hi' .           "Check whether the string 'hi' is element
                                         of aSet. Answer the boolean object (with
                                         value true or false) isItIn"

aSet remove: 'hi' .                      "Remove element from set"
```

An array has a fixed length and is accessed by integer keys starting with 1.

```
myArray ← Array new: 3 .                 "Create an array of length 3, and
                                         insert three strings by cascading:"

myArray at: 1 put: 'hi' ; at: 2 put: 'hallo'; at:3 put: 'GKS' .
```

The last two operations are equivalent to the literal representation of an array:

```
myArray ← #('hi' 'hallo' 'GKS') .
```

An OrderedCollection is a two-sided stack:

```
aCollection ← OrderedCollection new .          "After the last operation, only 'GMD'
aCollection addFirst: 'hi'; addLast: 'GMD' .   is left in the stack."
aCollection removeFirst .
```

For ordered collections and arrays, the binary message denoted by the comma-selector is used to concatenate them. By combination of the comma messages we can then create:

```
combinedSequence ← a, b, c, d .
```

A Dictionary is a collection of key/value pairs. The key must be unique. Such a key/value pair is an instance of Association. Here are some examples to illustrate the principle:

```
aDict ← Dictionary new .
anAssociation ← aDict at: 'a' put: 'hallo' .
aDict at: 'b' put: 'hi' .
aDict at: 'c' put. 'GKS' .
aString ← aDict at: 'b' .
aKey ← aDict keyAtValue: 'hi' .
aDict removeAssociation: anAssociation .
```

After insertion of an object into a collection, the object itself and not a copy of it, is contained in the collection. This will be explained by an example. Assume that an attribute was assigned to an object with the unary message with attribute: and that the message attribute serves for inquiring the attribute. We construct:

```
anObject attribute: 'green' .
aGroup ← Dictionary new .
aGroup at: aKey put: anObject .
anObject attribute: 'red' .
```

```
aValue ← aGroup at: aKey .
aValue attribute .
```

Because of the identity of the inserted object with anObject, the last method returns the value 'red'.

2.5.2.2 Blocks and Control Structures

A block is a sequence of expressions. Even a block is, somewhat surprisingly, an object in Smalltalk-80, specifically an instance of the class Block. A block expression consists of a sequence of expressions separated by periods and delimited by square brackets.

Control structures in Smalltalk-80 are evaluated by messages to instances of the class Boolean (or of its subclasses True and False). The arguments here are blocks. The most important control structures are *conditional selection* and *conditional repetition*. (Goldberg & Robson, 1983).

Conditional selection is provided with the message to a boolean object with the selectors ifTrue:IfFalse:, ifFalse:IfTrue:, ifFalse:, and ifTrue:. An example:

```
(1) myPolyLine color = 'green'
(2)   ifTrue: [ expression1. expression 2. ...]
(3)   ifFalse: [ expressions ] .
```

In (1) the equality message delivers as result the boolean constant true or false; depending on the result either the first (2) or the second block (3) is evaluated.

Conditional repetition is iterated depending on the truth value of a receiving block (see the example in 4.5.).

2.5.2.3 Enumerations

Collection classes provide a further construct that is very useful for programming: the *enumeration messages*. They are used to define do-loops, for example. To support the control structures associated with enumeration messages, a block can be supplied with a *block argument*. Syntactically, such an element is introduced by adding an identifier at the beginning of a block, preceded by a colon. The block argument is separated from the expression following by a vertical bar. As an example for an enumeration message, the do-loop is realized by sending the do: message to a collection. The argument of do: is a block with a block argument, in the following example identifyed by eachPrimitive. We begin with a set myPrimitives of objects, each assumed to understand the message color:.

The expression

```
myPrimitives do: [ :eachPrimitive | eachPrimitive color: 'green' ] .
```

applies the messages color: 'green' to each element of the set.

An ascending sequence of integers is also a collection. It can be created by sending an integer a to: message. So

```
1 to: 10 do: [ :i | ...statements ...] .
```

causes the variable i to be incremented from 1 to 10.

The messages select: and collect: are also useful. The *selection* message defines a subset of all elements of the receiver, if there associated block values evaluate to true:

```
detectAndGreenSet ← myPrimitives select:
        [ :each | (each detectable) and: (each color = 'green') ] .
```

The collection message allows to define a collection of the block values evaluated for each element of the receiver:

```
myContents ← myObjects collect: [ :each | each content ] .
```

2.5.3 Messages Understood by All Objects

Smalltalk-80 offers several useful messages that can be applied to all or almost all objects; a few of these messages will be introduced in this paragraph. Methods for evaluating the messages described here are defined in class Object or specialized in some of its subclasses

2.5.3.1 Comparison

There are two methods for testing the identity of two object identifiers, == and =. The value returned by these messages is either true or false.

```
a == b
```

results in true, if a and b represent the same object. As a rule, the results of

```
a = b
```

is implementation dependent and usually delivers true if the instance variables of two different objects are identical. So, for example, two different collections c1 and c2 may represent the same component, i.e., the expression c1 = c2 will be evaluated to true, if the identical object has been inserted as element:

```
c1 ← OrderedCollection new .
c2 ← OrderedCollection new .
c1 addFirst: 'GMD-F3' .
c2 addFirst: 'GMD-F3' .
```

Note that c1 and c2 are different objects, which may be edited independently, and as a consequence of being different, the expression c1 == c2 evaluates to false.

2.5.3.2 Testing Functionality

The functionality of an object may be tested in different ways.

```
a isKindOf: AClass .
```

returns true if the class of a is AClass or if it is one of its subclasses.

```
a isMemberOf: MyClass .
```

tests for direct membership. The inquiry message class passed to a, i.e.,

```
myClass ← a class .
```

returns the class of a. This method was used in the implementation description of the method intersect: in Rectangle in the way that the unary message class delivers the class, so that class method origin:corner: could be used for creating a new rectangle:

```
intersection ← (self class)
  origin: (origin max: aRectangle origin)
  corner: (corner min: aRectangle corner) .
```

Note that this method is different from

```
intersection ← Rectangle
  origin: (origin max: aRectangle origin)
  corner: (corner min: aRectangle corner) .
```

The last method would always create an instance of Rectangle, whereas the first method would consider the possibility of defining subclasses of Rectangle, and in this case the method class would deliver the intersection as instance of the receiver's class.

2.5.4 Multiple References, Copy Methods

Smalltalk-80 provides mechanisms that allow multiple use of same or identical information. Different variables may be used as identifiers pointing to the identical object. Such a reference may be replaced by a new one, if an object identifier appears on the left hand side of an assignment (←).

Even though the referencing mechanism is the normal means of naming in object-oriented systems, we mention it because it is useful for graphics systems. In object-oriented systems, graphics primitives are objects that can be modified by changing their internal state, e.g., by applying new attributes or coordinates. Primitives are repeatedly inserted into more complex aggregates to build up graphical object hierarchies. If the internal state of the object is changed, the new state is is shared by all components of the graphics system where a reference to the object was established before. That is, all variables that refer to the object in question now refer to its new state. This is a very elementary fact, but it should not be forgotten. To illustrate multiple reference by an example, we execute the following expressions where an object is inserted in a collection and then its internal state changed by

```
anObject attribute: 'green' .
aGroup ← Dictionary new .
aGroup at: aKey put: anObject .
anObject attribute: 'red' .
aValue ← aGroup at: aKey .
aValue attribute .
```

Because of the identity between the inserted object and anObject, the last method delivers by inquiring the internal state of aGroup returns 'red' although no update message has been sent directly to aGroup. If this strong coupling is to be avoided one must first create a copy of anObject and then insert the copy into aGroup.

Besides referencing from different "locations", e.g., instance variables of different objects to the identical object, three different copy operations are desirable for graphics systems. Two copy operations are already provided in Smalltalk-80 (deepCopy, shallowCopy); the third operation can be easily implemented, we call it deepGraphCopy.

The basic idea of all three methods is that a new object of the identical class is generated as copy; the copy has the same or identical internal state immediately after execution of the copy operation. Each of the individual objects—original and duplicate—can then be changed by passing messages to it without any effect to the other one. The three copy methods differ in the aspect that the relationships between their internal states are different.

2.5.4.1 Shallow Copy

The method shallow copy is defined by producing identical instance variables. As an example, a dictionary is created and two insertions using two objects are performed:

```
aHouse ← Dictionary new .
aHouse at: #left put: aWindow .
aHouse at: #middle put: aDoor' .
aHouse at: #right put: aWindow .
```

With the help of the shallowCopy operation, we now generate:

```
aHouse1 ← aHouse shallowCopy .
```

The new copy has identical instance variables, as shown in Fig. 2.10.

The duplicate may now be modified arbitrarily. We insert a new object into the duplicate using the symbol #left as key.

```
aHouse1 at: #left put: aNewWindow .
```

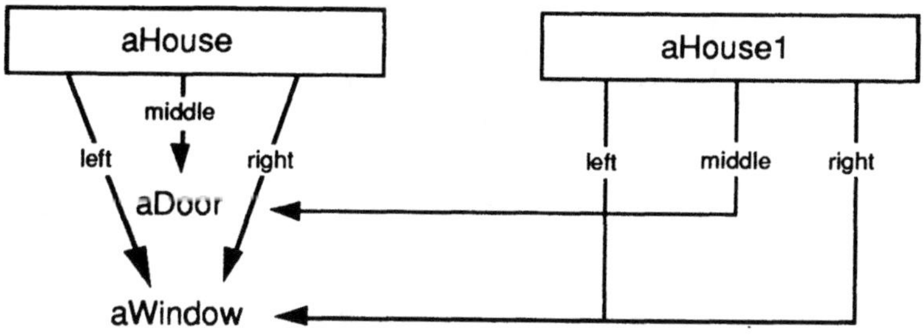

Fig. 2.10. Result of shallow copy. This type of copy operation delivers a copy sharing the instance variables of the original.

The last insertion results in the structure illustrated in Fig. 2.11.

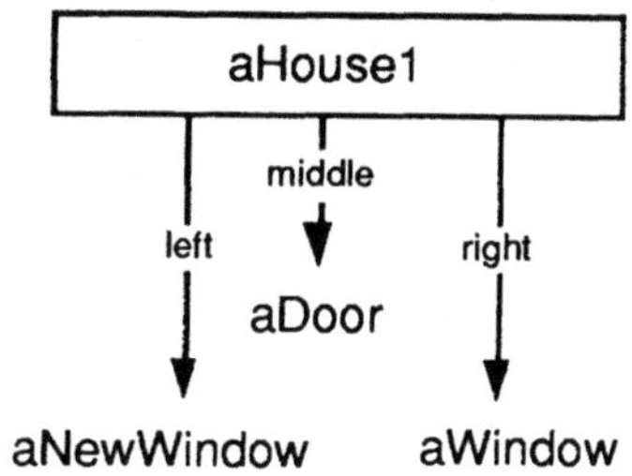

Fig. 2.11. New messages can be sent to a copy without any effect to the original.

If we now change the state of aWindow:

```
aWindow color: 'green' .
```

then the state of aHouse and aHouse1 changes at three points. Note that the same effect may be reached by the following operation:

```
(aHouse1 at: #right ) color: 'green' .
```

Shallow copy can be advantageously used in computer graphics when two different graphics objects have to share thè same geometric description (cf. 8.3.8).

2.5.4.2 Deep Copy

Deep copy creates a new object with different instance variables (only at a very deep level are elementary objects such as numbers shared). If we create:

```
aHouse2 ← aHouse deepCopy .
```

then we obtain the following picture. The fact that aHouse refers to the same window twice was not regarded by the operation.

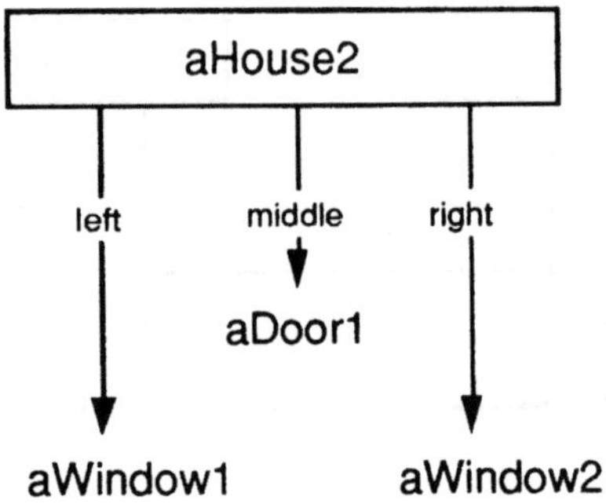

Fig. 2.12. Result of a deep copy, generating completely new objects as instance variables.

2.5.4.3 Deep Graph Copy

In computer graphics, we also need a variation of deep copy which checks whether several instance variables of the original share identical information and which keeps this in mind and uses this knowledge for reproducing this knowledge to the deep copy's instances:

```
aHouse3 ← aHouse deepGraphCopy .
```

The effect becomes quite clear in Fig. 2.13, which shows the difference from the deep copy operation.

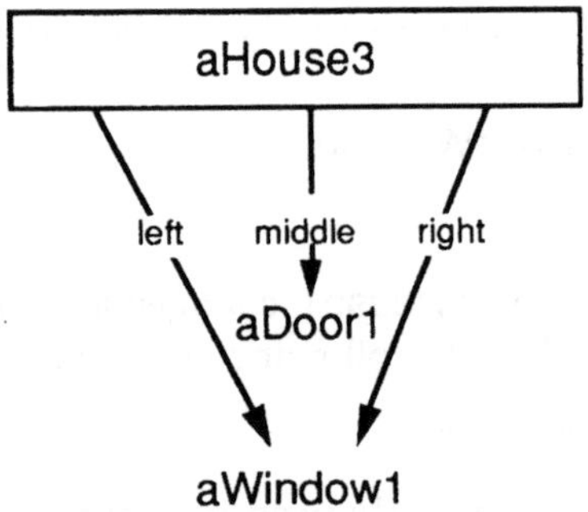

Fig. 2.13. Result of deep graph copy. The copy has its own instance variable and shares it in the same way as the original.

So the result of the following expression is true:

```
aHouse3 at: #left == aHouse3 at: #right .
```

In computer graphics, the last operation is the most natural operation for producing a deep copy of a graphics object hierarchy that maintains the knowledge about shared sub-hierarchies.

2.6 Summary of the Basic Concepts

The main characteristics of object-oriented programming can be summarized as follows:

- **Objects:** every entity in an object-oriented system is an object. An object may be regarded as a collection of its internal data, invisible from the outside, representing its present state. An object is addressed by one or several identifiers establishing references to it.
- **Messages:** objects are addressed by messages defined for the specific object. The object as a receiver of a message has different possibilities of reacting to a message. It may change its local state; it may send further messages to other objects (or to itself); it may return a value, i.e., another object, as a result.
- **Methods:** the reaction to receiving a message is to evaluate the method assigned to it.
- **Classes:** every object is an instance of a class and behaves as specified in the class definition (i.e., the methods are defined here). The class therefore describes which messages an object may receive and how the corresponding methods are evaluated.
- **Instance and class variables:** the internal state of an object is represented by instance and class variables. While instance variables contain information of an individual object, class variable are used for storing information common to all instances of a class and accessible by them.
- **Class methods:** in (most) object-oriented systems, classes are objects by themselves. Consequently, methods may define as well for classes.
- **Inheritance:** important characteristics of object-oriented systems are the inheritance mechanisms they provide. When creating a new class, classes from which inheritance is to be permitted may be defined. Inheritance means that both variables and methods are provided for instances of subclasses.
- **Hierarchical and multiple inheritance:** there are different inheritance mechanisms. With hierarchical inheritance, only one direct superclass from which inheritance is possible may be defined, resulting in an inheritance tree. With multiple inheritance several classes from which inheritance is possible may be defined for a new class, resulting in a directed graph describing the inheritance relations.

The above summary is valid mainly for all object-oriented approaches relying on the instance-class principle. There are however object-oriented system concepts that considerably differ from this. The *prototype-delegation* principle that will be discussed in Chap. 11. is an example for a substantially different object-oriented concept. Stefik and Bobrow (1985) lists over fifty different object-oriented approaches. There are, fortunately, a number of common characteristics in spite of the almost immense diversity. Most issues in object-oriented graphics presented in this book are based on the common characteristics, but the consequences for switching to a prototype-delegation system are discussed.

The common basic concepts of object-oriented languages are as follows:

- Each object may store its private information, which may change incrementally over time.
- Each object is defined by its own behavior, which is embodied in methods.
- Each object may communicate with other objects. Each object may request information from other objects.
- Objects may inherit behavior, i.e., they may import predefined functionality and possibly refine it.

3 Object-Oriented Interface Architecture

Although the architectural concepts presented here are not only applicable in the context of computer graphics, they are nevertheless relevant for the development of interactive graphics applications. Object-oriented application frameworks as a prefabricated implementation, realized in the form of a generic application, are an important aid for the developer in order to realize an executable application quickly. The Model-View-Controller model in Smalltalk-80, the MVC-triad, shows how a first version of an interactive user interface can be implemented, and how it may be improved without having to change any portions of code of the application behind the interface. In this sense the MVC triad can be seen as a new concept for modularization of interactive systems. Both concepts, the application framework and the MVC model, may be combined. They constitute an improvement for the design and implementation of interactive systems.

3.1 Application Framework as Generic Application

The examples, presented so far, for inheritance were concerned with reusing and possibly overriding predefined methods by creating subclasses. The result of such a process is a new class that can be used again in the same way. In this scenario, the following thought is in the foreground: use a given class to simplify the generation of a new one.

It may seem somewhat surprizing that inheritance can be use to modifying a dynamic process, i.e., a complete executable application, without directly changing its code. Based on this capability of inheritance—which we prove later—the following thoughts led to the idea of a *generic application*:

- A prefabricated executable application, adaptable by the application programmer to its special application, should be preferred to a "dead" set of subroutines.
- In an executable application the control module could be implemented by the producer of the framework, freeing the application programmer from the burden of implementing the most complex part of an application.
- The final application could then be constructed in an iterative process by modifying an existing application.

3.1.1 Disadvantages of Conventional Toolboxes

When a toolbox is used, only a set of existing routines (or classes in the object-oriented world) is made available. Applications programming then consists of the following steps:

- Writing a new main program that models the application's process as a whole.
- Using the toolbox to call predefined functionality implemented in individual submodules.
- In an object-oriented environment use of inheritance to benefit from existing functionality when designing new classes.

The disadvantage of the toolbox approach lies in the fact that the control module must be developed from scratch.

3.1.2 Modification of an Existing Application

How can object-oriented methods be used to modify an existing, executable application, as stated above? We illustrate the basic principle through an example showing (schematically) the management of a mouse event in different layers of the system. The example is adopted from the MacApp application framework (Schmucker, 1986).

Assume that an object-oriented, generic application "transports"—triggered by a mouse event—the position of the mouse from the screen to a window and from there to the actual application. The predefined classes involved in the mouse handling process are Screen, Window, and Application. All three classes own a method event:. We assume that the predefined methods simply perform a coordinate transformation, from screen coordinates to window coordinates, and from window coordinates to application (world) coordinates. In this manner the position is transformed from position1 to position2 to position3.

We now modify the predefined mouse handling process by the following steps. For the three predefined classes the respective subclasses MyScreen, MyWindow, and MyApplication are defined and the event: method is overridden for all these classes, as shown the description below. The desired application-dependent reaction to an event is implemented: for MyScreen overriding consists (in this special example) of analyzing the mouse position, and in deciding in case of several windows, which one should become the actual window. The actual window is used as argument of the predefined class method window: (of class Window), so that the right window may be inquired by screen using the predefined class method window of Window.

The following (fragmentary) overview of the implementation description, to be implemented by the application programmer, shows how the principle works.

Partial Implementation Description of the Application Programmer's Classes

class name	**MyScreen**	
superclass	**Screen**	
instance methods		
event: position1		"mouse event in screen coordinates, called by framework"

```
| actualWindow |

statements for my special application
such as definition of the actual window

Window window: actualWindow          "initialize class Window"

↑ super event: position1             "back to generic application"
```

```
class name          MyWindow
superclass          Window
instance methods

event: position2
                                    "mouse event in window coordinates,
                                    called by framework"

    statements for my special application

    MyApplication application: myApplication    "initialize class Application"

    ↑ super event: position2
                                    "back to generic application"
```

```
class name          MyApplication
superclass          Application
instance methods

event: position3
                                    "mouse event in world coordinates, called
                                    by framework"
    reaction of my special application to mouse event
    • • • here the code is found for the real special application • • •
    • • •
    • • •
```

As shown, after execution of the application programmers method, the generic application executes its own method forwarding the event to the object actualWindow. Note that the described procedure can be implemented in such a way that the application remains executable even if one of the subclasses is left out. In this case, the event is passed to instances that are initialized as a default.

The predefined application framework, which is hidden to the application programmer, may be implemented as shown by the following description.

Partial Implementation Description of the Predefined Generic Application

class name	**Screen**
instance variable names	actualScreen
instance methods	

event: screenPosition "Transform mouse position from screen coordinates into window coordinates, by inquiring the actual window's coordinate system"

```
| theWindow |

theWindow ← Window window          "inquire actual window"

calculate window position

theWindow event: windowPosition
```

---

class name	**Window**
instance variable names	actualWindow
instance methods	

event: windowPosition "Transform mouse position from window coordinates into world coordinates, by inquiring the actual application's coordinate system"

```
| theApplication |

theApplication ← Application application          "inquire actual application"

calculate application position

theApplication event: applicationPosition
```

instance methods for inquiring window

window "deliver actual window"

```
↑ actualWindow
```

```
class name                          Application
instance variable names             actualApplication
instance methods

event: applicationPosition          "mouse event in world coordinates deliv-
                                    ers error message if not overridden by
                                    subclass (or alternatively any thumb
                                    dummy application)"

    self error: ' must be overridden by special application'


instance methods for inquiring application

application                         "deliver actual application"

    ↑ actualApplication
```

Figure 3.1 shows the system components of the whole application. Note that in difference to traditional systems the predefined component, delivered by the producer, is an application, and the user defined portion is merely a set of subclasses, used in the same way as a subroutine package.

3.1.3 The Generic Application

A generic application used for designing real interactive applications must contain much more than is schematically shown in the last paragraph. All of the functionality common to (almost) all applications that should be developed for a given system should be predefined. Specific applications can then be implemented by using inheritance, adding new methods, and overriding existing methods of the generic application.

The power of a generic application can be explained by a metaphor: using an interface toolkit is like building a house from scratch, whereby a lot of guidelines have to be followed. Using a generic application is like starting with a complete standard house, already following the guidelines, and adding some specific modifications, as illustrated in Fig. 3.2.

The concept of an application framework has the following advantages:

- Guidelines for the user interface in a broader context can be not only written on paper, but can be implemented in software. Thus, a uniform interface can be guaranteed to a large extent, even in the case where different application programmers produce software for one system.
- The time required for implementing an individual application can be considerably reduced.
- Because there is a common framework, better integration and cooperation among different components is possible.

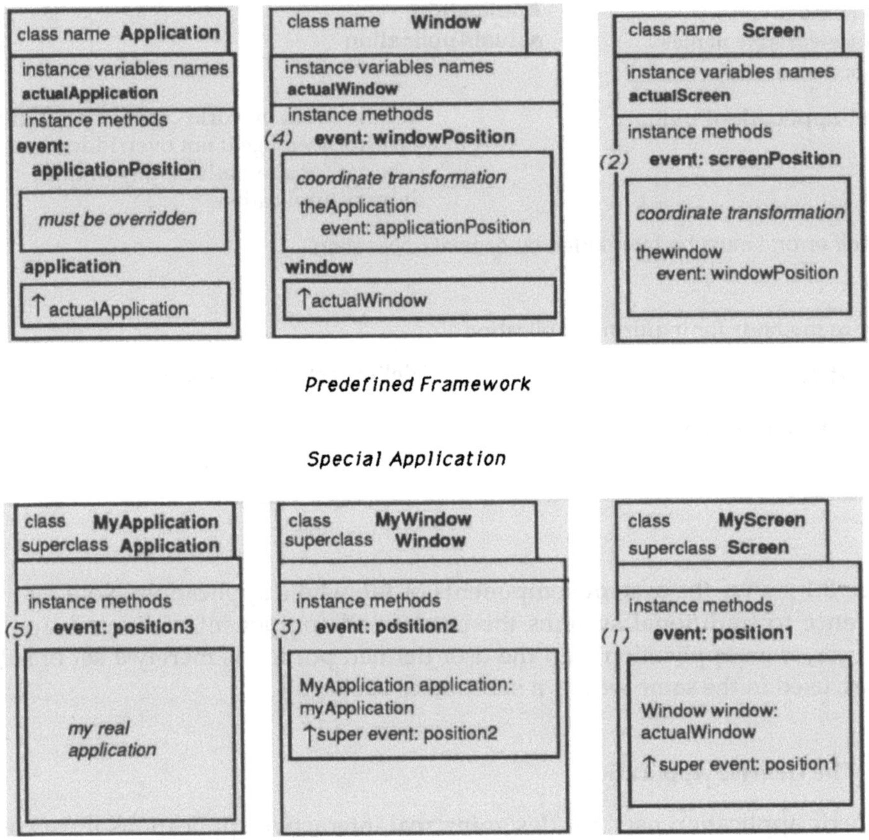

Fig. 3.1. Modification of an existing generic application application The illustration shows how a predefined application can be extended by subclasses defined by the application programmer. The attached numbers show the main control flow. It can be seen that the specific application part is automatically integrated in the generic application by addressing the event to super.

3.1.4 GINA – A Generic Interactive Application

The most well-known application framework is the generic application MacApp, implemented in Object Pascal. ET++ is its counterpart based on C++ (Weinand, Gamma, and Marty, 1988). We have followed through a similar development at our institute, called GINA (Generic Interactive Application) (Berlage, 1990). In the following, GINA is used to illuminate the functionality of current generic applications.

GINA is an object-oriented application framework written in CommonLisp (Keene, 1989). It is based on an interface between CommonLisp and the OSF/Motif software (Berlage, 1990). The concepts of GINA are similar to those of MacApp, and the resulting applications have a lot of similarities with typical Macintosh applications. The generic interactive application is executable from the beginning and provides a complete graphics user-interface, but lacks any application-specific behavior. New applications are created by defining subclasses of GINA classes and adding or overriding methods.

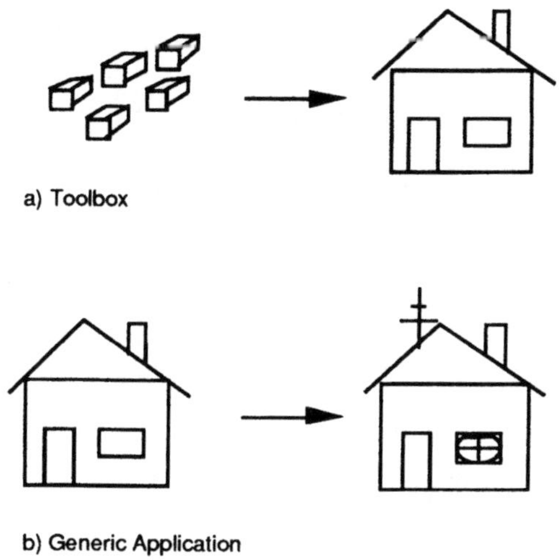

Fig. 3.2. Toolkit vs. generic application. In the toolkit approach, an interactive application must be built up from scratch. A generic application can be compared to order a standard house and add some specific components.

3.1.4.1 The Empty Application

New applications are developed starting with the (empty) generic application. The programmer can work with an executable application from the very beginning, and newly added features can be tested immediately. In connection with a powerful Lisp environment an incremental programming style is supported.

The empty application already contains a lot of functionality that can be inherited by other applications:

- A main window (shell) representing a document is displayed. It contains the names of the application and the document as a title and can be resized, moved, zoomed, and turned into an icon.
- The menu bar already contains the standard commands new, open, close, save, save as, revert, print, and quit.
- The window can be scrolled using the two scrollbars.
- Multiple documents, each with its own window, can be created.
- Documents can be saved in a file and existing documents can be opened again using predefined dialogs to select a file. The current size of the shell is stored automatically.
- Documents can be started from a *finder,* because they know which application can handle them.
- The document contents can be printed.

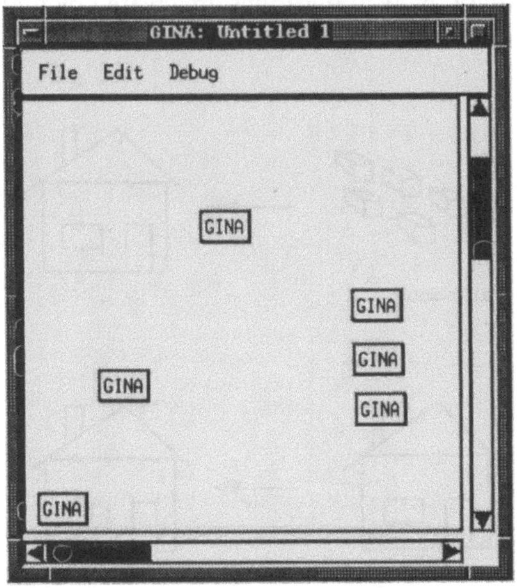

Fig. 3.3. Screen dump of the empty application. The standard functionality of a typical application is already implemented in the empty application. Only application specific differences to the standard application have to be coded. For example, commands for opening, closing, saving and creating new documents are already available. The programmer only has to write a method to translate the document contents into a stream of characters and vice versa. In addition the window can be scrolled using the two scrollbars, and complete handling of coordinate transformations between screen and window is supported by the empty application.

- The debug menu contains entries to inspect the current state of the most important CLOS objects that make up the empty application. Following the pointers to further objects, the complete internal state of an application can be inspected. Each widget shown at the surface can be inspected by a special mouse click.
- Finally, the window contains some buttons labeled "GINA", which will beep when they are pressed. The behavior of the buttons can be overridden by the application.

The functionality of the empty application reveals a certain common model on which many applications are based. It is closely related to the Macintosh application model. As the Macintosh shows, the model is sufficiently general to cover nearly all types of applications.

GINA also contains an application-independent undo/redo mechanism with unlimited history. The current application overrides the predefined command object by implementing an (application-dependent) undo method. The user can call undo- and redo-operations using the undo and redo entries in the edit menu. However, the history can become quite long and it may be necessary to go back a long way. Therefore, GINA also offers a history scroller as an alternative user interface.

Using the history-scroller, a sequence of commands can be replayed much in the same way as a video movie.

3.1.5 Generic Applications and Graphics Systems

As will become clear in 8.3.10.3 an object-oriented graphics system can be used without any problems together with a generic application. Such a graphics system consists of a set of predefined classes and methods, and its functionality can be used for specializing and adding methods in the context of a generic application. In particular, an integration of graphics systems into existing interface frameworks supporting window managers and menus is possible in a convenient way.

3.2 The Model-View-Controller Triad

The Model-View-Controller concept (MVC) is the most important concept in the Smalltalk-80 programming environment for designing user interfaces. Unfortunately the MVC concept is not discussed in the otherwise outstanding publications (Goldberg & Robson, 1983; Goldberg, 1984) since a special book planned for the design of user interfaces has not yet been published. In the meantime a small booklet is available, giving advice on how to use the concept (Krasner & Pope, 1989).

One of the objectives pursued by the MVC concept is a modularization of the system components—application, input, and output. The MVC concepts supports the idea of a strong separation between these three components, especially for creating different versions of user interfaces for one application.

The MVC concept is more than a pure concept. Because of its many predefined classes, it may be regarded as a elegant toolbox for interface design. Furthermore—due to its predefined communication paths between the different components—aspects of a generic application are also supplied by MVC.

3.2.1 Separation of the Interface

The statements listed in a typical interactive graphics application program can be distinguished into three types of code:

- code that handles the internal data and operations of the "actual" application, isolated from any display operations on the screen,
- code that is directly concerned with graphics output or input, i.e., the direct procedure calls of the graphics kernel's functionality,
- code for mediating between the application model and the interface. Mediating includes the initial construction of a display and the mapping of input operations as a result of user interaction into modified states of the application. It should be noted that the mapping process may be very complex and may include complex geometric modeling operations.

3.2.1.1 Problems with Traditional Systems

Let us consider a typical layer model where an application calls the functions of a graphics kernel by subroutine calls. The application program uses the existing graphics procedures for creating a graphics representation. Therefore, the implementation of the kernel's internal functionality is modularized and invisible. The application program doesn't need knowledge as to how the procedure renders the requested service. However, the *calls* of the graphics procedures (both for output and input) and the construction of the drawing—i.e., the transforming of states of the application into appropriate sequences of operations provided by the graphics kernel—belong to the code of the application program.

The mixture of different types of code—as is illustrated in Fig. 3.4— has serious disadvantages. It is often desired to design a new user interface or change an existing one of an existing and stable application. New or modified interfaces are required when first experiences with preliminary versions suggest an improvement of the interface. Usually, the application is to remain completely unchanged in its inherent logic. However, the style of presentation and the use of interactive modules, i.e., the mediating process must be modified. Therefore, it would be highly desirable to have an new kind of interface architecture, separating the code for describing an application from portions of code which are responsible for display construction and interaction.

Simple and well-known as the goal for achieving a modularization of the mentioned components may be, it may be difficult to fulfill as long as traditional systems are used. Traditional systems do not provide coexistent objects with flexible communication patterns and they fall short in advanced control mechanisms. What can be reached by using object-oriented systems is quite a lot better as we will show.

3.2.1.2 Separation of the Interface in Object-Oriented Systems

The result of this paragraph will be anticipated. Object-oriented systems provide a separation facility which works as follows:

- Representation of the application component and the display component (including the mediating component) as two separate objects in the sense of object-oriented systems.
- Realization of the application without any direct reference to the display component.

The separation can be reached in object-oriented systems through the following two steps, which will be described in detail by the example of the Model-View-Controller concept of Smalltalk-80:

- *Flexible communication* with mutual message passing between the two partners, application and display. This style of communication is possible because in object-oriented systems, objects may be coexistent, and mutual communication can be defined easily.
- *External handling* of graphics input and output. The term *external* was used by Szekely who explained and discussed the whole ideas of separation in great

detail (Szekely, 1987). Here the entire display of application objects is handled outside application objects. The basic idea is that application objects do not directly send messages to the graphics kernel system. Instead, they use trigger concepts such as dependency, introduced in 2.3.2.4; when the internal state of application objects has changed, an update of the display will be triggered without addressing the display objects. External input handling can be achieved if the application objects act as *receivers* for messages sent by the input devices, and not as senders inquiring input devices.

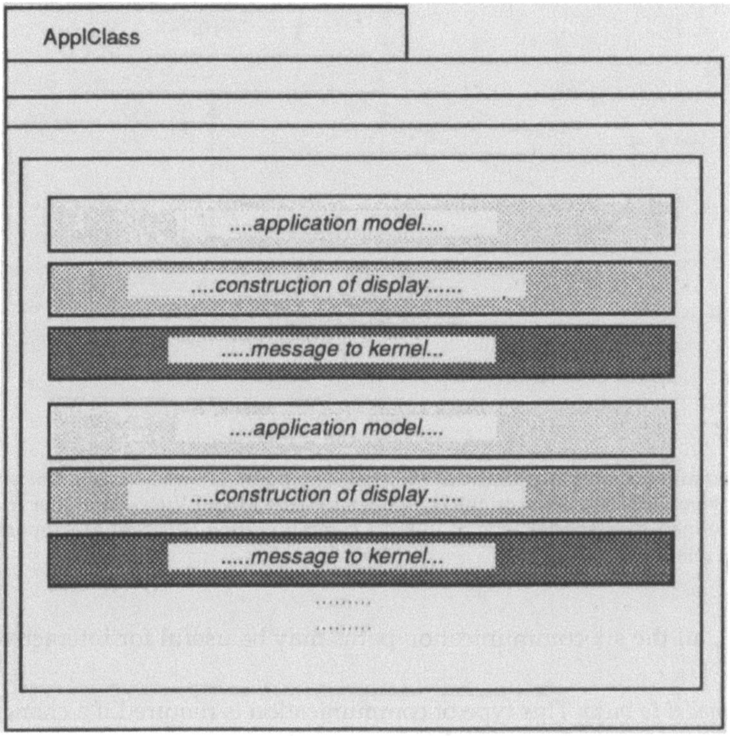

Fig. 3.4. Mixture of three different types of code in the application. In a traditional layer model the code of an interactive application program consists of three different parts: pure application-oriented statements, mediating between application and interface, and the direct calls to the graphics subroutine package. The mixture of code makes it very difficult to change or modify the user interface for a stable application.

3.2.2 Building up the MVC Triad

The various construction steps for establishing the MVC model will be described and explained by an example. The basic concept of MVC is the construction of a *triangle* (or more than one triangle) with

- an application object, called *model*,
- a presentation/mapping object, called *view*,
- a mapping object for input handling, called *controller*.

The next section will show how to program the communication between the individual objects. At first the communication between the individual components is described by qualitative examples. Figure 3.5 shows six communication paths between the components of the triad.

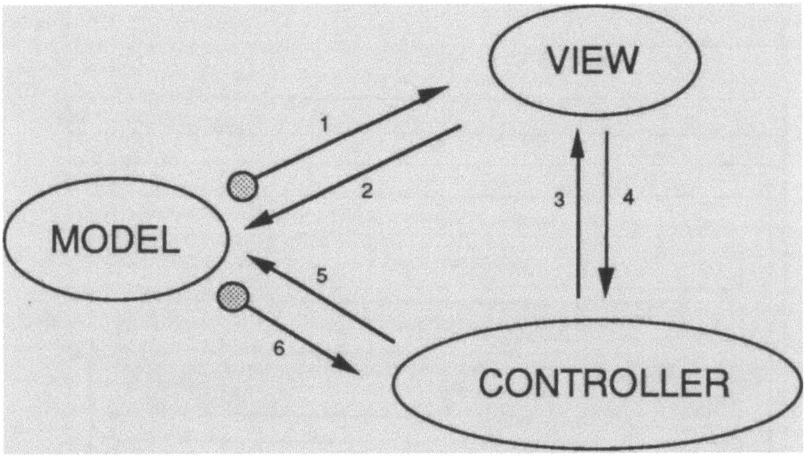

Fig. 3.5. Communication paths in the MVC triad. The figure shows six communication paths, which may be established between the components of the Model-View-Controller triad. Path 1 and 6 are defined by a special type of indirect communication (triggering) supported by the dependency relations.

In general, all the six communication paths may be useful for interactive system design.

1. *From model to view:* This type of communication is required if a changing state of the model requires a modification of the display. As mentioned this is done by triggering using a dependency relation.
2. *From view to model:* A view may inquire information from application required for a display construction.
3. *From controller to view:* A controller may effect the modification of a display (without having to use paths 5 and 1) due to an input. This may be useful if an input action (e.g., scrolling in a window) modifies the state of a view, without any change of the model.
4. *From view to controller:* A view may activate an input device dependent upon states in the presentation.
5. *From controller to model:* A controller may effect a modification of the model due to an input.
6. *From model to controller:* A controller may be influenced due to a modification of the model. For example, the sequence of menu labels of a mouse menu

controller could be permuted. This type of communication is not predefined in the programming environment. However, it can be realized easily as a dependency between model and controller.

3.2.3 Predefined Classes

For establishing the MVC triad, much support is given by the Smalltalk-80 environment. To avoid any confusion for the application programmer looking for a class Model, Smalltalk-80 does not provide any predefined class for the the model, because the model is completely application-dependent and must therefore implemented by the application programmer.

The class View is predefined in the environment with many useful subclasses to provide in particular everything required for constructing windows with specific types of content, e.g., text views, form views, list views.

The class Controller is also already available with many subclasses that support, for example, all input devices such as mouse, keyboard, menus. The Controller classes are correlated to the subclasses of View in the sense that they provide the style of interaction to control the associated views. For example, the class TextController supports text editing for TextView.

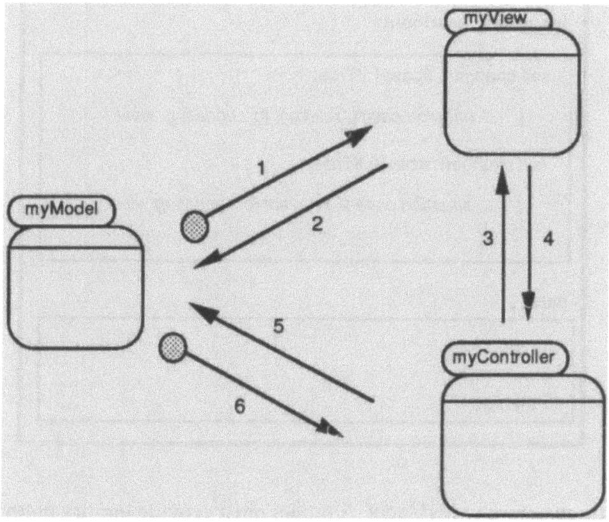

Fig. 3.6. The MVC instances. Smalltalk-80 supports predefined methods for the coordination of the three components of the MVC triangle.

3.2.4 Establishing Communication

For constructing an MVC triad, the following procedure is described in the next sub-sections:

- Three classes that will be called MyView, MyModel, MyController are defined by the application programmer together with their associated methods.
- One instance for each of the classes myModel, myView, myController is created.
- The instances are coordinated so that they know each other as required for message passing between them.

3.2.4.1 Constructing a Model Class

It was mentioned that there is no class Model and there is also no obligation to name such a class in this way. Therefore a class MyModel may be a subclass of any other class if this is useful. In the general case shown here, it is only a subclass of the most general class Object.

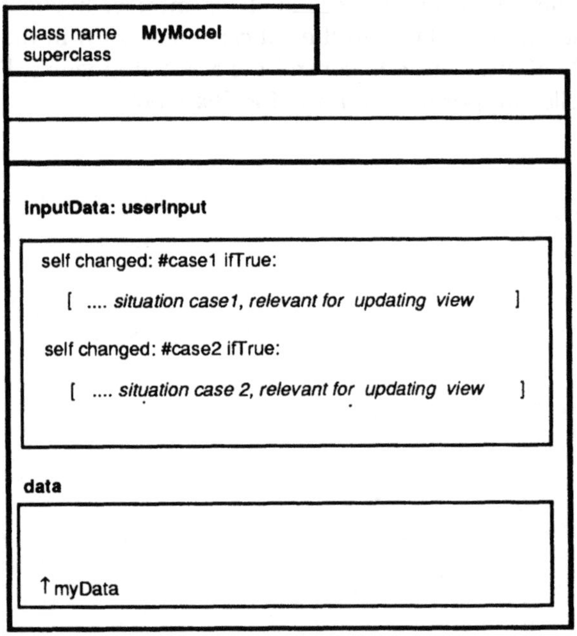

Fig. 3.7. Schematic structure of MyModel. A model must provide inquiry methods for delivering it own data as a source for the construction of a display, shown here by the unary message data. In addition it must be able to receive messages sent by the controller (inputData:). As a reaction it may trigger its dependent, the view, by a changed: message.

The following recommendations should be noted accordingly:

- The application class should not define the user interface concretely. Therefore any display message or a message to an input device (controller) must be avoided.

- If an update of the display or the construction of a new display is required—which may be caused by a new state of the model—the model should communicate with its view by a trigger message, sent to itself (in this way informing its dependent). To do this, a message like the following is sufficient:

  ```
  self change: #myNewState .
  ```

- The objects, in our example MyView and MyController, mediating between interface and application, have to inquire all information needed for display construction from myModel. All these inquiry methods have to be implemented as instance methods of MyModel, making myModel a receiver responding to messages sent by the interface components.
- As a result of the user interaction, the internal state of the model may be modified. This is usually done by sending messages from myController to the myModel. Therefore, the class MyModel must also provide methods for receiving the required information.

3.2.4.2 Constructing a Controller Class

A controller class, i.e., the class MyController in the actual example, must always be defined as a (direct or indirect) subclass of the class Controller. Through insertion into the inheritance chain, MyController may be specialized for its own specific needs and the inherited functionality of Controller may be used as well.

The essential form of specialization consists in mediating between user input and the model by sending messages to it. The existing subclasses of Controller make it quite simple to handle the user input, for example, to analyze menu selection or to control the mouse. Message passing to the model requires knowledge of the model's methods and can therefore not be predefined by the environment. Rather, the application programmer who will generally have programmed the model as well must take care that the corresponding messages are sent to the model.

For getting knowledge about the actual model, an inherited inquiry method (unary message model) is available. It is also possible, by applying the unary message view, to obtain the current View (myView). This is possible because the triangle will be established by View and the class View informs the controller about the other partners as shown in the next paragraph.

3.2.4.3 Constructing a View Class

The class View is of special importance to the whole MVC model. Apart from defining an instance, myView, View initializes all components of the triangle.

MyView is defined as a (not necessarily direct) subclass of View. An instance, myView of MyView, must provide an application-dependent method update: for reaction to changes of the model. The update method is responsible for the display of the modified state of the model. For this it may use the functions of any appropriate system to support the display of information, especially an existing (graphics) kernel system. In general information about the model is required for this display process, so that the model will be inquired by myView. The model can be addressed because MyView owns a method model for delivering the actual model instance.

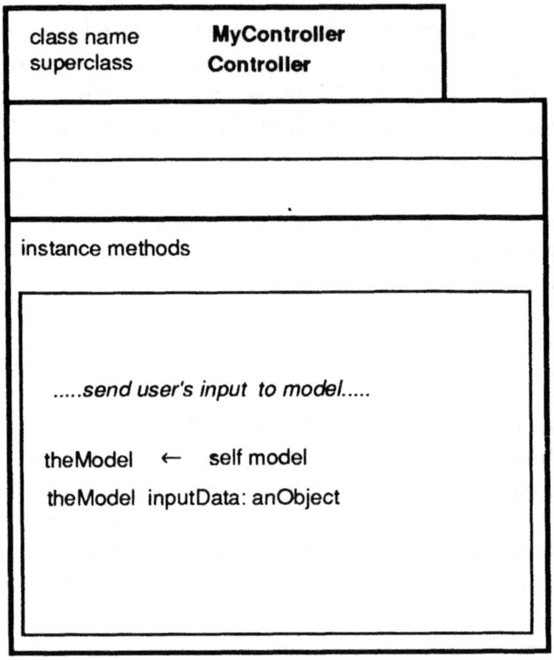

Fig. 3.8. Structure of MyController. A controller class may send input to the actual model as a reaction to user's input. It has knowledge about the model by access to an instance variable inherited by Model.

How will the whole triangle be instantiated, after the classes MyModel, MyView and MyController have been defined, i.e., after the application programmer has generated almost the complete programming code (except for the class methods of MyView)?

A class method of MyView—called open in this example—creates the instances myModel, myView and myController by simply using the message new (or any other method for creating new instances, as provided by one of the superclasses of the existing classes). Then the coordination of the triad is performed by a special class method (inherited by View) of MyView with the selector model:controller:.

Applying

```
myView model: myModel controller: myController .
```

establishes the whole triadic relationship. The programmer need not know the individual actions in every detail.

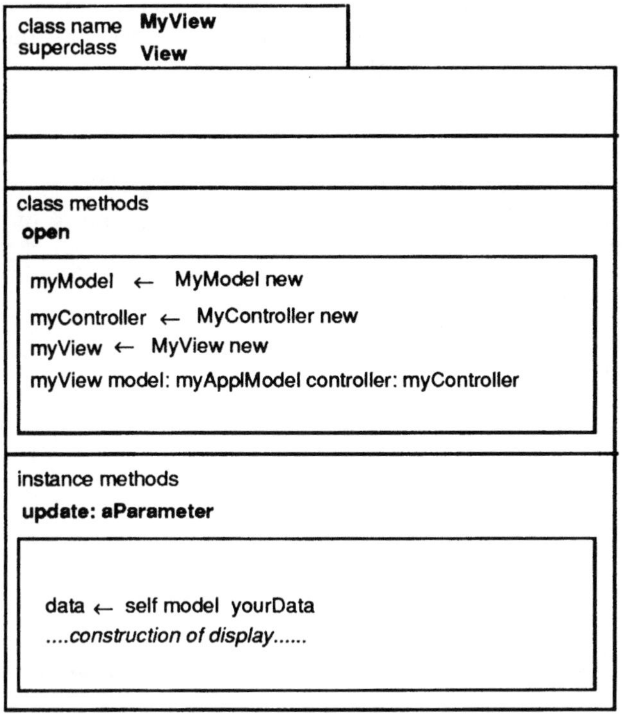

Fig. 3.9. Structure of MyView. The MVC triad will be instantiated by creating the model and view, and by establishing the relations between all three components by the method model:controller:, inherited from View.

The service provided by View includes the following steps, illustrated in the above Fig. 3.9:

- establishment of the dependency of myView and myController from myModel.
- information of myController about myModel and myView. They may be inquired by the messages model and view.
- information of myView about myModel and myController. They may be inquired by model or controller from myView.

Now the communication in the triangle is completely established.

3.2.5 The Example of a Counter

The following example, presented by Michael Hanus of the University of Dortmund and his colleagues in various tutorials—also documented in the MVC "cookbook" (Krasner & Pope, 1988)—shows the implementation of a minisystem in which the value of a counter may be incremented by the value 1 or decremented by 1. The interaction is controlled by menu options. This example is not only documented, but it also comes with the Smalltalk-80 system, a product of

ParcPlace Systems (Version 2.2 of July 4, 1987). We have slightly simplified this example (our view is subclass of StandardSystemView, and our controller is subclass of StandardSystemController).

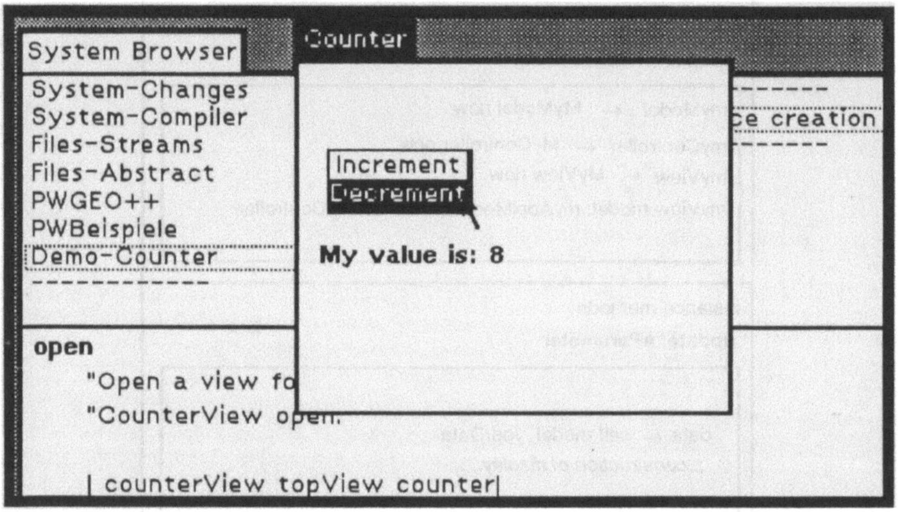

Fig. 3.10. The user interface of the counter examples. The counter view together with the pop-up menu is displayed as an overlay to the Smalltalk-80 System Browser, after evaluation of the open message.

3.2.5.1 The Model

The model is an instance of a user defined class CountHolder and consists essentially only of an instance variable value for representation of the counter.

If the model shows a situation which requires a modification of representation, a change: message is used. For inquiring, the method count is provided. It delivers the value of counter.

In addition, the model offers increment and decrement provided by the model's class CountHolder.

---

class name	**CountHolder**
superclass	Object
instance variable names	value
class methods	

new: aNumber "Create a new counter and initialize it with aNumber"

```
    | newCounter |

    newCounter ← super new.
    newCounter initialize: aNumber.
    ↑ newCounter
```

instance methods

"CountHolder methodsFor: operations"

```
decrement                          "Subtract 1 from the value of the counter"

    value ← value - 1 .
    self changed: #decrement


increment                          "Add 1 to the value of the counter"

    value ← value + 1 .
    self changed: #increment


initialize: aNumber                "Initialize the state of the counter to
                                    aNumber"

    value ← aNumber
```

CountHolder methodsFor: 'accessing'

```
value                              "return my current value"

    ↑ value
```

3.2.5.2 The Controller

The class CounterController delivers the controller component of the MVC triad. It is not described here in full detail. CounterController has inherited important features from the predefined class StandardSystemController. We concentrate on the aspects which are important for the MVC concept.

In an initializing step, a menu with the pop-up menu labels 'increment' and 'decrement', which are visible at the user interface, is assigned to the Controller. The menu selections activate "call-back" messages (called menu messages) subtract and add. Their corresponding methods call the model. This part of the example shows very well how to enrich an already existing menu by subclassing where knowledge about the protocol of the model is used.

---

class name	**CounterController**
superclass	StandardSystemController
instance variable names	*none*
instance methods	

```
"CounterController methodsFor: 'initialize-release' "

initialize

    super initialize.

    self:    yellowButtonMenu: (PopUpMenu labels: 'Increment Decrement')
      yellowButtonMessages: #(subtract add)


"CounterController methodsFor: 'menu messages' "

subtract                                    "Subtract 1 from the value of the counter"

    (self model) decrement

increment                                   "Add 1 to the value of the counter"

    (self model ) increment
```

3.2.5.3 The View

The view class SimpleCounterView is a subclass of StandardSystemView. The instance method update: defines the methods depending on modifications of the model. In general, one has to inquire the value (counter down or counter up or reset counter) of the parameter of update: and branch accordingly. Since, the presentation of the model is always the same, to display the current value of the counter, this type of branching is not required.

The message display is inherited. It uses the inherited message displayView, which is overridden (reimplemented) here. The value of the model is inquired in method displayView (value ← self model count). The representation is then done at the desired position in the view. This more technical detail, not relevant to MVC, will not be explained here.

The class method shows the initialization of the whole MVC triangle as described above. The instances are created and the dependencies are furnished through model:controller:. In addition, size, inscription and representation of the View is defined. The last expression of this category shows how the Controller may be inquired from aSimpleCounterView with controller in order to be opened.

---

class name **CounterView**
superclass View
instance variable names *none*
class methods

CounterView class methodsFor: 'instance creation'

```
open                                           "Open a view for a new counter"
                                               "CounterView open."

    | counterView counter |                    "temporary variables"

    counter ← CountHolder new: 0 .             "create model, view, define MVC triad"
    counterView ← CounterView new .
    counterView model: counter controller: (CounterController new) .

    counterView borderWidth: 2 .               "initialize view (not explained in
    counterView insideColor: Form white .      detail), open controller"
    counterView label: 'Counter' .
    counterView minimumSize: 120@120 .
    counterView controller open
```

CounterView methodsFor: 'displaying'

```
displayView                                    "Display the value of the counter in the
                                               counter view."
    | pos |

                                               "Calculate the absolute display coordi-
                                               nates from the coordinates of the view
                                               box."

    pos ← (self insetDisplayBox topLeft x +10) @ (self insetDisplayBox center y).
```

```
                                        "Concatenate the components of the
                                        output string and display them."

('My value is: ', self model value printString) asText allBold asParagraph
    displayAt: pos.

update: aParameter

    self display                        "display is inherited; it uses displayView,
                                        which was overridden above"

self emphasizeLabel                     "the label of the view is emphasized"
```

3.2.5.4 Comments

The example shows that nothing about the interface is coded in the application. If only the interface is to be modified, the displayView method and and nothing else must be replaced. Connections with a generic application can be seen in the establishment of the triad, which is coordinated by the predefined functionality.

Note that the controller with its menu messages actively sending messages as a reaction to user input to the application is also a new concept, compared with traditional approaches where input can only be inquired by the application layer.

4 Smalltalk-80 Graphics Kernel

We will present the graphics kernel of the Smalltalk-80 system and focus on the aspects that are relevant to the chapters that follow. In particular, Smalltalk-80 will be contrasted to GKS and PHIGS. In addition, Smalltalk-80 concepts offer ideas and suggestions for the specification of GEO++ in Chap. 8. The ideas are mainly derived from an analysis of the underlying object-oriented principles and not so much from the actual functionality of the Smalltalk-80' graphics kernel. An extended description of the Smalltalk-80 graphics kernel is presented in Goldberg & Robson, 1983.

The Smalltalk-80 kernel is a raster graphics system. It consists of a set of classes and methods. The internal implementation is fully transparent up to the pixel level. Therefore, the kernel interface as well as its internal implementation is available to the applications programmer. This is a wholly different principle from the one that governs GKS and PHIGS because both standards are based on a model where the kernel's implementation is completely hidden to the application programmer.

4.1 Output Primitives

Smalltalk-80 provides an individual class for every special type of primitive. Every single primitive can be addressed as an instance by a variable as object identifier.

The most important classes for output primitives are:

- The class Path, with its subclasses Spline, Curve, Line, Arc, LinearFit, Circle, where LinearFit corresponds to the GKS or PHIGS polyline, and
- the class Quadrangle for the representation of rectangles, a subclass of Rectangle.

4.1.1 Generation and Instantiation of Primitives

As a rule, a primitive is generated by sending the message new to its class. This creates a new, empty primitive instance (with at yet undefined coordinates). Coordinates may be assigned to a primitive by corresponding messages. *Partially instantiated* primitives may also be generated, i.e., primitives with partly empty coordinates, i.e., coordinates referring to nil. Along these lines it is possible, for example, to insert empty points into a linear fit and assign values to them later as shown below. Substantial advantages of late instantiation occur: one may construct graphics object hierarchies with empty or partially instantiated primitives and independently formulate algorithms (programs, rules, constraints) for the definition of relations between their coordinates. The evaluation of the dependencies, resulting in a complete instantiation, may be deferred until the hierarchy will be displayed.

4.1.2 Editing and Inquiry Methods

An existing primitive such as a linear fits may be edited by adding a coordinate to it. More precisely, this means that the primitive is edited, since the receiver is itself changed by such a message. Other possibilities exist to edit a primitive that are well suited for the interactive generation of primitives.

Beyond editing graphics primitives, the variety of ways in which geometric parameters can be set and inquired is remarkable. In this, the principle of minimality that governed the design of GKS an PHIGS was consciously abandoned. Some examples for editing and inquiring a linear fit are given, which supplement the examples for Rectangles listed above (cf. Chap. 2):

```
aLinearFit addLast: aPoint
```

adds a point,

```
aLinearFit at: 3: put: aPoint
```

replaces the third coordinate,

```
lastPoint ← aLinearFit last
```

returns the last point,

```
secondPoint ← aLinearFit at: 2
```

returns the second point.

4.1.3 Merge Constraint

Sometimes it is desirable to use the same point as a coordinate for different output primitives. This is possible in Smalltalk-80 because inserting a coordinate is implemented as the creation of a reference to the coordinate. With multiple references to the same object, immediate support of so-called *merge constraints* is directly established. If an internal state, for example a coordinate of a repeatedly used point, is changed, then all primitives which refer to this point are changed consistently. This is shown in Fig. 4.1. If such a multiple reference is undesirable the point in question must be replaced by a separate instance with the same value, i.e., a copy.

4.1.4 Examples

Two examples, one for a reference to a common point, and one for a partial instantiation together with a rule describing geometrical relations, are given.

4.1.4.1 Merge Point

As an example for primitives with common coordinates, which are called as *merge points* in Borning, 1981, one can define a quadrangle by

```
po ← Point x: 1 y: 1 .
pc ← Point x: 5 y: 3 .
aQuad ← Quadrangle origin: po corner: pc .
```

We create two lines by:

```
line1 ← Line beginPoint: po endPoint: pc .
line2 ← Line beginPoint: (aQuad bottomLeft) endPoint: (aQuad topRight) .
```

If we now change (not replace!) the point pc:

```
pc x: 3 .
```

then all values change in a consistent way, as shown in Fig. 4.1.

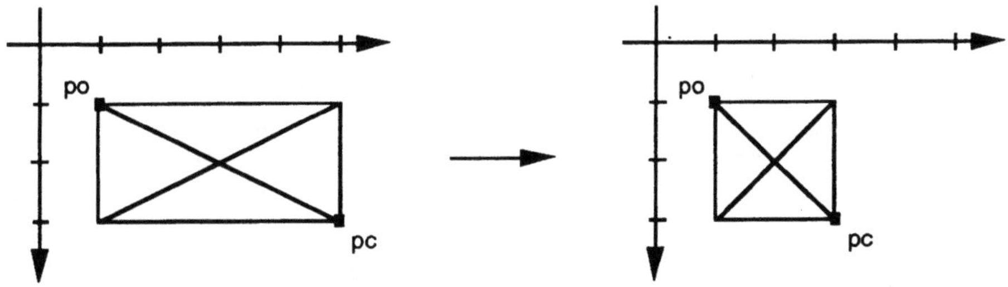

Fig. 4.1. Primitives with merge points. All points of the right hand side, the two end-points of the lines, and the corners of the quadrangle refer to the x-coordinate of pc. If pc is changed by modifying its x-coordinate all points on the right-hand side will change consistently.

4.1.4.2 Partial Instantiation

As an example of a partial instantiation, a linear fit is created with four instantiated points and the third point left uninstantiated. Moreover, the first and last points are merged:

```
aFit ← LinearFit new .
aFit add: (0@0); add: (1@3); add: (Point new); add: (3@1); add: (aFit at: 1) .
```

Next a rule relating the points is defined:

```
sum ← (aFit at: 2) + (aFit at: 4) .
(aFit at: 3) x: (sum x) .
(aFit at: 3) y: (sum y) .
```

As a result the third point is the result of adding the second and fourth point, leading to a parallelogram, as shown in Fig. 4.2.

If we now change the second coordinate:

```
(aFit at: 2) x: 2 .
```

and evaluate the rule again:

```
sum ← (aFit at: 2) + (aFit at: 4) .
(aFit at: 3) x: (sum x ).
(aFit at: 3) y: (sum y).
```

the parallelogram will be change consistently.

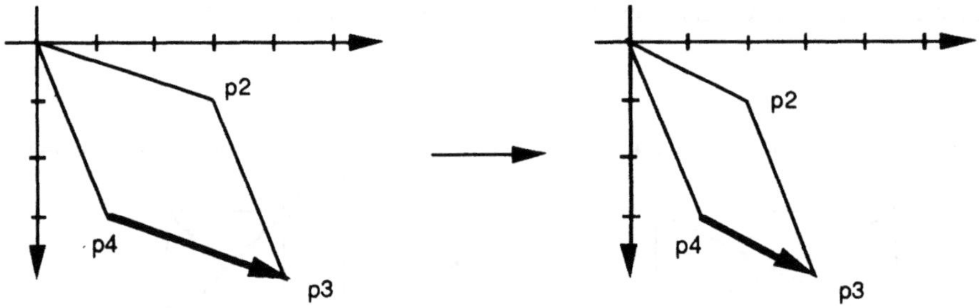

Fig. 4.2. For the partially instantiated linear fit a rule is defined, fixing that p3 is sum of p2 and p4. If p2 is changed then p3 will change accordingly, resulting in a new parallelogram.

The example has shown that partially instantiated primitives have the advantage that geometrical rules between output primitives may be described directly in terms of these primitives.

4.1.5 Derivation of New Primitives

Several methods are available for creating a derived primitive from an existing one. A primitive may be created by a transformation message which returns a new, transformed primitive and leaves the receiver of the message, the original primitive, unaffected. For instances of the class Path, a new instance may be defined by using enumeration messages, similar to those introduced in 2.5.2.3. The new primitive has the same attributes and the same number of points, but the values of them are determined by the block iteration. For example, the collect: method generates a new linear fit from an existing one; the value of the block is computed by adding a coordinate as an offset of the original point:

```
shiftedLinearFit ← aLinearFit collect: [:eachPoint | eachPoint + offSetPoint] .
```

4.1.6 Primitive Attributes

Since the Smalltalk-80 system was devised for black-and-white graphics on raster displays, attributes are available which refer to a primitive as if painted with a brush. The shape of the brush is defined by a black-and-white matrix, an instance of the class Form. In addition to the form, a destination is specified. The resulting display is defined by one of 16 rules that allow drawing a black-and-white point on a black-and-white destination. No special attributes are available, however, for defining specific linestyles.

Note that attributes are assigned in an object-oriented manner. Every object has individual instance variables for its attributes, which can be set and inquired in a variety of ways. It is not possible, however, to assign an attribute to a class variable. Since any instance of a class has access to the class variable of its own class or its superclasses, default values could be specified in this way. But, because the entire code is fully transparent, such handling of default attributes can be programmed easily.

4.2 Generation and Display of Graphics Objects

The Smalltalk-80 graphics kernel differs substantially in its functionality from GKS and PHIGS in the structuring of a graphics object hierarchy. If one calls GKS a one-level system because it supports a single layer hierarchy, and PHIGS a multi-level system, then the Smalltalk-80 kernel is zero-level. There is no predefined graphics object structure. Consequently, there is no pick operation, just individual graphics objects. Anything more complex than that must be implemented with the available programming tools, which are, however, very comfortable. Since there is no object structure, no editing of such a structure is possible. All operations refer to graphics primitives.

4.2.1 Posting

How is an object, i.e., a graphics primitive, displayed on screen? The basic philosophy of Smalltalk-80 requires that a primitive carry all information necessary for its own representation. It is passed to the object through appropriate messages. For an object to be able to display itself, the output medium must be selected (usually the instance Display, a global variable of the class DisplayMedium), along with the display attribute, i.e., the brush, and a clipping rectangle. Additionally, a modeling transformation can be defined that recomputes the primitive's coordinates. Also, display messages are available that require fewer arguments, e.g., when the clip rectangle need not be specified; in this case clipping occurs on the screen's boundaries. In a truly interactive graphics application, a view would be generated using the Model-View-Controller concept. Automatic clipping of the view is not supported, however. Therefore the view's inner rectangle must be inquired from the view and used as argument for the display message of every primitive. As pointed out above, all this may be modified and improved by programming, but it is not initially supported.

4.2.2 Graphics Input

The main graphics input device is the pointing device (mouse). Its coordinates may be inquired in different ways (continuously and after pressing or releasing a button).

4.2.3 Interactive Generation of an Output Primitive

The following example shows how a linear fit may be generated interactively. In the event of a mouse click triggered by the red button, the current position of the mouse is added to the graphics primitive. Then the system waits until the mouse is released.

Mainly the messages to the linear fit are of interest. A black form of size 4 by 4 is used as attribute of the output primitive. It is assigned an empty (i.e., consisting of no coordinates) linear fit by the message form:. The mouse position is appended to the linear fit with addLast:. For visual feedback of the intermediate state, the linear fit is displayed on the screen with displayOn:. The action is repeated until another mouse button is pressed.

```
aLinearFit ← LinearFit new.
aForm ← Form new extent: 4 @ 4.
aForm black.
aLinearFit form: aForm .
flag ← true.
[flag] whileTrue:
  [mousePosition ← Sensor waitButton .
  Sensor redButtonPressed
        ifTrue: [aLinearFit add: mousePosition .
              aLinearFit displayOn: Display .
              Sensor waitNoButton ]
        ifFalse: [flag ← false]].
```

4.2.4 Limitations of Hierarchical Inheritance

Inspection of the code for the class Path serves as a good example to illustrate the potential and limitations of hierarchical inheritance compared to multiple inheritance. The class Path is a subclass of DisplayObject. The class DisplayObject has several subclasses; for example Form. Path inherits from DisplayObject the methods for display, setting default values and others. On the other hand, Path is a sequence of points. So it has many in common with the class OrderedCollection, which supports handling of sequences. Since Smalltalk-80 knows only hierarchical inheritance, the functionality of OrderedCollection cannot be inherited by Path. For this reason, the property of being a sequence is supported by an instance variable of OrderedCollection with name collectionOfPoints. The assignment methods used above, as we know them from OrderedCollection, must each be individually implemented as a new (relatively small) method. Some examples of implementing the behavior of a sequence for Path follow.

---

class name **Path**
superclass DisplayObject
instance variable names collectionOfPoints form

instance methods

testing

at: index "Answer the point of the receiver's path at position index"

↑ collectionOfPoints at: index

first "Answer the first point of the receiver's path"

↑ collectionOfPoints first

at: index put:aPoint "Store the argument as a point on the receiver's path at position index"

collectionOfPoints at:index put: aPoint

In multiple inheritance, we can do without storing the coordinates in an instance variable defined explicitly for this. We would simply define Path as a subclass of both DisplayObject and OrderedCollection. Then Path is automatically *a-kind-of* collection and the above methods are automatically available. Figure 4.3 shows the hierarchy if multiple inheritance is used.

4.2.5 Comments

The Smalltalk-80 kernel is to some extent a typical representative for supporting graphics in object-oriented programming environments. Graphics kernels of this category provide graphics primitives, mechanisms for handling event input, and special complex graphics classes, for example, to generate windows, menus, and dialog boxes. Existing object-oriented kernels are transparent, and together with the potential supplied by inheritance they are very flexible.

Especially the numerous options of editing and inquiring output primitives and the object-oriented naming mechanisms offers high flexibility. As shown above, interactive generation of primitives is simple to realize. We should note that such operations can only be supported with a great deal of effort in GKS or PHIGS, since primitives are not editable. As will be shown in Sect. 9.6, particularly the generation of visual feedback during interactive editing is remarkably difficult to realize using PHIGS (or GKS).

Object-oriented kernels, however, do not provide a set of kernel functions for device-independent graphics programming that is sufficiently rich, complete and harmonized. Compared to GKS and PHIGS, they provide no model for the generation, maintenance, and long-term storage of graphics object hierarchies or other general purpose *graphics semantics*. There is no pick device which directly relates input to a graphics object structure. In short, they can be characterized as toolboxes, or kernels in a narrower sense,.and the should not been qualified as at complete *system*.

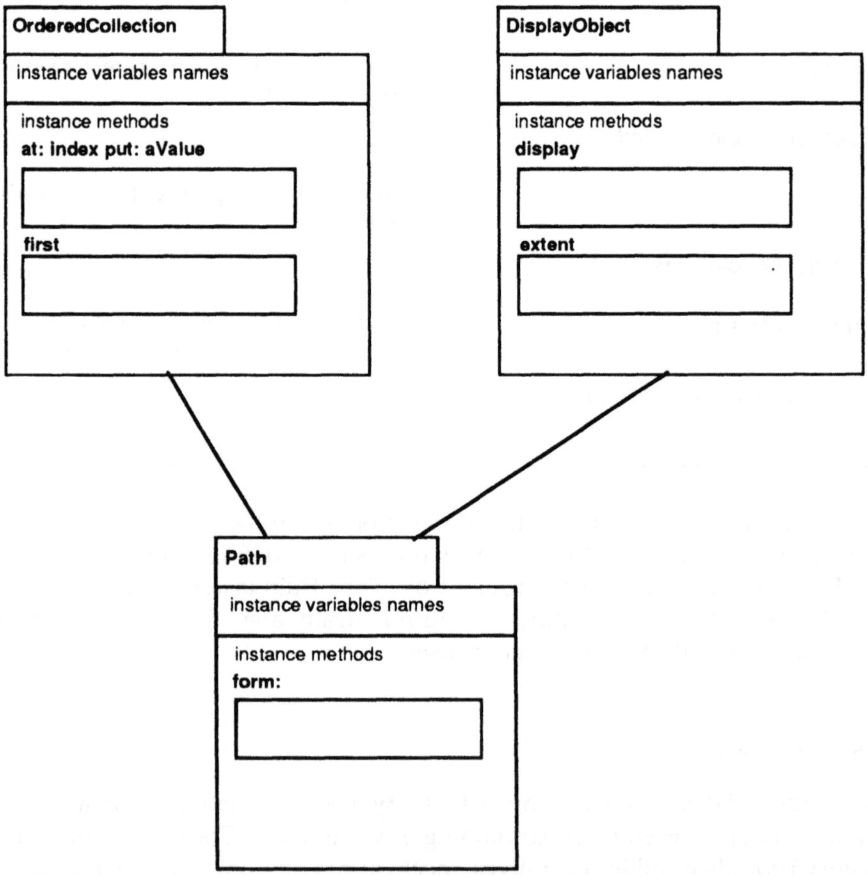

Fig. 4. 3. Path, organized as common subclass of OrderedCollection and DisplayObject. In multiple inheritance, the handling of geometric coordinates can be inherited from OrderedCollection; methods that allow access to the geometric coordinates do not have to be re-implemented in this case.

5 GKS and Object-Oriented System Design

In this chapter we will be looking at the graphics standard GKS through the object-oriented lens. Several differences between a traditional graphics kernel system as GKS and an object-oriented graphics system will be described. Simultaneously, we will introduce the goals of standardizing a graphics system. Some of the examples encompass an object-oriented modification of GKS, to aid in pointing out the differences between the traditional and object-oriented approaches. By no means do we propose a modified GKS as the graphics system of the future. It should be noted that much of what is said on the next few pages also applies to the standard PHIGS. But PHIGS will be analyzed in more detail in other chapters of the book.

5.1 Goals of Standardization

In defining standards in the field of computer graphics, one hopes to solve a number of relevant problems, such as the portability of graphics application programs. We wish to focus here on those graphics standards that are intended to support the applications programmer in implementing (interactive) graphics applications. There are of course other standards in computer graphics, with other goals (cf. Arnold & Bono, 1989).

The basis for supporting the applications programmer is the specification of an applications programmer's interface. At present two standards have been specified in this area: GKS and PHIGS (ISO, 1985 & ISO, 1989a). Work is currently in progress on PHIGS+, an extension of PHIGS that will support high performance graphics—especially rendering (lighting and shading).

The specification of a graphics standards comprises two major steps:

a) The functional specification of an interface for the applications programmer independent of a programming language.

b) The definition of special language bindings for important programming languages.

The specification of a standard is combined with the expectation that commercial firms will implement it that and will make it available for many important programming environments. The applications programmer can then employ the standard for his own projects.

The internal realization of such implementations are hidden *(principle of a hidden kernel)*. Even if it is technically possible, the programmer should not use or modify the internal code of the implementation, because they are not part of the standard. Otherwise the modifications would restrict portability of the application.

A strict boundary between applications programming above of the kernel and the internal hidden implementation divides the functionality of graphics programming as a whole into two worlds, so to say. One world is that of the application programmer who is restricted to the standardized interface, and the other world is that of the kernel's producer, who is completely free as to how to realize the standard.

For a standardized graphics kernel such as GKS and PHIGS, one expects a systematically organized functionality. That is to say, all functions should be available on the same abstract level. One criterion for the qualitative evaluation of an applications programmer's interface, provided by a graphics standard, is optimal support of the programmer's needs. In this, a standard should support anything that may be appropriate for the programmer (*principle of rich kernel*). Superfluous functions that do not belong in the hands of the programmer or minor utilities easily implemented on a higher level above the kernel should not be incorporated in the standard (*principle of minimal kernel*). The motivations for the entire procedure of defining a standard are described in detail in (Enderle, Kansy & Pfaff, 1987).

Fundamental goals in defining graphics standards functional descriptions are that they be application independent, programming language independent and device independent:

- The criterion of *application independence* refers to the functionality. The kernel is to reflect the average of the functions common to the important graphics application areas and should not contain components of a specific application.
- *Language independence* means that functionality should be defined such that interfaces (*language bindings*) to various programming languages are possible.
- *Device independence* refers to a definition of the kernel which may be described independently of specific device characteristics, achieved by an abstraction which is based on the concept of *logical devices* and the introduction of normalized device coordinates.

5.2 A Short Review of the Main GKS Features

We begin by compiling the important characteristics of GKS and concentrate on features of GKS that we will discuss in the section 5.3 and for which we will develop alternative approaches.

5.2.1 The GKS Layer Model

To integrate graphics kernel systems into programming environments, consider the *GKS layer model*. Figure 5.1 shows the layering of the individual levels. The operating system which manages graphics resources such as graphics output and input devices is on the lowest level. The graphics kernel system follows on the level above. The functionality of the graphics kernel is accessed by a language-dependent layer. Between the application programmer's own specific application and the kernel, an application-dependent layer may be implemented. This layer, which is not part of the standard, may add additional functionality supporting particular types of applications. In CAD applications, such a layer may support geometric modeling . In other applications, such as cartography, it may provide the programmer with special output primitives supplementing the kernel.

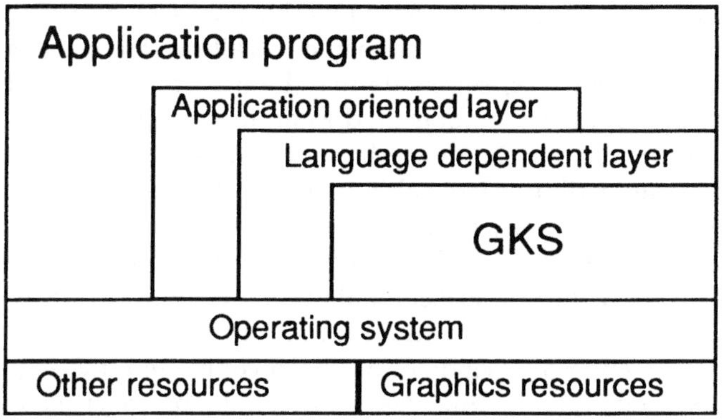

Fig. 5.1. GKS layer model. In the traditional layer model, higher levels will call the lower ones as subroutines. It is not possible for a component of the kernel to call routines written by the applications programmer and see them as receiver of a call.

GKS supports only a simple control structure. Upon calling a GKS function, the caller hands control to GKS. GKS provides then the specified functionality of the called procedure and returns control to the caller. Thus we have the typical subroutine control structure.

Two aspects are important for such procedure calls:

- After the application program has relinquished control to GKS, the execution belongs to GKS alone. The service provided by GKS consists of displaying graphics information as specified in the standard or modifying internal states of the kernel.
- During execution it is not possible to access resources that have been programmed by the application programmer. Therefore any control knowledge is implemented outside the kernel.

5.2.2 Output Primitives

GKS supports six types of output primitives: a line primitive, a point primitive, a text primitive, two raster primitives, and a general-purpose primitive to address special device characteristics. Graphics primitives may be inserted in segments. Output primitives are in never objects in the view of the application programmer: they are "produced" by specific subroutine calls transmitting geometrical coordinates to the kernel. There is no possibility to assign names to output primitives or to manipulate them as individual items.

5.2.3 Segments

A segment may be regarded as a collection of output primitives. Output primitives may be inserted into a segment. An explicit insert operation is not available. After a segment has been opened with the open operation, all subsequently generated output primitives are automatically inserted into the open segment. The process ends when the segment is closed by the close function. One can refer to *the* open segment, because at most one segment is allowed to be open at a time.

In contrast to primitives, segments may be manipulated as single entities. Segments possess an identifier, specified as an input parameter when opening the segment. Segments may be deleted, made visible or invisible. They may be provided with the attribute detectable or non-detectable. When a segment is detectable it may be picked by means of a graphics input device, for example the mouse. In addition, attribute highlighting is available for segments. Segments may also be inserted into other segments together with a transformation. All these operations are performed by using the segment identifier.

After the generation of a segment has been completed, the segment may no longer be modified. New primitives may neither be inserted nor removed. PHIGS provides far more facilities in this context, especially for editing of collections (*structures*).

5.2.4 Assignment of Primitive Attributes

Primitive attributes such as color or line type are set *modally* in GKS: an attribute, once set, is valid for all subsequently generated primitives until overwritten by a new attribute.

5.2.5 Conceptual Differences Between Primitives and Segments

There is an essential difference in GKS (and in PHIGS) between output primitives and segments. Specifically, the attributes for the two constructs are strictly separated. It is not possible to assign a primitive attribute to a collection of graphics primitives, i.e., a segment, by using its name nor can a segment attribute be assigned to an individual primitive.

If, for instance, an individual primitive is to be highlighted, then a segment consisting only of the primitive has to be defined. If on the other hand all the primitives of one segment should obtain a specific color, one must proceed dexterously: set the attribute at the beginning of the segment (immediately after its generation) and then invalidate the attribute by inserting a new attribute before new successive primitives are generated. It is not possible to use the segment identifier for this purpose.

We will later see that it makes much sense to minimize the differences between collections of output primitives (segments, structures, groups) and individual output primitives by assigning them essentially the same attributes, and by allowing editing of both constructs.

5.2.6 Graphics Input

Graphics input is returned by logical input devices in GKS. The most important graphics input device in the context of this book is the *pick device*. It returns the identifier of the identified segment (and possibly an identifier of a group) for segments with the attribute "detectable".

All input devices are inquired by the application program. The terminal operator can produce input after an input device has been activated. There are two modes for queries: direct query (input request) and the event query. In the event query, the data are collected asynchronously in a queue. They can later be requested from this queue. In both cases, the terminal operator's input causes no direct action. All actions are executed after evaluation by the calling application program.

5.3 The Structure of a GKS Program

To illustrate the structure of a GKS program, a typical series of GKS operations will be listed. We open a new segment, set a primitive attribute and insert two primitives, then the segment is closed.

```
NAME = 1
CREATE_SEGMENT(NAME)
SET_COLOR('GREEN')
POLYLINE(XARRAY,YARRAY,NPOINTS)
MARKER(XP,YP)
CLOSE_SEGMENT .
```

A segment attribute is set by using the segment identifier:

```
SET_DETECTABILTY(NAME,TRUE).
```

After activation of a pick device, the call

```
REQUEST_PICK (NAMEPICKED) .
```

returns the identifier of the picked object. Reaction to the pick operation may consist of highlighting:

```
SET_HIGHLIGHTING(NAMEPICKED,TRUE) .
```

A segment can be deleted by:

```
DELETE_SEGMENT(NAMEPICKED) .
```

Since the segment identifier is an input parameter, it will be managed by the application program. The application programmer has to ensure that the name is not in conflict with GKS rules. For example, identical names cannot be assigned to two different segments, otherwise an error with a corresponding error message is generated.

5.3.1 One-to-One GKS Language Binding for Smalltalk-80

To illustrate the difference from the object-oriented programming style, we will now follow GKS rules strictly and define a language binding of the above scheme for Smalltalk-80. We will then evaluate, how object-oriented the resulting language binding is.

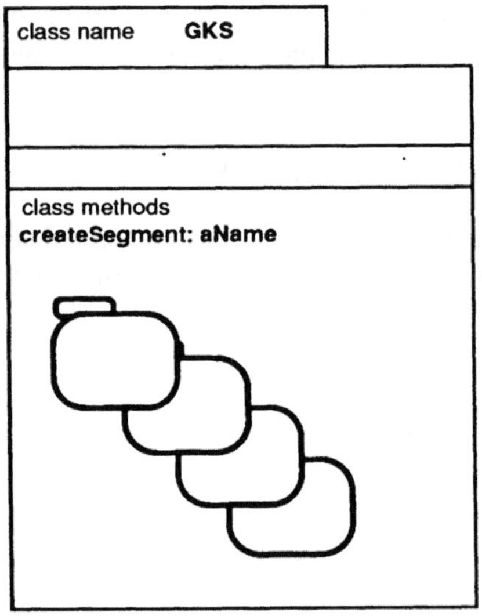

Fig. 5.2. A one-to-one language binding of GKS to Smalltalk-80 shows that segments, although intuitively considered to be objects, are hidden in the kernel and are not accessible by the application programmer.

Since the employed names are instantiated as *input* parameters, we may use them only as arguments of messages:

```
GKS createSegment: name
GKS color: 'green'
GKS polyX: xarray polyY: yarray
GKS pointx: xp pointy: yp
GKS closeSegment
GKS setDetectability: true forSegment: name
```

```
namePicked ← aPickDevice request
GKS delete: namePicked .
```

From the message sender's point of view, there is a class, say **GKS**, to which the above messages are sent. Its methods correspond to the functionality of GKS. Since only input parameters instantiated by the application may be employed for the above functions, the operations do not result in a new object as far as the sender is concerned. Similarly, inquiring the pick device can only return a segment identifier, which is then used as argument in the last expression.

In keeping with the GKS principle, no objects are created for the individual primitives or segments. We can therefore say that this (somewhat senseless) one-to-one translation causes segments to be created only as internal and hidden objects (of the class **GKS**) as is illustrated by Fig. 5.2. This example shows that a non object-oriented style of programming is indeed possible in Smalltalk-80: all functionality is placed into a single class (here GKS) and all the methods are defined for it, resulting in a degeneration of an object-oriented system.

5.4 Object-Oriented Modifications

An object-oriented modification of GKS is easily defined by applying some of the Smalltalk-80 naming principles to GKS; it will not, however, conform completely to the GKS standard. We first define classes for the most important graphics objects. Access to instances can then be provided by the assignment operator.

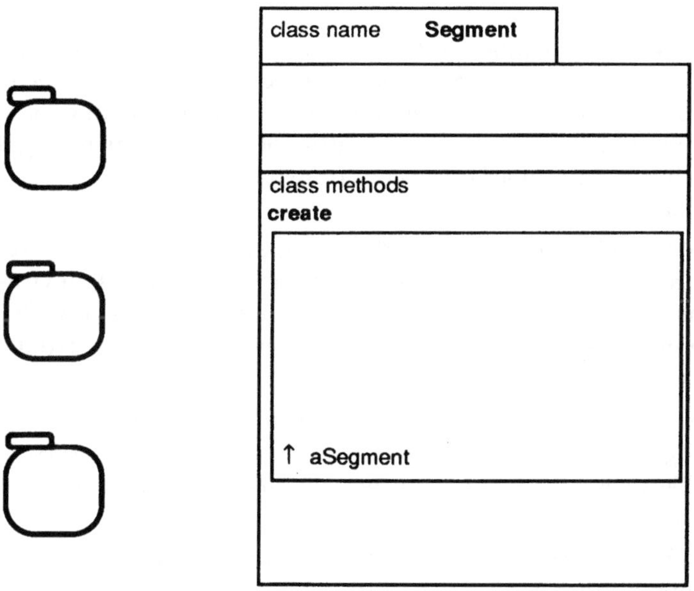

Fig. 5.3. Segments as instances of a class Segment. The example shows that Segment (as a class of the kernel system) generates segments as instances so that they may be accessed directly.

5.4.1 Segments as Objects

To provide the application programmer with segments as objects, corresponds to the object-oriented programming style. It becomes possible provided we supply segments as instances of a class Segment and making them referable by an assignment operation. Thus we obtain, for example, the following specification of segment operations:

```
aSegment ← Segment create
aSegment setVisibility: true
aSegment delete .
```

5.4.2 Output Primitives as Objects

If, by analogy with the Smalltalk-80 kernel, output primitives are also defined as instances of a class, it is possible to generate a new primitive, for example, as follows:

```
aPolyLine ← PolyLine new: coordinates .
```

By allowing the insertion of this object into several segments would then only be a small extension of GKS functionality:

```
aSegment insert: aPolyLine .
```

5.5 Guidelines for an Object-Oriented Kernel

If we continue in this manner and successively turn all the important entities in the graphics kernel system into objects, we eventually leave GKS behind by breaking out of its limited functionality. That is not the intention of this section. Rather, some guidelines for the specification of an object-oriented graphics system will be listed, and some conclusions drawn from them.

The guidelines are:

a) By analogy with the Smalltalk-80 kernel, all important items relevant to a graphics system (output primitives, segments, attributes, devices, transformations) should be available as objects of individual classes. They can then be referenced by identifiers, changed consistently, copied, grouped into collections, queried by inquiry methods, and more.

b) The kernel's functionality should be defined in such a manner that all objects are assigned their own information with their own methods. In addition, each object should be able to answer inquiries about its current state, for instance about its attributes.

c) The applications programmer's interface should be defined as classes, objects and method interfaces that are visible from outside. It should be possible to create subclasses for all these classes. The implementation of the entire functional specification should thereby remain hidden.

d) Requirements for flexible communication between application objects and kernel objects should be met, including the definition of call-back messages, a mechanism that will be explained below.

Following the above guidelines for the design of a graphics system will have a variety of advantages for handling important problems in graphics programming. With a few examples, we will illustrate that; there is no need to specify a graphics system in detail. In the sequel we assume only that an object-oriented graphics kernel is available that meets the requirements listed above.

5.6 An Extended Layer Model

The new mechanisms in object-oriented programming should lead to an extension of the traditional layer model, the *extended layer model*. The relationships between kernel and application, illustrated in Fig. 5.4 may be established as follows:

- The functionality of the graphics kernel may be used—by analogy with the traditional layer model—by application objects sending messages to the (non-internal) *transparent* kernel objects.
- Subclasses of the transparent kernel classes should be constructed to integrate additional knowledge (application-specific information/algorithms, geometric modeling) into them.
- Call-back messages should be defined so that instances of the kernel's classes (or subclasses) may send messages to application objects.
- The possibility of indirect communication between application and kernel should incorporate trigger mechanisms (as in the model-view-controller concept).

Before discussing the first two items, we remark briefly on the potential of communication by the methods mentioned in the first and last statement.

The traditional possibility mentioned in the first statement is used when objects that are not themselves of a graphics nature wish to use the functionality of the kernel. To these ends, the trigger mechanism we encountered in the MVC concept may be used to address the kernel indirectly. We have discussed this concept in Chap. 3 and illustrated its advantages. A graphics kernel can be aptly integrated into the MVC concept by causing display and interaction to take place in a view. Such integration is quite simple for a given application, so there is no need to enlarge on it.

5.6.1 Using Inheritance

Subclassing of the transparent kernel classes offers many possibilities to integrate additional functionality smoothly into an object-oriented kernel without violating the principle of hidden implementation. First, the principle is shown, then more complex and more precisely elaborated examples follow.

5.6.1.1 Subclasses for Output Primitives

We start with subclassing of output primitives. Two simple examples are presented, which show how new graphics methods may be integrated, and how application-specific knowledge may be included. We assume that Circle defines the class for circles and Polyline that for polylines.

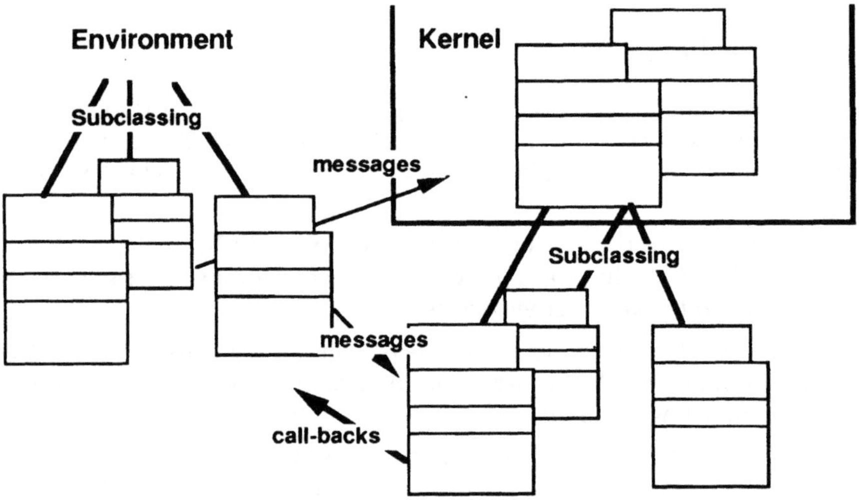

Fig. 5.4. The extended layer model. The classes of the hidden kernel can be used (in a traditional manner) by sending messages to them, preferably by using indirect addressing by triggering mechanisms. In addition, subclassing of the kernel classes is possible as well as subclassing of the predefined classes of the environment. Call-back messages can be sent to application classes supporting flexible mutual communication.

In the first case, we create a subclass NewCircle and define an additional method for the generation of a circle. It creates a circle based on three points supplied as arguments:

aCircle ← NewCircle point1: p1 point2: p2 point3: p3 .

The method is implemented by internally computing the center and radius and then sending the predefined kernel message center: aCenter radius: aRadius to self.

This method could quite easily be implemented in the traditional layer model by a procedure, calling the kernel's function. But subclassing results in a tighter integration of the new method in the kernel. If a set of extended primitives is created by subclassing, one could practically forget that the new classes were not originally part of the prefabricated kernel because all methods of Circle are inherited to the new primitive's class.

The second example is taken from the field of cartography. We wish to create a subclass ContourLine of PolyLine.

For ContourLine, methods for assigning and inquiring application data are defined, e.g., the assignment of height and its inquiry:

```
aContourLine ← ContourLine new: points .
aContourLine meters: 500 .
myHeight ← aContourLine meters .
heightInFeet ← aContourLine feet .
mySegment insert: aContourLine .
```

The advantage of subclassing is again strong integration—here of application data with graphics data. The implementation of the methods is absolutely trivial. Height, for instance, can be stored in an instance variable.

Again, inheritance provides strong integration. If, for example, our graphics kernel supplies an inquiry method for delivering all primitives (in the sense of is-kind-of) for a segment, the user-defined primitives are automatically returned, and they may be analyzed by the method class introduced in 2.5.3.2 and the selection method, introduced in 2.5.2.3:

```
aSetOfPrimitives ← mySegment primitives .
contourSubSet ← mySet select: [ : all | all isMemberOf: ContourLine ] .
```

The last example can only be implemented in a rather inelegant way in a system as GKS. Since an object has both internal methods and variables, many instances of the above type, each with an instance variable for storing the height, may coexist. For this reason, an object-oriented implementation is quite trivial, yet natural. In GKS we are forced to build a dynamic data structure for the management of the non-graphics information. PHIGS offers the possibility of inserting non-graphics application data into a graphics data structure to solve this problem—this rather inelegant mechanism could be used for administrating the height information (see Wisskirchen, 1986a).

5.6.1.2 Subclasses for Segments

Among the possibilities of using inheritance, the enrichment of graphics segments by geometric modeling algorithms is very attractive. In many applications of graphics data processing, complex geometrical functions need to be applied to objects before they may be displayed. Consider a cylinder which is ordinarily described by its height and radius. The geometric modeling process can be considered as an algorithm using the data for its geometrical description, radius and height, and the current transformation as input for the generation of primitives which may be used by the kernel for creating a segment. In the usual layer model this algorithm is part of an application-dependent layer, implemented as an intermediate layer between kernel and application.

A appropriate, consistent geometric modeling system may be seen as an application-oriented layer, if we integrate it in a system like GKS or PHIGS. The application above this layer should primarily use the functionality of this layer, and not the functionality of the kernel directly. That is why it communicates only with the cylinder in the example. In the application layer one wishes to set and change height and radius of the cylinder, move the cylinder, set it detectable or highlight it. In the traditional layer model the implementation of numerous, often trivial routines for bridging between the two worlds would be required.

In an object-oriented kernel we do not need an intermediate layer by utilizing the potential of inheritance for the specialization of graphics segments. For this purpose, we create subclasses of the class Segment for the various types of geometric objects. A subclass of Segment is then addressable by messages from the "application world". Its internal methods translate these messages into graphic primitives for the kernel system as shown by the partial implementation description below.

Taking advantage of inheritance allows us to concentrate on implementing the non-trivial part, that is the algorithm for geometric modeling. The numerous small bridges, handling of segment attributes, naming, deleting, inserting into other segments are inherited from Segment. The general strategy is illustrated in the following protocol, which includes some pseudocode. The geometric modeling algorithm generates the primitives needed for display as the following partial implementation description illustrates.

Cylinder as Subclass of Segment

class name	Cylinder
superclass	Segment
instance variable names	radius height

class methods

instance creation

radius: r height: h "generate a new cylinder by creating a segment"

↑ mySegment ← (super new) radius: r height: h

instance methods

radius: r height: h

radius ← r "set values of instance variables"

height ← h

mySegment open "create and open segment"

calculate primitives line1, ellipse1,...by modeling algorithm

mySegment insert: line1 "Insert results of geometric modeling into open segment"

mySegment insert: ellipse1

• • •

```
mySegment close
↑ self
radius
                                        "Answer radius"
↑ radius
insert: aPrimitive
                                        "override inherited method"
self error: "I'm a Cylinder, not a Segment"
primitives
                                        "override inherited method"
self error: "I'm a Cylinder, therefore I cannot deliver my components"
```

Since Cylinder inherits the usual methods from Segment, the usual segment operations such as assignment of attributes, deletion, transformation, insertion into a hierarchy may be carried out. If needed, these segments may be protected against undesired operations inherited from Segment by overriding and producing an error message, as shown for the insert method.

We could even interpret a cylinder as a *virtual* segment. Virtual means that a cylinder, although it may be handled as real segment, does not allow access to its primitives, as shown in the example above. It is even possible to implement a *lazy evaluation* where the specific primitives only existent while the cylinder is displayed (posted). This is an object-oriented speciality, because each instance of a cylinder is a combination of methods (procedures) and internal data, a construct which cannot be modeled in traditional languages, but which can be handled by its object identifier without problems in a hierarchical graphics system. This idea of a virtual segment has some similarities with Borning's so-called *virtual* part, where polar coordinates are transparent as components to the outside of an object, but are not represented internally (Borning, 1979).

In the above example the class Cylinder was created as subclass of Segment, an existing class of the kernel system. This decision has the consequence that we cannot integrate Cylinder into an hierarchy of non-graphics classes. Assuming, that Cylinder is a product in a product hierarchy organizable in classes, this cannot be modeled together with the previous defined subclassing, if only hierarchical inheritance is supported by the environment.

In object-oriented systems with *multiple* inheritance, both views of Cylinder, the geometrical and product oriented view, may be modelled. In this case a graph-like object hierarchy can be built up and the decision shown in Fig. 5.5 can be avoided.

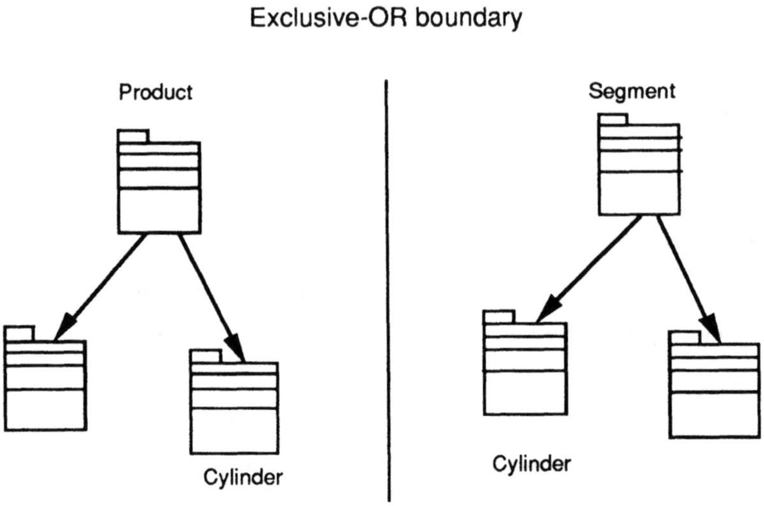

Fig. 5.5. Problems with hierarchical inheritance. For a cylinder which has a double nature (product-oriented and graphics-oriented), it must be decided, what type of nature should be supported by the system's inheritance tree if the programming environment supports only hierarchical inheritance. When multiple inheritance is supported, a mixture of the two aspects can be implemented by an inheritance *graph*.

5.6.2 Communication Between Application and Kernel

In an interactive application, we can differentiate between an application program, the graphics kernel and the user of an interactive interface. Depending on the type of the interactive application, there are different characteristics of the role to be played by the user and the application program.

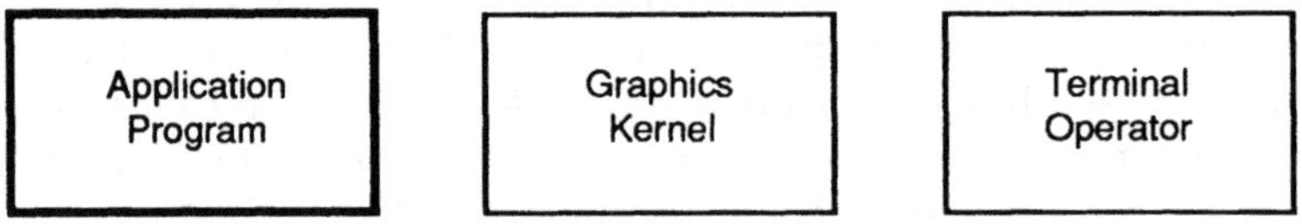

Fig. 5.6. Case of a predominant application.

In the first case, illustrated in the Fig. 5.6, the control of the interaction lies primarily with the application program. Upon request of the application program, the user enters data through an input device, the application program processes it and prompts the user again for data entry, if required. An application of this type could be a complex mathematical simulation in which the user enters simulation parameters upon request. The application program dominates here, and the application program is the master, whereas the user at the terminal could be considered to act like a slave serving the master.

A second case is also imaginable, however, i.e., the dialog is controlled by the user, and the application program plays a rather subordinate role in controlling the interaction.

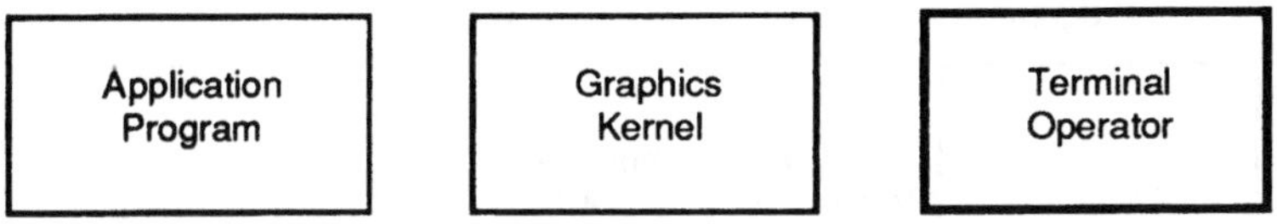

Fig. 5.7 Case of a predominant user interaction.

An example of such an application system would be an interactive graphics editor in which the application program plays primarily the role of a storage administrator for the objects generated by the user. Control of interaction, e.g., when and in which order which objects are generated, lies completely with the terminal operator.

The third case corresponds to a mixed form which is, of course, also imaginable. Interaction is partly controlled by the application program, partly by the user at the terminal. Such a mixed form in which the initiative varies from time to time may be the most frequent case.

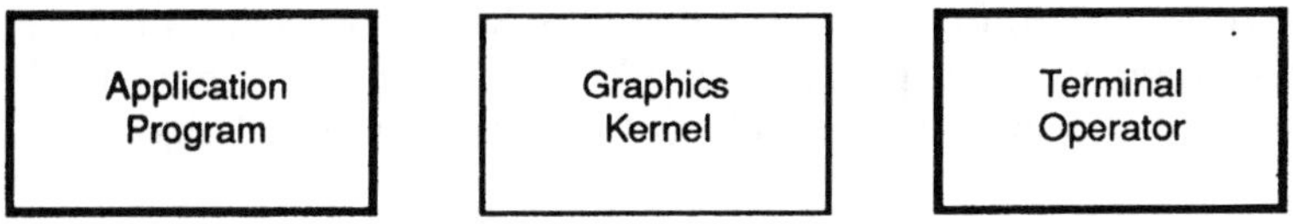

Fig. 5.8. General case of varying control between application and user interaction.

5.6.2.1 Requirements for the Architecture

Which requirements for the software architecture result from the last, the most general model?

a) If control of the dialog lies with the application program, we expect that the application program may call the functions of the kernel.

b) If control lies with the terminal operator, we expect that the software components activated by the user may call the appropriate component of the application program.

5.6.2.2 Control Structures in Traditional Systems.

As mentioned, in traditional graphics kernel systems the control lies exclusively with the application program. Therefore, option b) cannot be implemented. The application programmer must use tricks and roundabout ways to achieve the required functionality. Usually the application program calls an input device, analyzes the user's input and then branches to the appropriate part of the application.

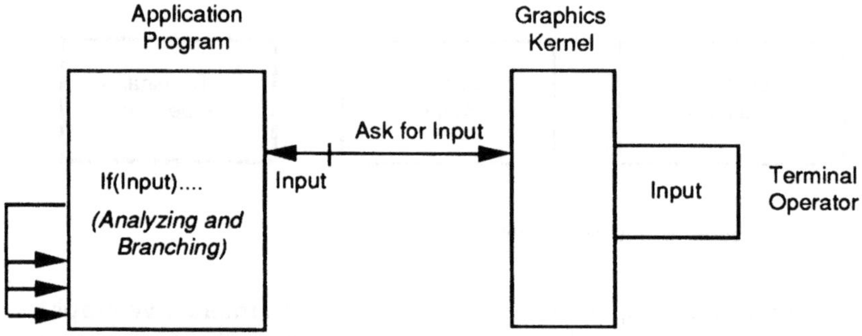

Fig. 5.9. Traditional input model. Input is requested by the application program. The application program calls an input device, analyzes the input, e.g., a menu selected by the user and then branches to the appropriate procedure.

5.6.2.3 Realization in Object-Oriented Systems

In an object-oriented environment, option b) can in fact be included. In reaction to an input operation, for instance a pick, the kernel can send a message to the picked object, which on its part can react by sending a message referred to as the *call-back message*, to an application object (or a graphics kernel object).

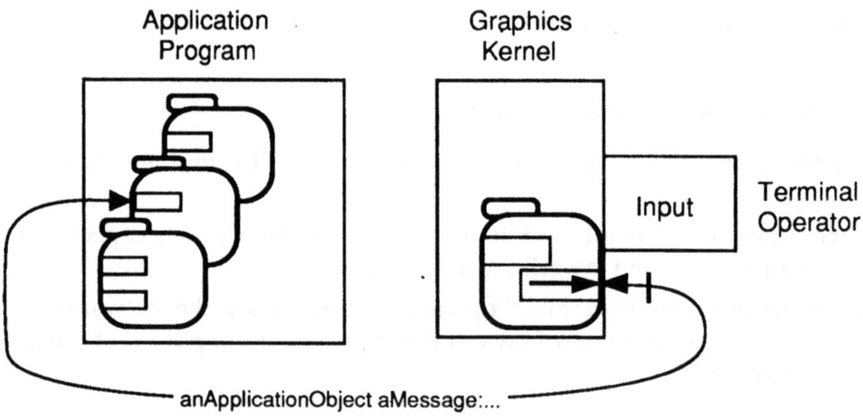

Fig. 5.10. Object-oriented input model. Picked objects of the graphics kernel may call application objects by call-back messages.

How can an object be informed as to the receiver and the type of message it should send as a reaction to a pick operation? Since we cannot modify the graphics kernel, we must find a way to associate this information with a picked object. Two possibilities for implementing this are:

- Create a subclass of Segment and override the method pick which is executed as a reaction to the pick operation. The situation is similar to the menu messages of the mouse menu controller in the Smalltalk-80 environment.
- Use an initialization message, sent to different pick candidates, which includes as parameters the receiver and the message pattern of the call-back message.

With these choices, the reactions of an interactive system to user actions may be modeled much more natural than in traditional systems, and it leads to a greater system transparency and modularity. The user activates an input tool, it refers to a graphics object, that in turn refers to an application object. Traditional systems, in contrast, demand a more control. A central dialogue evaluator, which has to be implemented by the applications programmer, analyzes the picked candidates or selected menu options, and branches to the appropriate procedure.

5.7 Assignment of Attributes

Let us consider the assignment of attributes in GKS and PHIGS and in object-oriented graphics kernels.

5.7.1 Attribute Assignment in GKS and PHIGS

In GKS, *segment-attributes* are set in an "object-oriented" spirit. An attribute is assigned explicitly to an object, in our case the segment, using an identifier. For an object-oriented language binding this implies that each object to which an attribute is assigned has a corresponding method at its disposal. If no attribute is assigned explicitly, a default assignment takes effect.

The assignment of *attributes for output primitives* is carried out *modally* in GKS. By this we understand that attributes are added to a status list that is implemented inside the kernel and from which the attribute values are transferred to the subsequently generated graphic primitives.

In PHIGS, only a few attributes relate to a structure as a whole and are assigned by using the structure identifier. For attributes which relate to graphic primitives, a concept differing from that of GKS is provided. Attributes are inserted into a structure and can thus seen as setting or changing a status. In contrast to GKS, the status is then applied to sequential element at structure traversal time, where the ordering relation is defined by the traversal rules. In a certain sense, this is also a modal allocation, but which can, in contrast to GKS, be changed dynamically.

5.7.2 Facilities of Object-Oriented Systems

Attributes may also be set modally in object-oriented systems, but we do not consider it to be desirable. Our goal is to be able simply to name the addressee of an attribute and thereby avoid temporal (as in GKS) or sequential (as in PHIGS) relationships (as in GKS or PHIGS, resp,). To have the application programmer assign an attribute to every primitive explicitly, would, of course, be unnecessarily complicated. To avoid this, an alternative would be to assign an attribute to another object, which stands for more than one primitive. Possible candidates for such objects are the primitive's class, or collections (in the sense of a part hierarchy) that contain the primitive. Essentially three options of attribute allocation are supplied by object-oriented systems. Of course, the may be applied in combination:

a) setting and modifying an attribute by a class method for a graphics primitive's class. The attribute could be represented (internally and therefore invisibly from outside) by a class variable which is accessed by the subsequently (in time) generated instances of the class (class attribute assignment). If one creates subclasses of the primitive´s class, this option may be extended to the class hierarchy.
b) If segments are considers as objects of a part-of hierarchy, then they are "containers" with output primitives or sub-segments as parts. Then even allocate attributes could be allocated to segments *(whole-part assignment).*
c) Since individual graphic primitives are objects, attributes may be assigned explicitly to them (*strict object-oriented assignment*)

This variety of options requires the definition of priority rules. We suggest that a) has lowest, b) middle and c) highest priority.

The following assignments may serve as examples:

```
mySegment ← Segment new .
PolyLine color: 'red' .
myPoly ← PolyLine new: nPoints .
myPoly2 ← PolyLine new: mPoints .
myPoly color: 'green' .
mySegment color: 'blue' .
mySegment insert: myPoly .
mySegment insert: myPoly2 .
```

The result, in keeping with our priorities, is that myPoly eventually has the color green, whereas myPoly2 is blue.

In the semantic net shown in Fig. 5.11 the relations between the different possibilities of assigning attributes are illustrated.

5.8 Summary

Starting with GKS, we described its functionality from an object-oriented point of view. Should we modify a graphics system as GKS such that all the important items we intuitively consider to be objects are made available as objects in the object-oriented programming sense, then we reap several advantages. Inheritance allows us to modify the kernel and combine it more elegantly with application-specific data and algorithms. We can realize more flexible communication between kernel and application. Furthermore, we can more directly assign attributes to visible graphics information.

We have not yet spoken of editable systems that support a multi-level hierarchy, it will be the topic of the following chapters.

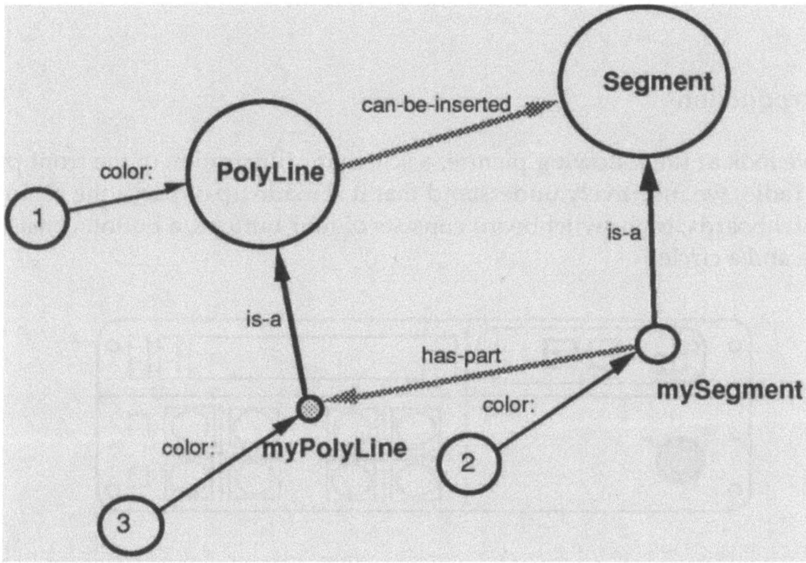

Fig. 5.11. Three different types of attribute setting, using object-oriented assignment. The highest proposed priority is (3), the direct assignment; the lowest is (1), which could be interpreted as a predefined default value for the class PolyLine.

6 Graphics Part Hierarchies

6.1 Introduction

When we look at the following picture, a schematic illustration of the front panel of a car radio, we intuitively understand that it is made up of parts: the radio has two switchboards, each switchboard consists of four buttons, a button consists of a square and a circle.

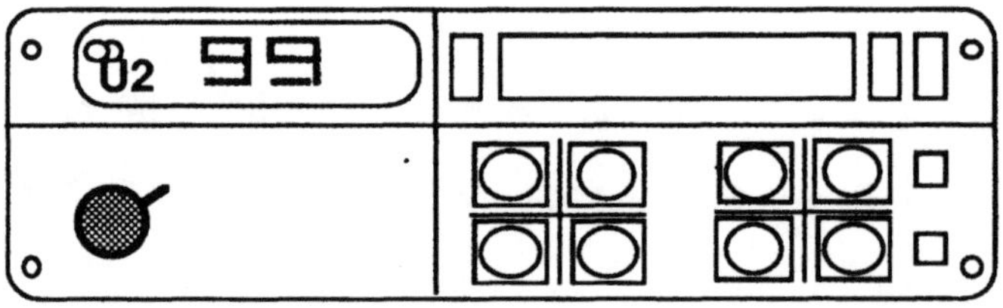

Fig. 6.1. Front panel of a car radio. With this drawing a part hierarchy is intuitively associated: the radio has two switch boards, each switch board consists of four buttons, a button consists of a square and a circle.

The organization of items in the form of part hierarchies is one of the most frequently used methods of modeling and describing phenomena in the real world. The idea behind this is that of constructing or describing complex objects through composition of simpler ones. It will reduce the overall complexity of a problem. Such organization of objects allows us to describe the construction of a whole from parts. Beyond this, the principle of re-using similar parts, i.e., parts with the same geometrical description, is often expressed in the context of part hierarchies. Part hierarchies play an important role in many areas of science and technology.

In computer graphics, part hierarchies are of interest wherever complex graphics representations can be interpreted as conglomerations of simpler parts—which is the case in most applications of graphics. An interactive graphics editor, such as MacDraw, is a typical application program based by the concept of composition: simple graphics primitives may be selected from a menu and grouped to form higher aggregates. Copy-operations serve to multiply parts and support the idea of the repeated use of objects having the same building pattern.

Part hierarchies are important in other fields of computer science, too—for instance, artificial intelligence. They are often used there in modeling and representing so-called world knowledge. We must note that a part hierarchy differs from a class hierarchy as understood by object-oriented programming. A class hierarchy expresses a behavior-relation, whereas a part hierarchy expresses a composition-relation. In the field of computer graphics, the word inheritance is sometimes used to express semantic aspects in connection with the part hierarchy. For example, one speaks of parts inheriting attributes from the structure they belong to. So the automatic transfer of characteristics of the whole to its constituents is called inheritance here. This use of the word inheritance is not to be confused with inheritance in the sense of creating subclasses. For this reason we will use the term inheritance only for latter sense, in the context of a part hierarchy we will speaking of *transferring* attributes down to parts of a hierarchy.

6.2 Part Hierarchies and Computer Graphics

In all those application areas of graphics which deal with structures that can be described naturally as part hierarchies, a graphics system that optimally supports the semantic aspects of a part hierarchy is highly desirable.

Consequently that such a system should provide for the representation of knowledge about the composition of a part hierarchy. In addition, it should offer the basic functions for their manipulation.

6.2.1 Requirements

The semantics of a part hierarchy are described by the operations that can be applied to the hierarchy. To a certain extent, their scope can be chosen freely. There exists, however, a hard kernel of operations without which it would be senseless to speak of a part hierarchy. If an interactive graphics system claims to support part hierarchies effectively, then we expect support in the following areas of functionality:

- Construction of a part hierarchy.
- Editing the hierarchy.
- Assignment and inquiring of attributes.
- Graphics input operations for the identification of parts of the hierarchy.

6.2.2 Criteria for Ideal System Support

Important criteria for the quality of a graphics system that supports a part hierarchy are naturalness and simplicity.

- Naturalness: the functional description of such a system by a programming language should be as close as possible to the semantics of the part hierarchy. Therefore, the graphics system must offer constructs that are intuitively related to the description of the part hierarchy.
- Simplicity: all frequently used operations for the manipulation of a part hierarchy should be supported directly. It should be possible to formulate each of these operations as a single expression, i.e., as an atomic action.

6.2.3 Combination With Other Semantics

It is important to note that computer graphics assists applications in which part hierarchies play a lesser role and where other semantics play a more important role. Typical examples are graph structures, such as Petri nets with nodes and edges, where the part hierarchy is "flat", but where complex semantics for modeling the neighborhood relations need be observed. Some of the semantic aspects can be abstracted from individual applications and may therefore be candidates to be supported by a corresponding kernel system. In other cases, however, the semantics are strongly tailored to the needs of an individual application. Consequently, supporting these directly through a graphics kernel system makes little sense. A graphics kernel system that can be combined with additional tools to model general semantic aspects in easily will be the optimal solution. Such support can be provided, for example, by help of new capabilities (rules, constraints) for the formulation of relationships between graphics objects —relationships that would be difficult to describe in the terms of a part hierarchy. In almost all cases that we are aware of, other semantic aspects occur in combination with part hierarchy. Therefore, the ease with which a graphics system that supports part hierarchy can be extended is an important aspect to be studied.

6.2.4 Manipulation of Part Hierarchies

The following examples illustrate some typical tasks that should be supported by a graphics system. We will be returning to these examples below, when we compare GEO++ with PHIGS.

6.2.4.1 Construction of a Hierarchy

In constructing a hierarchy, the main task consists of composing a complex part hierarchy from predefined building blocks. To this end, a graphics system provides output-primitives on the lowest level. It should also be possible, though, to store previously constructed parts in a library and access them when needed. In above example, it would means access to already existing buttons, to the construction of a switchboard (where using a button four times and defining its four positions are important operations), and to the construction of the front panel (using the switchboard and the other needed parts).

6.2.4.2 Assigning and Changing Attributes

Next to constructing the part hierarchy, it is often necessary to assign a new attribute to parts of the hierarchy, or to change an existing attribute. It may be necessary to change the attribute of an individual part, for example a specific button on the radio. On the other hand, we may wish to add a new attribute to all eight buttons on the front panel at once. This latter operation require that the system "knows" that all eight buttons on the radio are based on the same building block. An interesting question in this context is how the graphics kernel supports access to an individual part—say, a specific button—, as opposed to access to the building pattern button.

6.2.4.3 Editing of Parts in a Part Hierarchy

The requirements of interactive graphics also demand support for editing a part hierarchy. Similar to the assignment of attributes, operations for changing a geometric description (editing a building pattern) and operations for changing an individual part (editing a part) should be offered:

- When a geometric description is edited, a pattern that is generally re-used several times is changed, so that all parts that are based on this description change. Moreover, to complete replacement, operations we expect: modification of a building pattern, insertion of additional geometric information, and deletion of existing information.
- When a single part is edited, only a specific object should be changed. We expect to have available, therefore, functions for the modification of the geometric description of individual items.

6.2.4.4 Interactive Access to a Part

The manner in which a graphics kernel system supports the programming of the interactive access to a part are important aspects of interactive graphics. It should be possible, with simple means, to set a part or a set of individual parts detectable, and to define the reaction to the pick.

6.2.4.5 Interactive Construction of a Part Hierarchy

If a part hierarchy is created interactively by means of a graphics editor, then additional operations, beyond aids for the construction of the hierarchy, are needed. They must be able modify the organization of the part hierarchy. As we will point out in 6.3, MacDraw, for example, offers functions for grouping a set of existing primitives or groups, and for ungrouping such a group. Functions like these should also be easily programmable by using a graphics system.

6.2.4.6 Binding a Part Hierarchy Into an Internal Application

The examples so far have been concerned only with operations that affect the part hierarchy directly. Frequently, however, such a hierarchy represents the user interface of a non-graphics application. For example, a construct like the front panel could be used as an interface for an application behind. The user may then manipulate the displayed buttons of the front panel using graphics interaction techniques and thereby control an application process "Play the radio". A graphics system must obviously fulfill requirements that ease the support of the communication between system and application.

6.2.4.7 Naming and Navigation

One prerequisite for simplified description of the functionality is an elegant and simple concept for naming in a part hierarchy. Not only naming of individual parts, collection of parts, and geometrical descriptions, but also navigating through the part hierarchy. So it must be possible, with simple means, to reach the descendents of a part and to access the ancestor chain of a part.

6.3 MacDraw and Part Hierarchies

In this section, we take a look at the graphics editor MacDraw or more specifically, its successor MacDraw II and concentrate on the aspect of handling part hierarchies by this editor. A single interactive application is not sufficiently comprehensive to extract the main requirements for a graphics system—which has to be an appropriate application programmer's interface for nearly all graphics applications. But there are two reasons why MacDraw could serve as a prototype candidate to offer suggestions for a graphics system:

- MacDraw is widely used and provides a style of interaction that may be considered to be state-of-the-art.
- The functionality of MacDraw—regarded as a graphics editor which supports the generation and editing of "hierarchical" structure—has much in common with the broad class of CAD-type applications that are supported by interactive computer graphics.

When referring to objects in this section, we understand them in an intuitive sense as entities of a MacDraw application. They motivate an analysis of their behavior and a search for their common and distinct properties—with the aim of implementing classes and instances which correspond to them as genuine object-oriented components of a graphics kernel.

6.3.1 Main Features

MacDraw supports a number of object types such as polylines, circles, ellipses, rectangles, and curves.

A set of primitives can be gathered into a group. Existing groups may also be treated as elements of a set and again be collected in a group, resulting in a multilevel hierarchy that may be interpreted as a part hierarchy.

Attributes may be applied to individual primitive or to a group. One or several single primitives or single groups can be selected with the mouse, and they will be highlighted automatically. The set of all selected items created in this manner is called an *ad-hoc set*. Attributes can be assigned to an ad-hoc set. An ad-hoc sets differ from a group by its life-time: it exists only while the objects are selected.

In a group, on the other hand, knowledge of the complete hierarchy of elements is retained—reaching to the lowest level of the hierarchy, the primitives. This can be studied when a sequence of ungroup operations is applied to a selected group, as shown by Fig. 6.2. Ungrouping is an operation directly applicable to the selected items; the result of one ungroup operation is the set of all "children" of the selected ad-group.

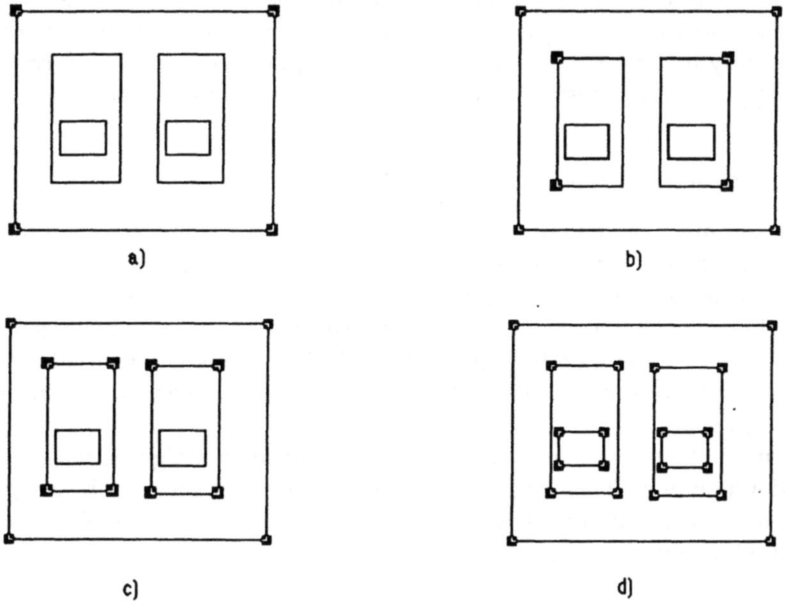

Fig. 6.2. Ungrouping a multi-level hierarchy. Three steps are required for a complete ungrouping of the part hierarchy. The activation points in b), c), and d) show that group a) knows about the complete hierarchy.

To sum up, MacDraw knows *three* different types of aggregates that can be assigned attributes:

- an individual primitive,
- an individual group, and
- an ad-hoc set.

6.3.2 Semantics of the Part Hierarchy

The semantics of the part hierarchy, i.e., the functions that can be applied to a primitive, a group or an ad-hoc set are more or less defined by the following operations:

- assign attributes,
- cut (delete), paste (add), copy,
- duplicate,
- generate a new primitive,
- edit.

These operations can only be applied to the highest level of the hierarchy. In other words, it not possible to apply an operation to an individual member of a group. Should it be necessary to do so, nevertheless, for example, to assign an attribute to an object, the group in question must first be ungrouped, i.e., destroyed; after having assigned the attribute, the modified group must be established by selecting appropriate objects and applying the group operation. Consequently it can be stated that MacDraw supports the following concept of managing part hierarchies: multi-level grouping and "top-level" editing.

6.3.2.1 Assignment of Attributes

Direct assignment of attributes is achieved according to the *point-and-act* principle. First, an object (group or individual primitive) is picked with the mouse. Then the desired operation is applied to the selected object in this case the attribute, chosen from a menu, is assigned. Since any chosen set may be defined by multiple selection, its members coincide with the "pointed" information so that point-and-act means that an attribute can be assigned to an ad-hoc set in a simple step (cf. Fig. 6.3).

One might be tempted to interpret this direct form of assignment as an object-oriented assignment. This would be a mistake, however, because the assignment applied to an selected objects is automatically chosen as a new default which is valid for all newly created primitives.

6.3.2.2 Cut, Paste, Copy, Duplicate

MacDraw also supports cut-and-paste operations for selected objects as is customary in the Apple Macintosh community. If a selected object is pasted or copied, the new object inherits all attributes of the original (except the position). The same is true for the duplication operation.

MacDraw does not support a concept for a multiply referenced object or a geometrical description used in different contexts with the feature that an edit operation applied to it will modify all of its occurrences. A copy or duplicate is always a deep copy in the language of Smalltalk-80 and knowledge about common ancestry is lost.

6.3.3 Generation and Editing of Primitives

Creation of a new primitive occurs after a primitive of a given type has been selected from the menu bar on the left; it is performed by the operations supported by the functions of the mouse and it consists mainly of adding new points, selecting existing ones, and move them.

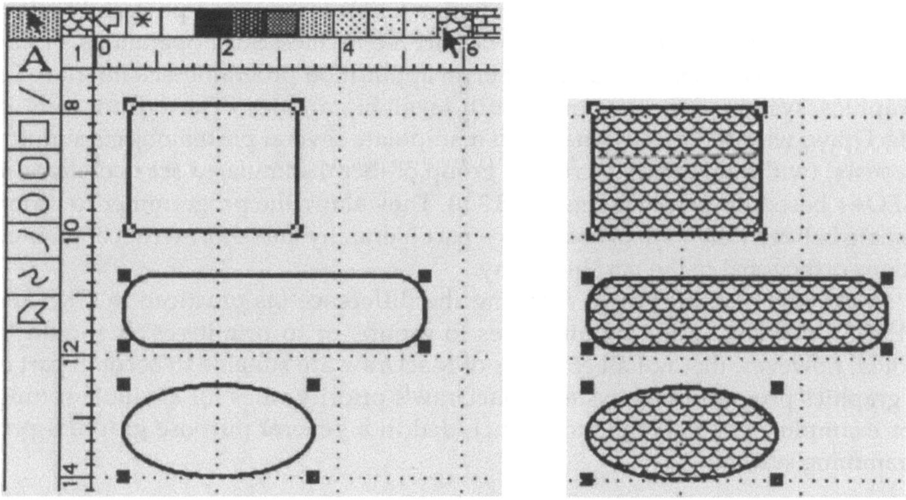

Fig. 6.3. Assignment of an attribute to a set of selected objects. After selection of a set of objects (ad-hoc set) an attribute is assigned to this set, resulting in the set displayed at right-hand side.

A group can either be ungrouped or deleted as a whole. So if a group is to be modified, say by replacing one of its elements by another this can only be achieved by the following steps—similar to these already mentioned above in the context of attribute assignment—: the group must first be disbanded, then the element to be replaced must be deleted, the new one added, and a new group generated by selecting an ad-hoc set and applying the group operation to it.

Beside creating primitives from scratch, existing primitives such as splines or polylines can be modified; for example, to change the position of a coordinate point of a polyline or a knot of a curve, as illustrated in Fig. 6.4., is legal.

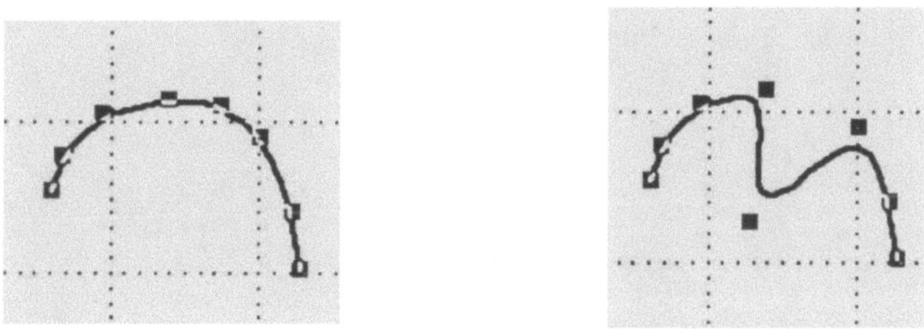

Fig. 6.4. Modification of a curve. A knot of a curve can be selected and moved, resulting in a modified curve.

6.3.4 Discussion

MacDraw's functionality led us to incorporate functions into GEO++ that may be seen to a certain extent as adoptions. The group/ungroup operations of

MacDraw, for example, can also be found in GEO++; they are a powerful tool for the construction and reorganization of part hierarchies. Such operations should be available as elementary functions in an application programmer's interface for graphics system that supports multi-level hierarchies. The ad-hoc sets of MacDraw, with their functionality to manipulate several picked objects simultaneously, (without having to create a group of them) stimulated set operations in GEO++ based on graphics sets (cf. 8.3.5). They allow the programmer to differentiate between the objects bound in a part hierarchy and short-term conglomerations orthogonal to the part hierarchy.

MacDraw also motivates reducing the difference (as practiced in GKS and PHIGS) between assigning attributes to groups or to primitives. It should be noted, however, that not all concepts of MacDraw are suitable to become part of a graphics programming system. MacDraw's priority rules for attribute setting, for example, are too simple to be included in a general purpose graphics programming system.

7 PHIGS and Part Hierarchies

In the next few chapters we will be discussing in greater detail both the object-oriented kernel system GEO++ and the graphics standard PHIGS (Programmer's Hierarchical Interactive Graphics System). PHIGS is the graphics system that especially supports a part hierarchy by handling multi-level structures. Unfortunately, there is hardly any literature on PHIGS that allows an in-depth analysis of some of the problematic points available. Such an analysis is important, however, in order to master identified weak points by introducing object-oriented design principles. We do not wish to denigrate the work of those who defined PHIGS years ago by stressing these critical points. But developments in the field of interactive programming have since progressed. The object-oriented paradigm is gaining more and more ground and, as we shall see, almost necessarily and naturally calls for the revision of some basic principles of PHIGS.

7.1 Drawbacks of the GKS Model

As mentioned already, GKS supports only a single-level hierarchy. There is an exception, as it is possible to insert a pick-Identifier into a segment. Therefore, the graphics information for an interactive pick-operation can be structured into two levels. So if a user interface with multi-level structures is to be implemented by using GKS, the applications programmer must construct and administer his own part hierarchy and then map it into GKS. Needless to say, this is a very tedious process. In addition, only a restricted possibility of changing the single-level segment structure is supported GKS. New segments may be added and existing ones may be deleted, but it is not possible to change the content of a segment. The use of GKS as a kernel for implementing non-trivial interactive applications is nearly impossible.

7.2 Motivation for an Extended Functionality

The weaknesses in GKS, clearly pointed out to the need for a new graphics standard, a programming system that directly supports the construction and modification of hierarchical graphics structures. As a result, PHIGS was defined and standardized. PHIGS supports:

- A multi-level data structure with the help of which part hierarchies can be constructed;
- a reference mechanism that allows multiple use of a construct, called *structure*, without having to duplicate its geometric description;

- an editing mechanism that allows not only the manipulation of structures as a whole, as in GKS, but also the manipulation of single elements (including output primitives, attributes, transformations, identifiers) within a structure.

Almost all operations supported by PHIGS can be interpreted as semantic operations for construction and editing of a graphics part hierarchy. PHIGS does not, however, offer a comprehensive high-level concept for the manipulation of such hierarchies. It is confined to elementary editing functions: in an open structure, an element can be inserted, a structure element may be removed, and a sequence of elements can be copied into the open structure from an existing one. Any desired transformation of one graphics part hierarchy into another one can be achieved with these elementary operations.

Nevertheless, for many of the operations on a part hierarchy that occur frequently in graphics interaction, much of effort is necessary to describe them by a series of PHIGS functions. PHIGS has no mechanism that supports the consistency of a hierarchical graphics data structure, i.e., that could point out inconsistent states in a structure. This is solely the responsibility of the applications programmer. We will be discussing the disadvantages resulting from this in more detail, as we wish to reach tenable alternatives by using object-oriented concepts.

7.3 PHIGS Components

The fundamental concept for the management of graphics information is the structure. The most important information about the definition of a graphics object, including references to other structures, is stored in a structure. A structure together with its substructures are called a *structure network*.

7.3.1 Construction and Editing Structure Networks

The construction of a structure is initiated by the command *open structure*. A *structure element* may comprise different kinds of information such as output primitives, attributes, transformations, identifiers, and references to substructures. For every function call that concerns the construction of a graphics object, an element is generated and inserted in the structure. A structure is defined and edited as follows:

- A structure is organized as a linear list; its elements are incremented with an integer element pointer.
- Only one structure may be open at any time.
- Insertion always occurs at the current element pointer, that is initialized to 1 when a new structure is generated and automatically incremented by every insertion of an element.
- When an element is deleted, the current element pointer is decreased by one, when an element is replaced, it is held constant.
- Arbitrary positioning of the current element pointer within an open structure is legal, any element of the sequence may therefore be edited directly.

- More complex editing operations that affect several elements are also available. For example, all elements between two element pointers can be deleted in one step.
- By inserting *label elements* into a structure, there is no need, generally, to employ integer element pointers; operations such as deleting between two labels are supported instead.

7.3.2 References to Substructures

An *execute structure* element may be inserted into a structure. Its parameter is the name of another structure which can be referred to. in this manner. The reference process builds a structure network in the form of an acyclic directed graph (cyclical references are illegal). The graph can be considered to be an organization scheme.

7.3.3 Posting

After selecting of an appropriate output device, the operation *post* is applied to a structure for displaying it. Display is achieved by expanding the graph by sequential traversal, i.e., its elements are processed sequentially until a reference is encountered; invocation of a reference results in an interruption of the sequential processing and leads to branch to the referenced substructure. This substructure may itself contain references, so that several levels can be processed. When a referenced structure has been completely traversed, a jump return to the calling structure occurs and sequential processing of the invoking parent structure continues at the element after the execute structure element (cf. Fig. 7.1.). We call the resulting sequence the PHIGS *traversal list. The traversal list is an abstract concept only* and it cannot be accessed by the application programmer.

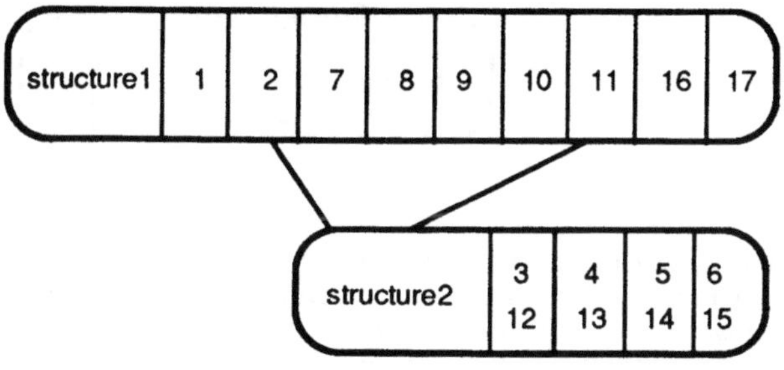

Fig. 7.1. PHIGS traversal. In the example, a substructure is invoked twice, resulting in a traversal list of seventeen elements. This list is only an abstract concept and cannot accessed by the programmer.

Several structures may be posted without first deactivating previously posted ones. Both posted and unposted structures may be edited.

7.3.4 Assignment of Primitive Attributes

During traversal, the attributes valid at the position of the execute element are transferred to the child structure. If a substructure is repeatedly invoked from within a structure—in PHIGS this implies that may occur at several positions in the parent structure—then different attributes and transformations are usually transferred down to each occurrence. In effect, the called structure may be displayed with individual characteristics (different attributes and transformations).

The following rules, illustrated by an examples in Fig. 7.2, govern attribute-setting in PHIGS:

- For a structure to be displayed, at the beginning a complete set of attributes is inherited from the environment. The set is valid until an attributes are encountered by the traversal process.
- If an attribute element is found in a structure, the currently valid attribute (of the same type) is replaced and the new attribute becomes valid for the following elements in the traversal process.
- If a substructure is referenced within a structure, then the current state of all attributes are saved and the substructure is called.
- The set of attributes is transferred downward, but changes when new attributes are encountered in the substructure.
- Upon return of traversal into the calling structure, the saved set of attributes is valid once again.

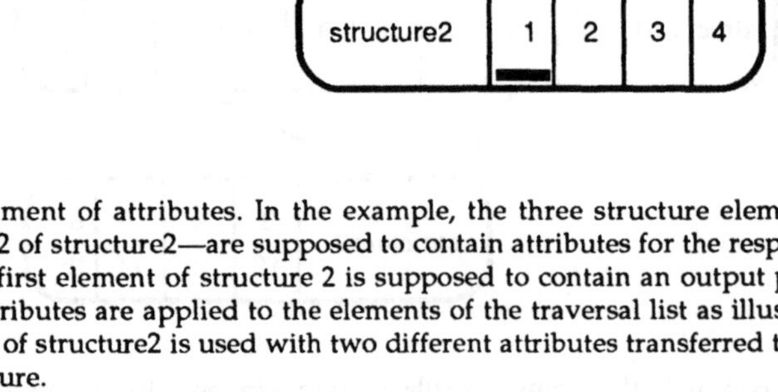

Fig. 7.2. Assignment of attributes. In the example, the three structure elements—1 and 5 of structure 1, and 2 of structure2—are supposed to contain attributes for the respective linewidths 1, 2, and 4.; the first element of structure 2 is supposed to contain an output primitive. During traversal, the attributes are applied to the elements of the traversal list as illustrated. Note that the first element of structure2 is used with two different attributes transferred to it by the invoking parent structure.

It should be noted that *no output primitive in a structure owns any attribute* because output primitives are represented by structure elements which may be used in different contexts. Attributes are only applied to visible information during traversal time, when posting a structure. This information cannot, as mentioned, be accessed by PHIGS functions. Referring to an attribute of an output primitive really means, that the attribute is applied to a primitive at a certain state of the traversal process of a structure network.

7.3.5 Transformations

The transformation pipeline in PHIGS has a device-dependent and a device-independent part. The device-dependent part, which we will not be discussing further here, comprises a projective transformation and a device transformation. The device-independent part consists of a single type of transformation, the *modeling transformation*, which may change during traversal of a structure network.

The modeling transformation is defined by a 4 x 4 matrix. It is handled much like a display attribute. When it is called by the application program, a corresponding element is inserted at the current element pointer of the open structure. It can be specified whether a modeling transformation inserted into a structure is to replace the previous one (local replacement) or to be multiplied with it at traversal time. In the latter case, one can choose between right and left multiplication. Furthermore, there is the option of setting the transformation absolutely (global replacement). As with display attributes, the modeling transformation is transferred downwards; transformations applied to a substructure have no upward effect. Also, as with display attributes, the transformation valid before an execute expression is reset upon return to the calling structure.

7.3.6 Visibility, Detectability, Highlighting

The concepts for manipulating the attribute types visibility, detectability, and highlighting has been substantially extended in PHIGS. In contrast to GKS, where these attributes can only be assigned to an entire segment, they may be set very flexibly in PHIGS with the aid of a powerful though somewhat unwieldy naming concept:

- A special structure element *add-names-to-set* allows a set of names to be inserted into a structure. They are assigned to the elements following in the structure during traversal time, much as attributes. Next to adding names, a set of names can be deleted from a structure with the special element *delete-names-from-set*.
- The two operations mentioned above can be used to assign a set of names to any primitive at traversal time.
- The assigned names may be used to define a *filter* for each of the three types of attributes, called *visibility filter, highlighting filter*, and *pick filter* respectively. A filter consists of two sets, an *inclusion set* and an *exclusion set*.
- All output primitives are initialized with the default values visible, non-detectable, and not-highlighted.
- In order for a traversed output primitive to be detectable, for example, one of its names, assigned by the name-set statement to it, must occur in the inclu-

sion set for detectability. In addition, none of its names may be members of the exclusion set.

Suppose, that for the structure network displayed in Fig. 7.3 the first element of structure1 is defined as an add-names-to-set element and the element 6 of structure1 as a remove-names-from-set element:

```
OPEN STRUCTURE (structure1)
SET ELEMENT POINTER (1)
ADD NAMES TO SET({ First, Second })
SET ELEMENT POINTER (6)
REMOVE NAMES FROM SET ({ Second })
```

When a pick filter will be defined by:

```
SET PICK FILTER ({ First, Second },{ Second })
```

then all output primitives used in the *traversal* list (see Fig. 7.1) between 1 and 17 will become detectable, because the name First is valid for all list elements. When we change the filter by:

```
SET PICK FILTER ({ Second },{ Second })
```

then only primitives with traversal list elements between 1 and 9 are detectable because this is the range where Second is a member of the current name set.

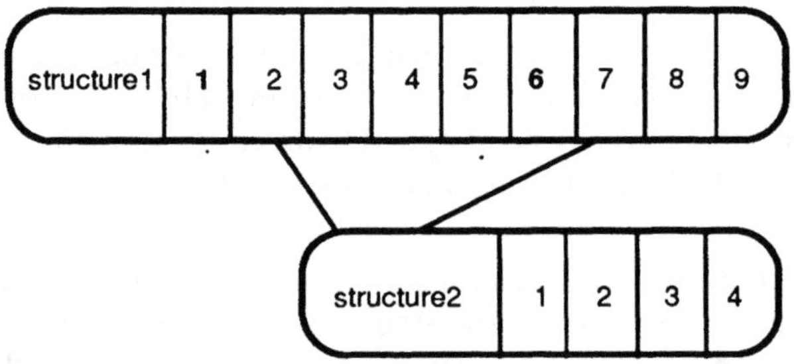

Fig. 7.3. Name sets in PHIGS. After insertion of a add-names-to-set element at position 1 and a insertion of a remove-names-from-set element at position 6 of structure1, filters may be defined for controlling highlighting, detectability, and visibility in a flexible manner.

What is the motivation for this apparently quite complex flexibility? In GKS, only segments have names and therefore attributes considered can be applied only to entire segments. This means that attributes such as visibility can only be controlled on the segment level and the visibility of parts of segments cannot be changed. PHIGS, on the other hand, allows defining and changing attributes dynamically and orthogonally to the organization of the structure network. The idea behind this principle is that *graphics requires structuring possibilities that are orthogonal to each other*. In meeting the resulting requirements, it cannot suffice simply to assign attributes to a structure as a whole.

We agree with this view, but find the solution offered in PHIGS to be quite complicated. It results in a naming concept that is hard to oversee and difficult to handle, as shown by our examples in Chap. 9. To look ahead to the next chapter, we would like to point out the following. In GEO++, every visible output primitive and every group of such primitives in a part hierarchy has exactly one unique name. All attributes are assigned directly to the visible information in an object-oriented way using this name. This allows attribute assignment in accordance to the part hierarchy, usually by a single operation. For filtering out specific sets which are *orthogonal* to the part hierarchy we allow to collect primitives, parts and groups into an ad-hoc set and assign attributes such as detectability (and even primitive attributes such a linestyles) to this set. We feel this substantially simplifies the flexible assignment of the attributes discussed here, without restricting flexibility (cf. 8.3.5).

The following is important to note:

1. In a complex multi-level graph the PHIGS filter concept is not powerful enough to define that to any predefined subset of the traversal list an attribute could be assigned valid for this set and invalid for the rest.
2. A slight modification of the definition would, however, enable this. The modification could be formulated in the filter is defined in the manner, that it is described by a set of sets, where the elements are and-predicates for names, for example:

   ```
   SET PICK FILTER ({ (Name1,Name3, Name7), (Name20, Name7) })
   ```

   i.e., an object is detectable if its name set is ecactly defined by Name1, Name3, Name7 or by Name20, Name7.

7.3.7 Interaction

The input tools of PHIGS are close in functionality to those of GKS. Available are locator, valuator, text input, and pick. After an activation, these input tools can be inquired directly or from an event queue. Because all tools are invoked by the application program, control and analysis is always at the responsibility of the calling program. Consequently, there are no input tools that can be combined with call-back messages.

We are especially interested in the pick operation. It is the input function that refers to the graphics object structure. As mentioned above, name sets together with a filter cause individual primitives to be detectable. Further, because of multiple referencing of substructures, there is usually no element in a structure that directly corresponds to a picked object in PHIGS. For this reason the pick operation returns a pick path that allows to analyze what visible object on the screen, corresponding to an element of the traversal list, was picked. The exact definition of the pick path is described in the examples of 9.1.

For a primitive to be picked, it must be detectable, which can be specified by a corresponding filter. Only a primitive can be picked, not a higher aggregate. If for example the circle in the top left button of the radio is picked and an echo is desired by highlighting of the whole button including the square, then this must be decided outside of PHIGS in the application program. The pick tool only signals the fact that the circle or the square in the top left button was picked. In other words, PHIGS has no knowledge that a whole group may be detectable as it is provided by the MacDraw interface. Consequently, in PHIGS, a group cannot be assigned a mouse-sensitive area that is different to the union of the areas of its components, and for which an individual highlighting method may be sensible, as MacDraw has shown.

7.3.8 Centralized Structure Store

PHIGS structures may be stored in a data base and then reused later. A few administration routines are provided for storage and retrieval. We will discuss some of the questions of managing graphics object structures in PHIGS and GEO++ in Chap. 12.

7.4 Modeling Part Hierarchies in PHIGS

In PHIGS, segments can be built in advance and kept in a data base until they are needed. The part hierarchy is represented compactly as a graph. If a structure is changed, all structure networks using it change as well. Through the transferral of attributes in the structure hierarchy, it is possible to establish multiple references to a substructure and yet display its content with different attributes in each occurrence. The compact representation of a graph in PHIGS has some severe limitations in the sense that it does not allow to define individual attributes for every node of the traversed graph displayed as tree on the screen (see 9.5).

Because the result of a posting operation cannot be accessed from within an application program there is no addressing scheme for parts, i.e., PHIGS knows no parts. In the special case of a directed graph without multiple references, this graph is degenerated to a tree. Then the accessible PHIGS structure corresponds directly to the nodes of the tree. If one attempts to model the front panel of the radio in this way, one obtains eight structures for the buttons instead of a just one and knowledge about the similarities in the geometrical description of the buttons is lost. A modification of the geometrical description of a button (editing a building pattern) must be managed by the application program, i.e., in a layer above of PHIGS. So PHIGS forces to deal with the phenomenon that information about an individually displayed object is only available by the pick path because it contains the necessary information about the calling hierarchy and the element pointers of the execute elements. This fact makes it very difficult to assign an individual attribute to a displayed and picked object in a PHIGS hierarchy (c.f. 9.4). We will return to these problems when we compare the alternative approach, GEO++, with PHIGS.

8 GEO++

In order to develop ideas for an object-oriented graphics system for the manipulation of a part hierarchy more tangible, we introduce the system GEO++ (Graphics System with Editable Objects, Version 2). Previous (incomplete) specifications of GEO++ have been described in Wisskirchen, 1986b, concentrating on a modification of the PHIGS structure concept, and in Wisskirchen, 1989, introducing the overall concept of GEO++, but less complete and without considering the potential of inheritance.

With GEO++ we hope to demonstrate how the object-oriented approach may be exploited to reach a new specification of a graphics kernel system supporting part hierarchies.

In this introduction we concentrate on specification and handling of the graphics object hierarchy of GEO++. We omit details such as device selection, activation of devices, querying of device description tables, listing individual graphics primitives. As far as these are concerned, GEO++ does not differ crucially from PHIGS. We demonstrate and motivate the functionality of GEO++ with the help of the radio example. Beyond this we hope to illustrate the potential of the GEO++ concepts by comparison with PHIGS, especially in Chap. 9. Our goal is to show concretely what advantages the use of a few concepts taken from the object-oriented world can bring for the specification of graphics systems.

8.1 Goals and Motivation

GEO++ should represent a synthesis of the concepts from the object-oriented design philosophy and the rich functionality specified in traditional systems such as PHIGS.

Many aspects of GEO++ were stimulated by object-oriented systems and the graphics kernels incorporated in them. This finds expression especially in the requirement that visible graphics units should exists as objects in the sense of object-oriented programming, i.e., they can be addressed by name, they carry their own information (attributes), and they keep methods for the assignment and querying of this information (*principle of locality*).

To a much higher degree than in traditional graphics systems, the construction and update of graphics data structures, therefore can be described as the applications programmer "feels" them: as the editing of objects that can be displayed. Programming becomes easier and unwanted side effects are avoided.

8.1.1 Integration in the Extended Layer Model

The purpose of GEO++ is to use it by the applications programmer as a predefined kernel. The kernel's internal implementation must remain hidden and should not be modifiable by the applications programmer. The applications programmer is not allowed the same freedom as he has in the Smalltalk-80 environment, where he can (and in some cases must) modify internal methods.

The principle of a hidden kernel has the advantage that the manufacturer of the kernel system may implement the internal components according to his own notions, including the effective implementation of time-critical operations in hardware. Here we adhere to the same principle as in GKS and PHIGS.

GEO++ should be embedded in the extended layer model, discussed in 5.6. To summarize:

- The functionality of the graphics kernel may be used by application objects sending messages to the (non-internal) *transparent* GEO++ objects.
- Subclasses of the transparent GEO++ classes may be built for integrating additional knowledge into these subclasses.
- Call-back messages may be defined so that instances of the kernel's classes may send messages to application objects.
- The idea of indirect communication between application and kernel should be maintained by incorporating trigger mechanisms as they were described in Chap. 3.

8.1.2 Support for Part Hierarchies

Comfortable handling of graphics part hierarchies is one of the central goals for the design of GEO++ leading to the motivation to support the requirements listed above in Chap. 6. in the most natural and simple way possible. GEO++ attempts to express what is generally accepted as an elementary operation for the construction and modification of a part hierarchy as a single, atomic function. Conversely, every function in GEO++ should be easily interpreted as an operation on a part hierarchy, so that a smooth translation into the semantics of part hierarchies is possible.

Another motivation for incorporating as much as possible of the semantics of a part hierarchy in GEO++ concerns the reduction and early detection of programming errors. The more knowledge about the structure and functionality of a graphics part hierarchy is incorporated in the system, the more easily misconceptions and programming errors may be detected.

A challenge for a graphics system handling multi-level part hierarchies is to arrive at an optimal synthesis for supporting two different aspects. First, the system must make optimal use of the geometric description *common* to (repeatedly used) parts. Secondly, the system should allow to model the *individual* aspects of these parts as well.

8.2 GEO++ Model

The overall, static structure of the GEO++ part hierarchy may be described as follows:

- In GEO++ a part hierarchy is represented as a *tree*. For example, the tree representing the radio and the relationships between the individual nodes and the visible graphics parts is shown in Fig. 8.1.
- A tree has a highest node, the *root*, which represents all visible objects of a single part hierarchy. Such a tree (named group) is an instance of the class Group of GEO++.
- Each subnode is an instance of the GEO++ class Part (or of a subclass of Part), representing the visual objects of the sub-hierarchy in the given hierarchy. Note that the information assigned a node (root or part) encompasses all of its sub-parts.
- Each part has essentially two main components, a geometrical description, the *content*, and a set of *part attributes*.
- The content of a part consists of a *building pattern*, i.e., an instance of Group or an instance of an output primitive class.
- Each group may define it own part hierarchy and may be posted on a selected display medium.
- Different parts may share one and the same building pattern, while a part's attribute can be seen as the parts own individual information.

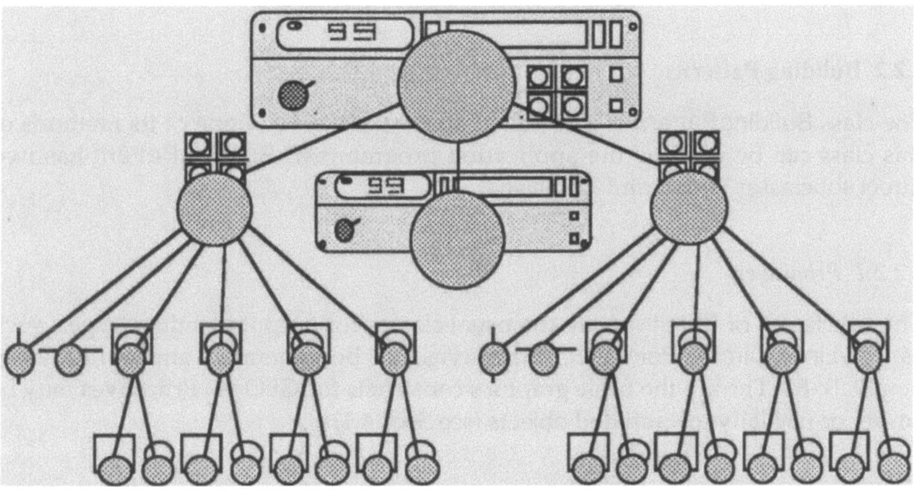

Fig. 8.1. Representation of a car radio's object structure. A node is an (unordered) set containing exactly the subnodes as elements. The leaves of the tree are single-element sets consisting of a graphics primitive. Each node corresponds with an GEO++ object, called part. Each part can be addressed directly and is owner of all attributes required for display and interaction. In addition, a GEO++ hierarchy knows about the same geometrical description used for equivalent parts such as, for example, the eight buttons.

In the following, the part hierarchy will be described more detailed—beginning with the static aspects, and to be followed by the dynamic aspects of the hierarchy (creating, navigating through, and editing).

8.2.1 Parts

A part cannot be understood as isolated—it is always integrated in *exactly* one part hierarchy. The root of the hierarchy (containing all information about the hierarchy) is known to a part and may be inquired by the unary method root.

The content of a part may be inquired by content delivering a building pattern. A part knows its content, but a content has no information about the parts that refer to it as content. Attributes of a part may be inquired by attributes delivering a collection of class Dictionary with the different types of attributes as values. Values of attributes may be nil. Besides the usual attributes, a transformation is also associated with a part and will be treated as an attribute. Because there is a unique connection between a part and its root, we can distinguish between a *global transformation* between a part and its root and a *local transformation* directly associated with a part as an attribute. The default value of the latter is the identity transformation.

Two parts p1 and p2 (even with different roots) may contain identical building patterns, i.e., when inquired by content they will deliver references to one and the same object. In this case they are called *geometrical equivalent*, which can be tested by evaluating the boolean expression:

```
(p1 content == p2 content) .
```

8.2.2 Building Patterns

The class BuildingPattern is a so-called abstract class, i.e., none of its methods of this class can be used by the application programmer. BuildingPattern has two direct subclasses Group and Primitives.

8.2.2.1 Primitives

The subclasses of Primitives are the usual classes for output primitive types, such as PolyLine, Circle, Point, etc. Primitives can be generated and edited as in Smalltalk-80. The are the basic graphics constructs for GEO++. Primitives may be empty or partially instantiated objects (see Sect. 4.1).

8.2.2.2 Groups

Groups stand for collections of primitives and other groups; and they play the role of segments in GKS and structures in PHIGS. By sending new to Group an empty group is created. It can be filled with graphics information by inserting primitives or existing groups. It should be noted that only groups or primitives (building patterns) may be inserted. The order in which they are inserted is irrelevant. In contrast to PHIGS, GEO++ has no horizontal sequential organization as it is defined by the integer element pointer of a PHIGS structure. The insert operation in GEO++ returns an access key, which we call indicator. Repeated insertion of a building pattern is allowed; this produces a new indicator every time. It is not allowed to insert a group into itself or to generate cyclic relations.

8.2.3 Construction of Parts and Navigation

By repeatedly inserting building patterns, the tree shown above may be generated. The *indicators* delivered by the insertion methods may be identified with the edges of the tree. The nodes of the tree can be addressed by appropriate navigation from the root. This is done in two steps:

- generation of a *path* as an instance of GEOPath by appropriate concatenation of indicators, and
- sending this path as an argument of the message part: to the root.

The result of this message is a part of this root. A part may be inquired by path delivering back the access path. Indicators are also instances of GEOPath with length one. GEOPath is subclass of OrderedCollection introduced in 2.5.2.1 and inherits many useful methods from it.

Besides this, there are more ways to navigate in a tree spanned by a root especially methods for reaching deeper parts from intermediate parts (cf. 8.3.3).

8.2.4 Attributes

Every node in a tree can be individually assigned an attribute of any type (color, line type, detectability, transformation, etc.). An attribute for the root is called a *group attribute*. The attributes for the adjacent nodes are *part attributes*. Moreover there are *attributes for output primitives*, so that one can speak about attributes for building patterns. Attributes for building patterns may be overridden by part attributes when they are used as content. For priorities between conflicting attributes see Sect. 8.3.4.2. The idea for the priority rules is, that the more specific an object is, the higher is the priority of an attribute, assigned to it. So, an attribute assigned to the root of a hierarchy has low priority, whereas an attribute assigned to a part which is a leaf in the tree has highest priority.

Note that:

a) a part attribute has no influence on the content of this part.
b) a part attribute at most influence the visual representation of its own subtree in the hierarchy of its root.

In particular, part attributes do not change any geometrical equivalence relations!

The advantages of this concept are discussed in detail in Chap. 9. We have the following problem in PHIGS. In order to assign an attribute for only one button of the radio in PHIGS, we must avoid inserting it in the structure for button. But, when we insert it in a higher structure, it affects the visual representation of more than one subtree of button. Therefore, in this case the PHIGS graph must be reorganized, *disbanding geometrical equivalences*.

8.2.5 Editing

In contrast to setting attributes, editing means modifying the geometric information of an object. GEO++ supports editing operations for groups, primitives and parts.

If a building pattern has to be changed by editing it effects:

- the part hierarchy, spanned by the building pattern itself, and
- all hierarchies, where it is used as content of a part.

Editing of a part may be done by inserting a building pattern, deleting a subpart or by replacing its content (and higher operation such as grouping and ungrouping). The effect of part editing is:

- Creation of a new building pattern, which becomes the new content of this part.
- (automatic) creation of a new chain of building patterns as content of the ancestor parts in the hierarchy..

It is important to note that the previous building patterns are not destroyed because they may be used as contents of other parts and possibly in other hierarchies.

Editing a part results in a replacement of its content. A side effect of this is the replacement of the contents of all its ancestor parts: new contents are created. We call this process an *individualization*. The new contents do not differ from the old one in their attributes. The part attributes of the ancestors also remain unchanged. After part editing, the new contents differ from the old ones only in those components whose paths are sub-paths of the changed part. So all geometric descriptions that have not changed during part editing retain their equivalency relations.

Because the parts in the ancestor chain have now new contents they are removed from their previous equivalence classes.

The part editing process may become clear by the example 8.3.6.4. Though the effect is not simple to describe, because so many other parts are affected by one part editing operation, the definition is very logical and conclusive. One main idea behind a part hierarchy is: if a part changes, then so does the whole, and the whole is defined by the ancestor chain.

8.3 Functional Overview by an Example

In the following, the most important GEO++ operations with the aid of the radio example are illustrated. We show the complete construction of the part hierarchy, the assignment of attributes and the more important editing operations. Inheritance in not used here, but will be demonstrated in Chap. 10.

8.3.1 The Insert Process

The part hierarchy of the radio is been built up by using the insert operation. The two primitives for circle and square are created with:

```
square ← PolyLine points: sqPoints
circle ← Circle center: cPoint radius: r .
```

Then a new, empty group is defined:

```
button ← Group new .
```

The following primitives are inserted into it:

```
s ← button insert: sq
c ← button insert: circle .
```

As a result of the insert operations the two indicators s and c are delivered. As usual in Smalltalk-80, one can do without the left arrow ← if one does not need the indicators.

We now construct the switchboard with its four buttons. The two polylines poly1 and poly2 are inserted into a new group to indicate the horizontal and vertical borders between buttons. button is inserted four times using the insert-and-apply-attributes operation, whereby four different transformations are used as attributes. The effect of the transformations is defined as a concatenation from root to leaves. So tr1,..., tr4 are instances of the class LocalTransformation that defines this special type of transformation.

```
switchBoard ← Group new
c1   ←   switchBoard insert: poly1
c2   ←   switchBoard insert: poly2
tl   ←   switchBoard insert: button attribute: tr1
tr   ←   switchBoard insert: button attribute: tr2
bl   ←   switchBoard insert: button attribute: tr3
br   ←   switchBoard insert: button attribute: tr4
```

Assumed that the radio was modeled with the exception of the two switchboards. So now only the switchboard must be inserted twice with different transformations:

```
left    ←   frontPanel insert: switchBoard attribute: ltrans
right   ←   frontPanel insert: switchBoard attribute: rtrans .
```

The result of these insertions is an object hierarchy corresponding to the tree of Fig. 8.2 showing the tree-structure of the radio, modeled in GEO++. Geometrically equivalent nodes are symbolized by the same pattern in the inner circle. The outer ring of the nodes is left white as place-holder to display part attributes introduced below.

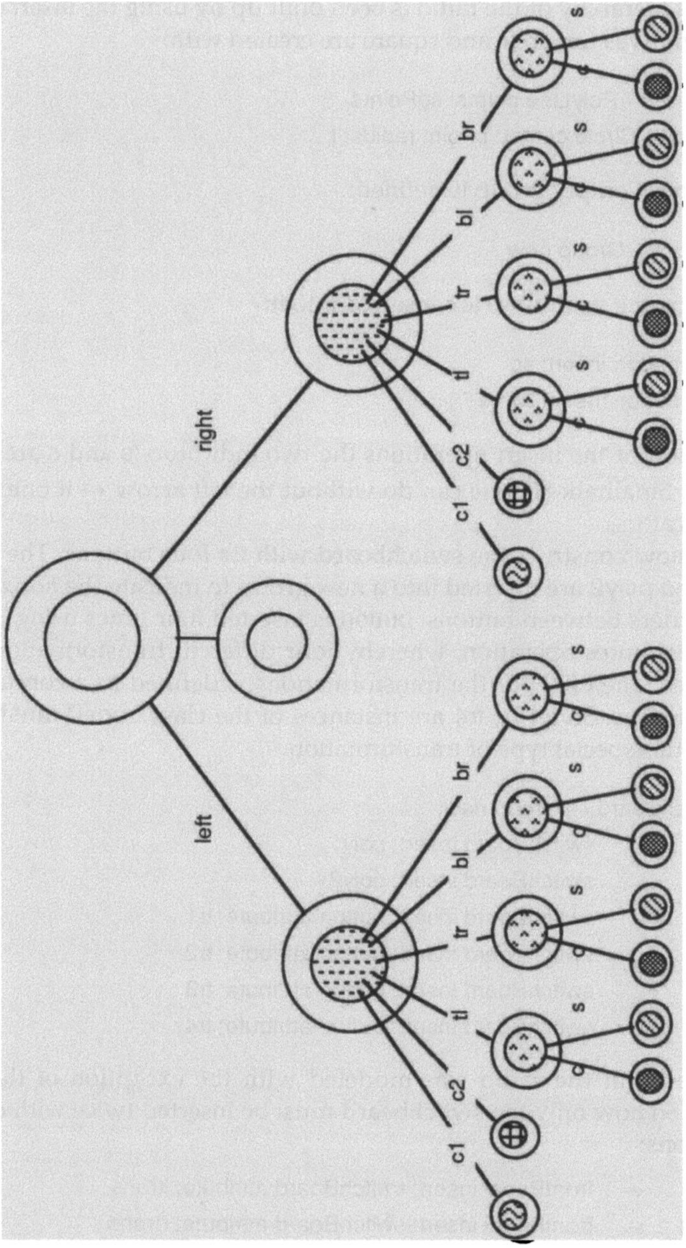

Fig. 8.2. Tree structure of the radio's front panel modeled by GEO++

8.3.2 Parts

Until now we have restricted ourselves to operations concerning building patterns, i.e., aides for the construction of a structure. Now operations are introduced that apply specifically to the sub-nodes of a tree, the parts.

8.3.2.1 Navigation in the Tree Using the Path

If one defines a path for beginning at the root of the tree, one can walk along this path. The result of such migration is a node relative to the starting point. Formally, this migrating is done by calling a function that creates a part. A part knows its path, its root and its content, i.e., the building pattern used in its node. A path is a sequence of indicators, as mentioned before. In our implementation a path is an instance of GEOPath, which itself is a subclass of OrderedCollection, predefined in the Smalltalk-80 environment and introduced in 2.5.2.1. An indicator is an instance (with length 1) of GEOPath. As the comma is available for concatenation in this context, we can concatenate paths in a simple manner. We always put parentheses around concatenated paths to make them more readable even though the Smalltalk-80 parsing rules do not require this in most cases.

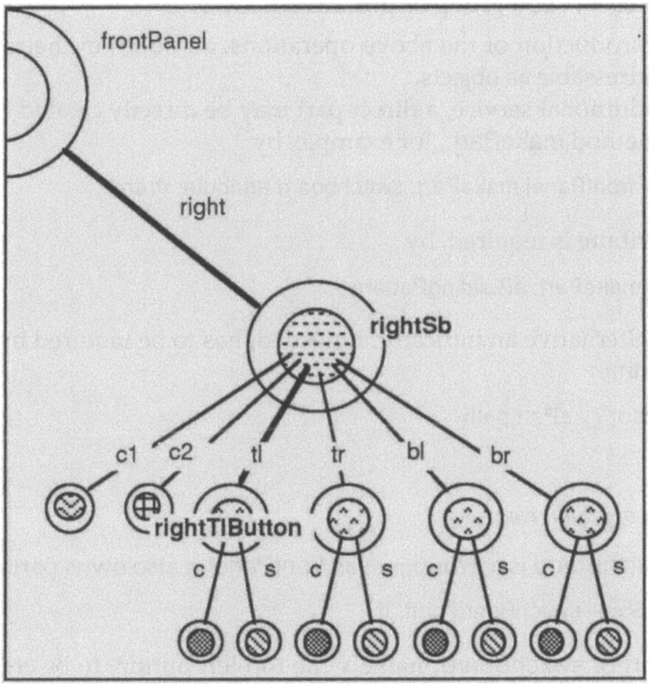

Fig. 8.3. Parts in the tree. Instances of Part correspond to the nodes of the tree modeling the part hierarchy of the radio with the group frontPanel as root.

8.3.2.2 Creation of aPart

The following operations will create parts (as instances of Part) for the root frontPanel:

```
rightSb ← frontPanel part: (right )
rightTlButton ← frontPanel part: (right , tl) .
```

The part rightSb corresponds to the right switchboard of the front panel, the part rightTlButton corresponds to the top left button in the right switchboard of the front panel. The first part, rightSb with a path of length one, is named *direct part*. Figure 8.3 shows the parts defined above with its paths.

Conceptually, a node in the tree is addressed by using its path and "walking" to it starting from the root; from the point of view of object-oriented programming, the method part: creates a part as an object. In a strictly sense, only after a part was created one can speak of a node. The following points should be observed, are important and are therefore mentioned again:

- A part must always be regarded relative to its root, in this case frontPanel.
- The root has knowledge about its parts and can be seen as their owner.
- The path of a part can be inquired from within the part by sending the message path to it.
- A part's content may be inquired using content. This returns the building pattern used, i.e., a group or primitive.

With the introduction of the above operations, all nodes in the represented tree are now addressable as objects.

As an additional service, a direct part may be directly created by an insertion using the method makePart:, for example, by

```
aPart ← frontPanel makePart: switchboard attribute: rtrans
```

or, if no attribute is required, by

```
aGroup makePart: aBuildingPattern .
```

Using this alternative an indicator, if needed, has to be inquired by an additional message path:

```
anIndicator ← aPart path .
```

8.3.2.3 Part of a Subgroup

Because switchBoard is a group just as frontPanel it also owns parts. The message

```
tlButtonSb ← switchBoard part: tl
```

causes a part of switchBoard, namely the top-left button, to be created. The root of this part is a subgroup of frontPanel. It would be wrong to say that tlButtonSb corresponds to two nodes in the frontPanel tree above. In fact, tlButtonSb can only occur in a tree that has switchBoard as root, as shown in Fig. 8.4. But it is right to say that a modification of this part may have an effect on the group switchBoard—which may produce effects on the two buttons, because it is used as content of two parts of frontPanel.

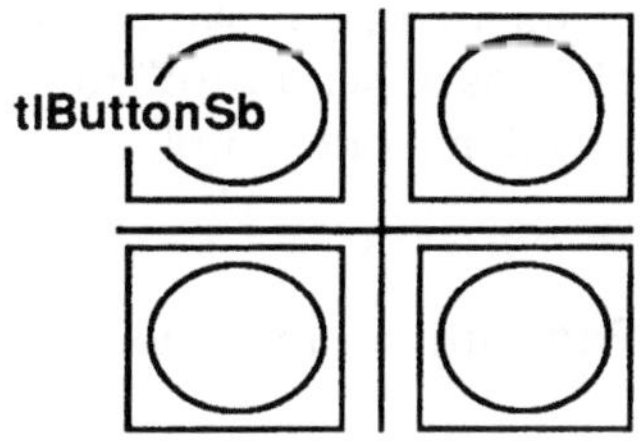

Fig. 8.4. Part of switchBoard. The part tlButtonSb is defined as part of switchBoard used as content in two parts of frontPanel. If tlButton is modified this effects switchboard and all part hierarchies where this group is used as content.

8.3.3 Navigation

To fulfill the most important needs of computer graphics, more comfortable methods for generating and addressing parts and navigation between them are needed. The method above only returns a single part by following a path beginning at its root. We will describe several additional operations in the following.

If we have already generated a part, a sub-part may be created by appending a supplementary path.

```
aSubPart ← aPart part: incrementalPath
```

creates a new part with the same root as aPart, using a path that corresponds to an extension of aPart's path with the supplementary path incrementalPath. When we create for example the following part:

```
rightTlCirclePart ← frontPanel part (right, tl, c)
rightTlButton ← frontPanel part (right, tl) .
```

Then we these parts coincide, so that this comparison results in true:

```
rightTlCirclePart == rightTlButton part: c .
```

The method parent returns a part's direct ancestor in the part-chain, so that the following identity holds:

```
rightTlCirclePart parent == rightTlButton .
```

GEO++ also offers operations that return a set of parts (as an a-kind-of Set):

```
allSubParts ← aPart subParts
children ← aPart children
allParts ← aRoot subParts
myChildren ← aRoot children .
```

The definition is quite obvious, it coincides with the navigation in the tree. So, the following method delivers all subnodes of the example's tree:

```
radioParts ← frontPanel subParts .
```

Beyond the query operations mentioned above, a qualified search of parts is also possible. We use the symbol #* as a "wild card" for this, standing for all indicators allowed for use in this position. For example,

```
someParts ← aPart part: (a, #*)
```

delivers all sub-parts of aPart with an incremental path of length 2 beginning with a.

The comfort offered for collection classes in the Smalltalk-80 environment (collect:, select: ...) allows the implementation of more complex search operations in a set of parts by simple means.

8.3.4 Attributes for Primitives, Groups and Parts

An attribute may be assigned to a primitive, a group or a part. The attributes highlighting, detectable and visible are applied together with a device identifier, so that their values can be set device-dependent, just as in PHIGS. We will omit this parameter in the following as it is not necessary to the understanding of this book to distinguish between different devices. We practically always have a single interactive device as active device.

As mentioned, the transformations used in this book are considered to be attributes. They can be seen as modeling transformations in PHIGS terminology.

8.3.4.1 Definition of Attributes

In accordance with object-oriented philosophy, attributes are created as instances of the class Attribute or its subclasses. This means they have a identifier with which their contents can be referred. So a new and empty attribute instance can be created by:

```
anAttribute ← Attribute new
```

A new attribute with specific line style is instantiated with:

```
boldStyle ← Attribute lineStyle: 'bold'
```

An instance of Attribute can carry more than one attribute. The class Attribute also has its own methods for assigning attributes. So the following is possible:

```
anAttribute lineStyle: 'bold'; color: 'red' .
```

In keeping with the GEO++ goal of offering rich functionality, there is a great degree of flexibility in assigning attributes. We allow attribute information to be set without previously instantiating an object of the class Attribute. It is possible, for example, to assign an attribute to a part in the following manner:

aPart color: 'green'
anObject at: aRelativePosition
anObject moveRelative: deltaPoint .

An object of the class Attribute would then be returned only by an appropriate inquiry message. Even in this case there is a variety of possibilities, such as:

(1) anAttribute ← aPart attribute
(2) aColor ← aPart color
(3) aLineStyle ← anAttribute lineStyle.

(1) delivers a complete set of attributes, that afterwards may be inquired for attributes of a specific type as in (3).

8.3.4.2 Priorities for the Assignment of Attributes

GEO++ knows many different types of attributes. This variety is caused by introduction of the part concept besides primitives and groups. Therefore careful thought needs to be given to the scope of attributes and the definition of priority rules. We now demonstrate in greater detail the extent to which an attribute has effect. It should become clear why we have defined these rules as will now be described. In the following example, we describe the effect of attributes in the context of the tree generated by frontPanel.

General rules for a tree generated by a group as its root are:

- Part attributes have higher priority than building pattern attributes.
- When an attribute is set for a part, the part's content remains unchanged. That is to say, the building pattern describing the part's geometric characteristics, and any attributes associated with this building pattern are not affected.
- Attributes for a part of a subgroup are handled as group attributes of the subgroup.

An example: the three expressions

(1) rightTlButton linewidth: 3
(2) button linewidth: 2
(3) tlButtonSb linewidth: 1

produce the following results:

1. The linewidth of the top left button of the right switchboard is set to three. This is a part attribute, which has highest priority. The content of the part, i.e., the group button, is not changed.
2. The expression (2) affects the group button. Because of lower priority compared to (1), only seven buttons change.
3. The part attribute of the switchboard's part (see Fig. 8.4), which affects button and has higher priority as (2), changes the top-left button of the switchboard. From the point of view of frontPanel, it is a group attribute. Because of (1), it

only changes the top-left button on the *left* switchboard in the tree generated by frontPanel.

The results of these operation, which are independent of the sequence in which the above attributes were applied, are shown in Fig. 8.5.

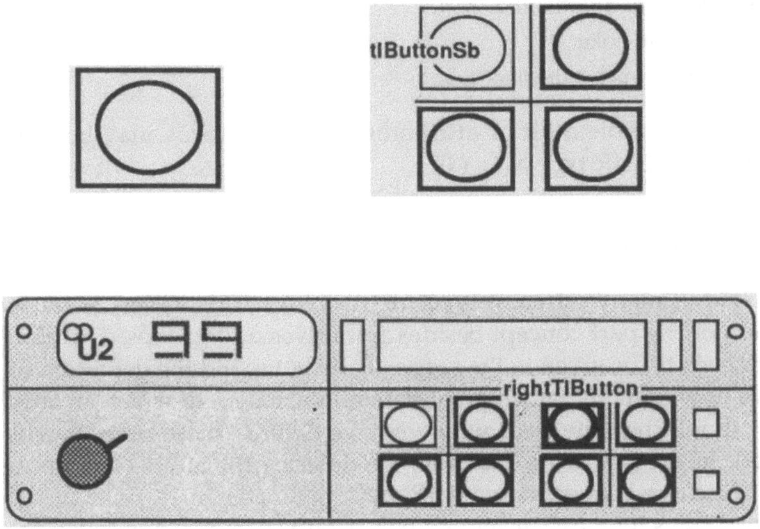

Fig. 8.5. Priorities for attributes.

8.3.4.3 Transferring Attributes Down

Next to priorities between different types of attributes, a procedure for the transfer of attributes in a part hierarchy must be defined. An attribute is only transferred down to parts of the part hierarchy and does not change the contents of the subparts, regardless of whether it the attribute is a group attribute or a part attribute, as shown in Fig. 8.6.

As will be demonstrated in 9.4, it is very difficult to inquire and change attributes of a picked object in PHIGS, because searching for an attribute and controlling all the effects and side effects of an attribute is a very complex task. Inserting an attribute into the structure of the picked primitive may have dangerous side effects, as the structure on this level may be used in other contexts as well.

Our situation in GEO++ is substantially better, because the nodes of the tree defined as parts are only known by the root of the hierarchy and are completely unknown by the contents. So we can define an attribute query method for each part individually. This simplifies programming of interactive attribute modifications to a surprising degree, also shown in 9.4.

For a group, the inquiry method

aWidth ← aGroup linewidth

returns either the default value for the linewidth or the value that was set in an explicit assignment to this group.

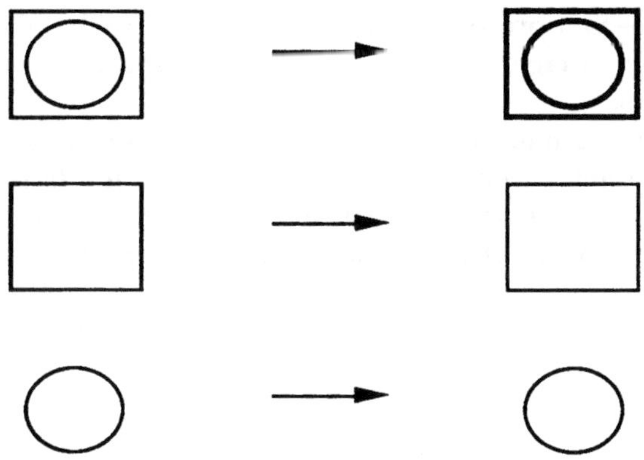

Fig. 8.6. Transferring attributes down. When we apply an primitive attribute to a group or part the visual representation of the subparts is changed, but the content of the subparts remain unchanged.

For a part, the query

aWidth ← aPart linewidth

also returns the linewidth that was transferred down to it. This is precisely the linewidth of its visualization. So a part is truly the owner of its attributes, and because there are different priorities for part and building pattern attributes, the part knows (internally) whether the attribute valid for it was acquired as a part or group attribute or even as a default value.

8.3.4.4 Rules

The rules that govern transferring down attributes depend on the type of attribute. The traditional primitive attributes and the visibility attribute are transfered down if the priority rules allow this. A group attribute is successively transfered down to the parts if only default attributes exist there. If another attribute is encountered in this process, then transferring down ends at that part (and does not continue on to sub-parts). A part attribute is successively transfered down as long as there are only default and group attributes. If a part attribute is encountered, transferring down ends there.

So if we extend the above example with the operation

circle linewidth: 1

we obtain the result that only those circles in frontPanel receive a this linewidth for which no other part attribute was transfered down from above. In our case this means that six of the eight circles obtain linewidth 1. The top-left button in the right switchboard, and the top-left button in the left switchboard were already defined by assignment of a part attribute.

It might be noted that the above example has been made complicated on purpose in order to demonstrate the effect of priorities. As a rule, one would progress in steps—first preparing all groups in the way that they are to be used as content, and then creating the part hierarchy and ascribing individual attributes to its parts.

The detectable and highlighting attributes are not transferred down as shown in Fig. 8.7. *In this manner we can set an individual button detectable without having its sub-parts detectable, as well.* Should we wish all sub-parts of a part to be detectable, we would have to address them individually or apply a set operation (see Sect. 8.3.5).

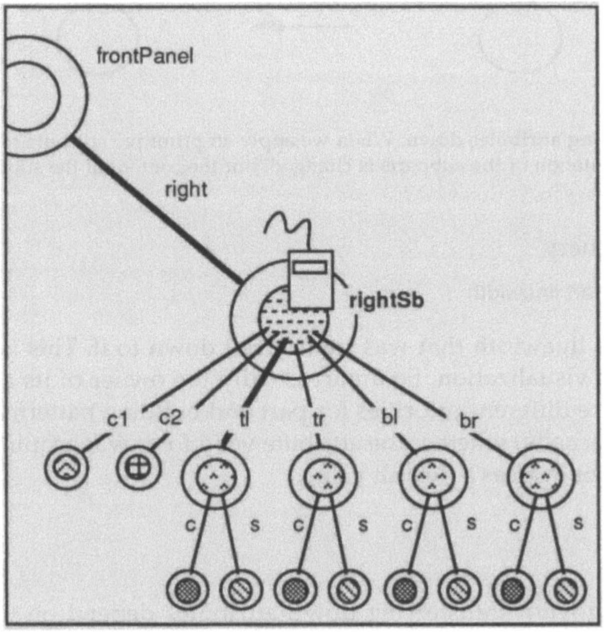

Fig. 8.7. Attribute detectable in a part hierarchy. The attribute detectable is defined for a part and it is not transferred down. In this example the right switchboard is detectable but none of its children (similar to MacDraw) and in contrast to PHIGS.

We still have to think about how transformations are to be handled in the part hierarchy. Since there is no sequential organization of the children of a root or part, their transformations do not affect each other. So transformations only apply from top to the bottom. The usual case is a downward concatenating transformation, which most closely fits the semantics of a part hierarchy. In the previous examples, the transformation matrix aTransformation is multiplied to the current transformation when a message of the type insert: anObject attribute: aTransformation is used. The current transformation is built up by a series of such multiplications from the root to bottom. It makes sense to allow access to both the current modeling transformation and the one assigned directly to a part, i.e., aTransformation. We do not discuss further methods of setting transformations (absolutely replacing, concatenating to the directly assigned one).

Note that the insert:attribute: operation used repeatedly in our example is simply shorthand for two operations, namely, creation of a part with the indicator returned by insert: as path and a subsequent assignment of an attribute in our case transformation) to the part.

The following two operations, for example, have the same effect:

```
tl ← switchBoard insert: button attribute: tr1
```

and

```
tl ← switchBoard insert: button
aPart ← switchBoard part: tl
aPart attribute: tr1 .
```

8.3.5 Set Operations

Quite a few of the methods introduced so far return a set of graphics objects as result. The method children, which returns a set of parts, is a typical example. Because it makes sense in many cases to assign each of these elements an attribute, we will now define some utility methods for sets whose elements are instances of Group, Primitive and Part. The implementation of these methods with the tools available in Smalltalk-80 is absolutely straightforward. Therefore, they need not be part of a predefined graphics kernel. Note that in PHIGS filters are introduced to assign attributes in a flexible manner; Brodlie et al. have proposed, as an extension of GKS, a selection mechanism similar to SQL for enquiring sets of graphics primitives and assigning attributes to them (Brodlie et al., 1989).

First we define the subclass GraphicsSet of Set. This allows us to make use of the existing methods for Set in the Smalltalk-80 environment. The class GraphicsSet may have building patterns as well as parts as elements. We define BuildingPatterns and Parts as subclasses of GraphicsSet. We now name a few exemplary methods for these classes.

For an instance of GraphicsSet the method attribute: is defined that returns self and assigns to every element of the set the attribute used as argument:

```
aSet attribute: anAttribute .
```

The query method

```
myAttributes ← aSet attribute
```

returns an instance of Set that contains the attributes of the receiver's elements. For an instance myParts of Parts, we define

```
myBuildingPatterns ← myParts content .
```

One should note that the above operations can only be applied to an (unordered) set if the result is independent of the sequence in which this set is processed. This is guaranteed by our rules for the assignment of attributes, the querying of contents, etc. The fact that the above operations are defined for sets allows even an internal implementation that processes the elements of the set in parallel.

8.3.5.1 Example for a Set Operation

The semantic difference between a set myParts as an instance of Parts and a part myPart, which also owns "elements" (namely its children) has the following aspects:

- The set myPart may consist of arbitrary parts, even parts with different roots. In other words, elements may be collected in a way *completely orthogonal to the part hierarchy.*
- The definition of attribute assignment is different. This is true both of the traditional primitive attributes and of detectability, visibility and highlighting.

Let us construct a small example for this. Assumed that a switchboard has buttons that consist only of a circle. tlButtonSb designates the top-left button of the switchboard:

```
tlButtonSb ← switchBoard part: tl .
```

Assume further that this button has been assigned a shading attribute shad1. Then the following situation exists here: one circle is filled with the shading attribute shad1. Because of the priority rules,

```
(1) switchboard attribute: shad2
```

now fills only the three remaining circles with shading attribute shad2. The alternative

```
(2 (switchboard children) attribute: shad2
```

is a set operation, which fills all four buttons with the attribute shad2, as shown in Fig. 8.3.

8.3.5.2 Graphics Contexts as Filters

The above operation allows the insertion of a part into a set and assignment of an attribute using the above above assignment. This can be done either immediately when the part is generated or at any later time. Using the general set operations and the selection methods supported by Smalltalk-80, it is possible to implement filter operations as offered by PHIGS through a single operation. For instance, to make a specific subset of parts detectable, one collects them in a set, for example, one creates a set mySpecialParts and defines:

```
mySpecialParts detectable: true .
```

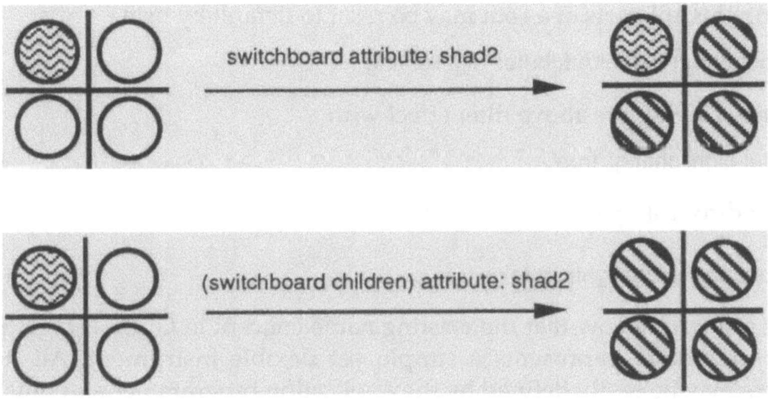

Fig. 8.8. Set operation. The first example shows that a part attribute has a higher priority than a group attribute. The second operation assigns an attribute to a set of parts, overriding the attribute assigned previously for the top left button with root switchBoard.

We have used the above mechanism without exception in our examples because it relies on a simple and transparent principle. However, it may have smaller disadvantages in some applications. These lie in the fact that the above expression extends the set of detectable objects in the system. If one wants to set the objects that were previously detectable to non-detectable, one must do so explicitly with an additional expression.

For this reason, one *could* define an additional utility function in GEO++. This would implement a filter mechanism to reset a selected attribute of all objects to its default state, and then use an inclusion and exclusion set:

```
myHighFilter ← HighFilter in: myNewParts out: someOtherParts .
```

Now exactly the difference set would receive the attribute highlighting: true.

The difference to PHIGS would here be: every object owns *only one, its own* name, but can be used in *different contexts* (context being modeled here by a corresponding set). Being an object, every part has this name automatically and receives all messages addressed to it by this name. Because the part hierarchy and the flexibility of the navigation and inquiry operations support arbitrary granularity down to individual graphics primitives, name sets as in PHIGS are not necessary. So in contrast to PHIGS, GEO++ supports *object* sets, and not name sets.

Because GEO++ and Smalltalk-80 allow easy construction of the above difference set with the method using the "–" as selector

```
mySet ← myNewParts – someOtherParts
```

it is suggested that only one alternative be offered. This supports resetting arbitrary attributes to their default states:

```
aGraphicsSet defaultAttribute: attributeTyp .
```

Following this, all parts of a root may be reset to default by using

```
(aRoot parts) defaultAttribute: 'highlighting'
```

and then achieving the above filter effect with

```
mySet highlighting: 'true'
```

The second-to-last operation is the same as

```
(aRoot parts) highlighting: false .
```

The last examples show that the existing name concept in GEO++, together with the set operations, represents a simple yet flexible instrument. All these alternatives may be easily defined by the application programmer and must not be part of a predefined kernel.

In Sect. 5.7 we have discussed the possibility to assign also attributes to a class for applying them to instances created subsequently. It is not very sensible to use this concept for a GEO++ specification, when implemented in a genuine object-oriented environment. As the section about inheritance will demonstrate, subclassing of Group and Part will be used comfortably for modeling specific applications. In this context, anyway, initialization methods for classes will be defined that will create non-empty objects as prototypes for an application. In this method, class variables for holding attributes could be introduced easily.

8.3.6 Editing

In contrast to setting attributes, editing means modifying the geometric information of an object. GEO++ supports editing operations for groups, primitives and parts.

8.3.6.1 Editing Building Patterns

The following rules are defined for the editing of building patterns:

- If a building pattern is edited, it affects all nodes of every tree in which it occurs as content.
- Such editing, however, leaves the part attributes for all parts that own this building pattern as their content unchanged.

The two rules can be summarized as:

- Editing a building pattern does not affect geometric equivalence, cause all equivalent parts owning the building pattern as content change consistently.

8.3.6.2 Editing a Group

The most important operation for editing groups directly, i.e., for sending messages to them, is the insert operation discussed previously. Beyond that there is only one other, namely the empty-group operation.

8.3.6.3 Editing Primitives

The most important operations for editing primitives change the geometric coordinates of a primitive. An example for this is the addition of points to a polyline. For this we refer to the Smalltalk-80 graphics kernel.

8.3.6.4 Part Editing

A building pattern can be placed into a part by an insert operation. A part may be deleted or its content can be replaced by another content. The visual effect of part editing is quite easy to understand, as the following examples show. However, the effect is not very simple to describe.

When a part is edited it is provided with a completely new content. The same is true for all parts of its ancestor chain. (The previous content of the part chain still exist as a building pattern, because it may be used by other parts.) The root of the part is only slightly modified in the sense that one of its part chains has been changed. The new contents created for the ancestor parts may be interpreted as a shallow copy of the old content, followed by a replacement of the modified subpart. The part attributes of the modified ancestors parts remain unchanged. So all geometric descriptions that have not changed during part editing retain their equivalency relations.

As an example, we will label the button rightTlButton with some text. We assume the button was previously set to bold and the text primitive dx appropriately initialized with string 'DX'. Then

```
tx ← rightTlButton insert: dx transform: aTransf
```

causes the desired labeling and the following picture (Fig. 8.9) emerges.

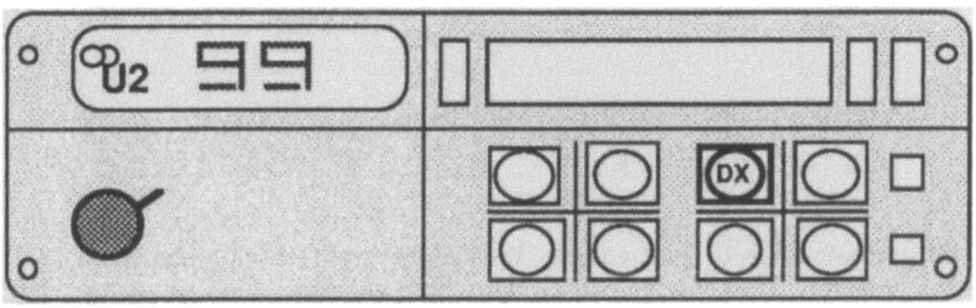

Fig. 8.9. Part editing with the effect that a button has changed. The button is bold because the part attribute is still valid.

The resulting GEO++ tree is shown in Fig. 8.10. At first glance, it may seem surprising that all parts in the ancestor chain have changed. But we must consider the fact that a new right switchboard has been created together with the new button. It implies that the content of the right switchboard may be inquired from this and used as a new "product" in many other part hierarchies. Nevertheless, the two switchboards have many identical building patterns. All this coincides exactly with the semantics of a part hierarchy as we see it.

Some other operations offered by GEO++ for part editing are:

aPart delete

aPart replaceContentBy: aNewBuildingPattern .

While the insert operation creates new parts, these last two destroy or replace parts. An additional part editing operation is

aPart individualize .

This operation does not change the visual display of the hierarchy, but it has the same effect, that new contents are defined in the ancestor chain and the geometrical equivalence is disrupted.

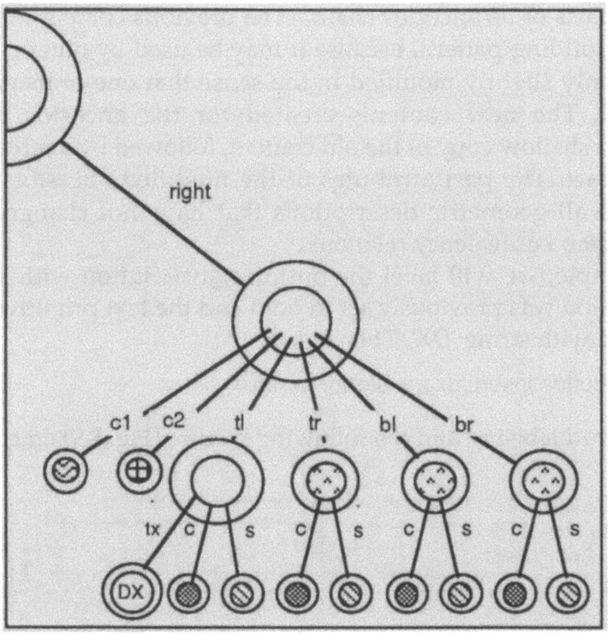

Fig. 8.10. Individualization by part editing. We see that rightTlButton has changed. It now has three parts as children. This change causes the whole ancestor chain to change. The ancestor parts have lost their fill pattern and group operations for the old unchanged groups sb and button will no longer affect myButton and its parent chain. One should note that the new nodes have retained many sub-nodes that are still in their old equivalence classes.

8.3.6.5 Editing Endnodes

In the special case of leaves, i.e., when the part's content is an output primitive, a part can be edited just as the output primitive. So a part whose content is a polyline can be edited in the same way possible for an instance of PolyLine:

rightTlSquarePart ← frontPanel part: (right, tl, s)

designates the top left part of the right switchboard. This is a polyline. So a coordinate can be added:

```
rightTlSquarePart addLast: aPoint .
```

The last operation uses the same coordinate system as the parts content, i.e., the output primitive square. Furthermore, it is possible to add to the part a point computed by concatenation of the transformations in the part hierarchy. Such a point corresponds (with the exception of the window-viewport operations not handled here) to the point returned by a pointing device (locator). So the following type of editing is also possible:

```
tlRightSquarePart addTransformedLast: aTransfPoint .
```

Since part editing, as mentioned above, creates a new content that can be inquired by the part, the added point is automatically recomputed into the part's coordinate system.

Querying a part's individual coordinates is also possible:

```
aCoordinatePart ← tlRightSquarePart at: 1 .
```

One should note that this operation is defined in such a way that it considers a coordinate as a kind of part. Attributes may be assigned to it as, for example, the attribute detectable, so that a single coordinate can be picked. Not only parts whose contents are polylines, but also the nodes of splines can be changed in this way. Such an individual point,however, cannot be transformed; it can only be replaced with a new point:

```
tlRightSquarePart at: 1 .put: newPoint .
```

This replacement causes individualization; a new content is created.

8.3.7 Partial Instantiation, Merge

Similar to PHIGS, GEO++ allows also the insertion of an empty group into a second one. Beyond this, empty or only partially instantiated output primitives can be used similar to the Smalltalk-80 kernel.

It is possible to generate empty or partially instantiated primitives. So the following operation is allowed:

```
aPolyLine ← PolyLine new: 10
```

generates a polyline with ten empty points whose values are nil. Some or all coordinates can then be instantiated by editing. Empty or partially instantiated primitives allow the construction of graphics object hierarchies and independently the formulation of algorithms (programs, rules, constraints) for the interplay of their coordinates.

The Smalltalk-80 technique of inserting the same point into different primitives can also be used to an advantage in GEO++. If for example, the circle is deleted from the group button and a line with the coordinates of two opposing points of the square is defined, then automatically two merge points ar created by :

```
line ← Line first: (square at: 1) second: (square at: 3)
button insert: line .
```

8.3.7.1 More Complex Part Editing

One of the operations often used in computer graphics has the goal of dissolving a part and transporting its contents "upwards". To reach this, we introduce the *ungroup* operation, similar as it is provided by MacDraw.

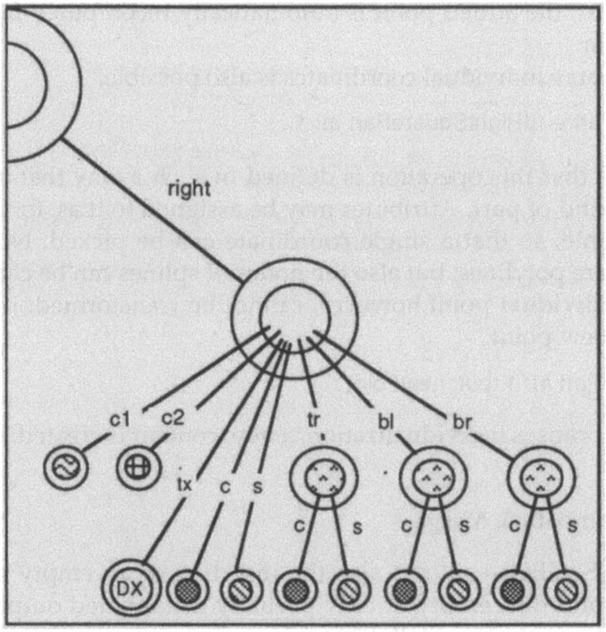

Fig. 8.11. Effect of the ungroup operation. In the ungroup operation, parts are "lifted". New parts are created and the tree is organized as shown. Ungroup does not affect the visual representation on a display medium.

In the example myButton is ungrouped, whereby the resulting new parts are returned as an instance of Parts, i.e., a set.

```
aPartSet ← rightTlButton ungroup .
```

rightTlButton dies, i.e., it cannot accept any messages without producing an error. The above operation causes the group assigned to myButton's parent part to receive additional children. The sub-tree that was previously rooted in myButton is deleted. This means that the tree is restructured as shown in Fig. 8.11. There is a one-to-one correspondence between aPartSet and the previous set defined by myButton children. This relationship can be established over the appropriate paths. Two parts that correspond to each other have, by definition, the same content and part attribute. This means that the visible representation is not changed. Detectability and highlighting, on the other hand, do change because the button myButton no longer exists in the part hierarchy.

The grouping function serves as a kind of inverse function to ungrouping. It has the purpose of grouping together a subset of a part's children to form a new part. If aChildrenSet is a subset of a part's children, then

newPart ← aChildrenSet group

generates a new part newPart. The attributes are defined in such a way as not to change the visible representation. The parts take their attributes with them. So newPart has no attributes of its own.

8.3.8 Copy Operation

In the context of GEO++ two of the copy operations introduced in Chap. 2 are most sensible. For a group, the method:

coypyOf Group ← aGroup shallowCopy

is defined in the way that the new group has the identical information in it, in the sense that all contents, all paths and all attributes are identical. The parts are not (completely) identical because they deliver a different root, the copy, but this is the only difference between them. It should be observed that the copy may be edited completely independently of the original group.

The method:

coypyOf Group ← aGroup deepGraphCopy

is defined in the way that the new group has the identical paths, but otherwise different objects are instantiated with the same values. Compared to deepCopy the same geometrical equivalence relations hold as in the original group. This means: if two parts of aGroup share the identical content, then the two corresponding parts of the copy will share it as well.

Analogous copy methods are defined for output primitives, but will not be considered here.

8.3.9 Graphics Input

We only consider the pick operation because it alone has influence on the graphics object structure. Only objects that are in the state "detectable" may be picked.

An object picked by the user is always a part (or the entire posted root itself). So if we assign the attribute detectable: true to a group , all posted parts that have this group as content may become detectable (in accordance with the priority rules for attributes). A pick may be requested or evaluated by an active part, i.e., a part with an associated call-back message.

8.3.9.1 Request Pick

After activation of a pick device, querying the device returns the picked object:

```
pickedObject ← Pick request .
```

Of course, only parts with the attribute detectable can be picked. A reaction to the pick operation could then be, for example,

```
pickedObject color: green .
```

This last action is executed if it is obvios from the context of the interactive dialogue makes that the picked object is to receive this attribute. In many cases however, the reaction depends on which part was picked. There are two ways to compare the part returned by a pick device with an existing one. One can either compare directly:

```
pickedPart == myButton ifTrue: [.....]
```

or one inquires the path and uses it for comparison:

```
pickPath ← pickedObject path .
```

GEO++ provides query facilities, which allow requesting other criteria for the analysis of a picked part's characteristics, such as attributes, geometric position, its root, subparts, ancestors, primitives etc.

In any case, the calling program queries and processes the picked information.

8.3.9.2 Pick and Call Back Messages

The second use of the pick operation causes execution of a specific preprogrammed message, assigned to a part. The assignment of such a call-back message is supported by two appropriate messages. The operation

```
aPart receiver: anObject
```

defines the receiver of the call-back message, and

```
aPart defineCallBack: aSymbol
```

defines the message selector of the call-back message.

If the first message is not applied, the *root* of the part becomes defined as the receiver by default. To enable the root to accept the message and the type of message is not predefined by GEO++ itself, then a subclass of Group has to be defined for the root with an appropriate method to make the root able to understand the call-back.

Let us make the call-back principle clearer with an example. If a call-back is defined by:

```
myButton defineCallBack: #play
```

and the button is picked, then the receiver object gets the message play: pickedObject

where pickedObject refers to myButton.

The motivation for the default regulation, sending the message to the root of the part, is that the root knows its individual parts and it can decide (if supported with appropriate methods) what is to be done when a button is pressed. Typical reactions to a call-back message are to change the representation of one or more buttons, to switch the detectability state of its parts, or to send messages to application objects, depending on the state of the dialogue.

The user may, after sending the message request to the pick device, pick a part, using an appropriate input device, say the mouse. As a reaction, the message picked will be sent to the picked part. If this part has been assigned a call-back, a corresponding message is sent to the receiver of the call-back message. Otherwise, the picked part is returned as the value of the request message, as defined above, and control is passed back to the sender of the request message.

We note here that it makes sense to vary the method executed by a part depending on the state of the dialogue. If defineCallBack: is sent again to the same part with another message pattern, or if a new receiver has been defined, then the reaction to pick changes accordingly. The message invalidate to a part causes the call-back message to be withheld. In the event of a pick, control is returned to the sender of the request message restoring the conventional case of request pick.

In order for a part to send its call-back to an object other than its root, this can be done by specifying a new receiver with the message

aPart receiver: aNewObject .

Further flexibility can be achieved by specializing the message picked of class Part by overriding it for a subclass of Part. The internal implementation of this message is hidden. However, the well-known trick of overriding this message in a subclass of Part and then using super picked can be used to specialize it, without violating the principle of information hiding. One could for instance, ensure by this that the instances of the special subclasses of Part could react with a special type of highlighting. All this is in compliance with the object-oriented motto that all knowledge about an object be implemented within that object as far as possible.

Since we use the mouse as pick device in GEO++, we need further methods for the class Part. We require that the.mouse send the message pickAreaIn if it moves into that part's pick-sensitive area. Upon leaving this area, the message pickAreaOut is sent (if no pick has been executed; otherwise control would be elsewhere). These two messages have no effect in the default implementation. They could however be overridden in a subclass of Part, for instance to cause visual feedback by attribute modification when these areas are entered or left.

For the reader interested in the internal implementation of GEO++ it is noted that the message perform , introduced in 2.3.2.3 will be used by the internal method pick of class Part for sending the call-back message in this way:

anObject perform: aSelector withArguments: (Array new at: 1 put: self) .

In this case, anObject is the instance variable of Part instantiated by the above message receiver:, and aSelector is the selector of the call-back message, together with self (the picked part) as argument.

8.3.10 Additional Remarks

The following functions are mentioned here for sake of completeness. They play no substantial role in the context of this book.

8.3.10.1 Inquiry Operations

Additional inquiry operations are, for example, querying a part according to geometric criteria, such as the extent rectangle or the pick-sensitive area, or the individual coordinates of graphics primitives. We will not discuss such operations in further detail.

We note here that if graphics code is to be spread across several modules in GKS or PHIGS, values of the kernel's states must be passed on in parameter lists or global variables. In GEO++, system states are inquired in a object-oriented fashion. An example: if an active part sends a reference to itself to another module (i.e., an object of an application-oriented class) by a call-back message, then the part may be asked by root to deliver its root. The root can then be inquired, and if it is wished, the complete state of the part hierarchy (subparts, contents, attributes) could be delivered by it.

8.3.10.2 Subclassing of GEO++

Inheritance has not been used here, so that most of the GEO++ functions described up to this point could also be defined for traditional environments. Only the call-back mechanism is not available in traditional programming languages and could cause some problems.

It must be noted that these remarks are only valid with respect to the overall GEO++ functionality. To exclude inheritance would of course lead to severe limitations and to a completely different system architecture for an interactive graphics application based on the traditional layer model. Subclassing of GEO++ merits its own section (see Chap. 10).

8.3.10.3 GEO++ and Object-Oriented System Architectures

How can GEO++ be integrated in the specific architectural concepts mentioned in Chap. 3—the idea of the generic application, provided by an object-oriented application framework, and the MVC concept?

Embedding a graphics application using GEO++ as kernel in application frameworks requires nothing more than inheritance so that predefined "empty" applications may be overriden.

For applications as CAD applications requiring display and interaction in windows embedding of GEO++ in the MVC triad could be realized by in the following steps: GEO++ methods may be seen as a set of additional methods for objects owned by a view. These objects are part hierarchies; the ownership could be arranged by instance variables of an application programmer defined subclass of View. The controller concept must be slightly extended by considering call-back messages as controller messages. Instead of defining an instance of a controller class, the messages are directly sent by parts to the application. For the application object receiving these messages nothing need be modified. Indirect addressing (triggering by change:) is a mechanism of the environment and can be applied as before.

For non-window-oriented applications, graphics kernels could be used for designing complex interaction-objects (widgets) such as menus. Also for this type of problems a functionality as it is defined by GEO++ could be very useful. In particular, call-back messages for connecting interaction objects to applications and subclassing for special widget classes (which are themselves subclasses of Part) are well suited for more "intelligent" interaction objects with knowledge about special application types.

9 Programming Examples

The following examples should convey a feeling for the differences between programming in GEO++ and programming in PHIGS. We begin with examples taken from "Understanding PHIGS" (Brown, 1985). They have been modified slightly in order to fit into a consistent example "Office Layout Application", well known example for editing a graphics object hierarchy, first used in the standard text-book (Foley & van Dam, 1982). For the PHIGS examples, pseudocode is used. There follow some examples with our radio and consideration about interactive generation of primitives using PHIGS.

All of the PHIGS identifiers used in the following are of type integer (as defined in the PHIGS document for Fortran language binding) and are input parameters. So every identifier used has previously been assigned a value. These initializations are omitted in the following; they involve additional programming effort. All of the transformations used in the PHIGS examples are set as local replacement transformations. This means they only have downward concatenating effect in the hierarchy and do not affect transformations set later for the same structure.

9.1 Office Layout Application Programmed With PHIGS

The office layout application concerns the programming of a small graphics editor to be used for designing the layout of an office floor plan. The user interface is shown in Fig. 9.1.

We have modified the example slightly by changing the dialogue strategy to the *point-and-act principle*: we first select a graphics object and then apply an operation to it (add, delete, move, rotate), also a selected object will be highlighted. A very detailed formulation of this example (the study of which will cost the reader some effort) was necessary to demonstrate precisely the differences between GEO++ and PHIGS. The yield of these efforts lies in the fact that the reader gains substantially more insight into both PHIGS and GEO++.

9.1.1 Construction of the Screen Layout

The example in "Understanding PHIGS" describes the construction of a screen layout (Brown, 1985, p.p. 109-112). A rectangular area (Screen) is divided into a work area (Work) and a menu area (MainMenu). The menu itself is divided into a text menu (MyTextMenu) and an icon menu (MyIconMenu). The components of the icon menu, the office furniture, are already existing structures loaded from a data bank. We do not discuss this point further, as it is of no great importance in our context and there are no crucial differences between PHIGS and GEO++ as far as storage on external media is concerned.

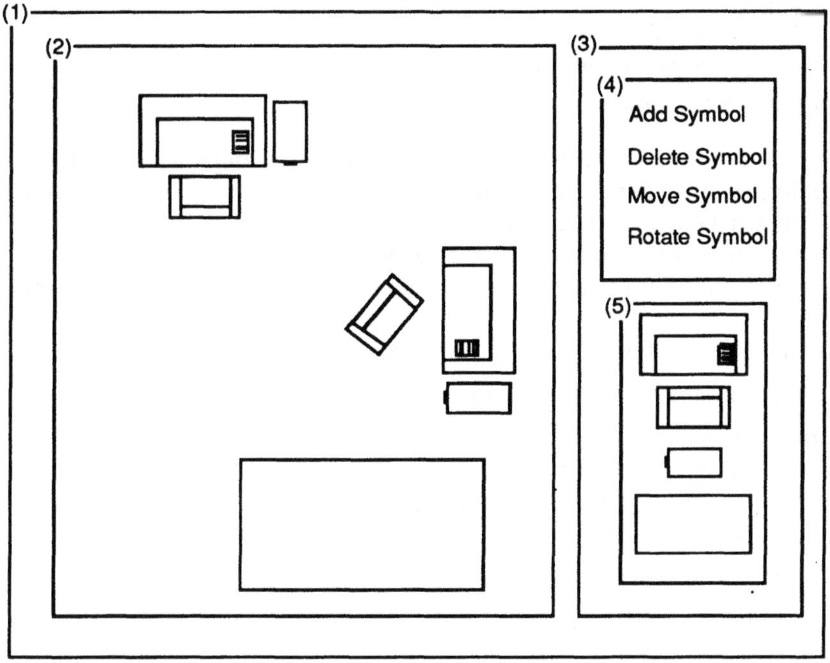

Fig. 9.1. Office Layout Application. The user interface of the Office Layout Application is shown. Dialogue guidance is supported in the rectangular menu on the right. This menu consists of two sub-menus. The icon menu in the lower right hand corner allows selection of predefined icons and their positioning in the work area with the operation Add Symbol. An object in the work area on the left can be picked and then deleted, moved or rotated.

The construction starts with the highest structure, the screen (1), named by the integer identifier Screen, consisting of the rectangle confining it and references to its substructures, MainMenu (3) and Work (2).

```
OPEN STRUCTURE (Screen)
  RECTANGLE (point1,point2)
  EXECUTE STRUCTURE (MainMenu)
  EXECUTE STRUCTURE (Work)
CLOSE STRUCTURE
```

Next, we wish to construct the main menu (3). Besides the bordering rectangle and references to the two substructures, we insert two pick identifiers, One and Two, into the structure. With the help of these, we can determine in which area of the screen a pick has occurred by comparing them to the identifiers returned from a pick operation.

```
OPEN STRUCTURE (MainMenu)
  RECTANGLE (point3,point4)
  SET PICK IDENTIFIER (One)
  EXECUTE STRUCTURE (MyTextMenu)
  SET PICK IDENTIFIER (Two)
  EXECUTE STRUCTURE (MyIconMenu)
CLOSE STRUCTURE
```

The set of detectable objects in our example changes depending on the state of the dialogue. In order to implement this dynamic change of detectability, we must construct corresponding name sets. In preparation, the strings for the name sets of the sub-menus to be constructed, MyTextMenu (4) and MyIconMenu (5), are inserted into these structures. These name sets control detectability and highlighting.

On the basis of these thoughts the following is done for the text menu:

```
OPEN STRUCTURE (MyTextMenu)
  ADD NAMES TO SET ({MyText})
  TEXT (X1,Y1,'Add Symbol')
  ADD NAMES TO SET ({'DeleteTransform'})
  TEXT (X2,Y2,'Delete Symbol')
  TEXT (X3,Y3,'Move Symbol')
  TEXT (X4,Y4,'Rotate Symbol')
CLOSE STRUCTURE
```

The menu with the predefined icons, which are themselves structures, is constructed in the same way. An ergonomically sound dialogue design demands that a selected graphics object be highlighted as reaction to a pick action. Therefore we will realize this demand for an icon selected from the icon menu. To prepare for this we assign a name to each icon. One "ADD NAMES TO SET" element and one "REMOVE NAMES FROM SET" element must be inserted into the structure MyIconMenu for each icon. We have done some indenting of the pseudocode to improve readability. The name MyIcons will later be used to set all icons detectable. The twice-indented names Desk, Chair, FileCabinet, Table will be used for highlighting after an individual icon has been selected. As a helpful trick we have used the same integer identifiers in the name sets and the execute statements. This will make it easier to coordinate the information of the pick path with that of the highlighting filter.

```
OPEN STRUCTURE (MyIconMenu)
  ADD NAMES TO SET({MyIcons})
      ADD NAMES TO SET({Desk})
          SET TRANSFORMATION (t1)
          EXECUTE STRUCTURE (Desk)
```

```
        REMOVE NAMES FROM SET ({Desk})
        ADD NAMES TO SET({Chair})
            SET TRANSFORMATION (t2)
            EXECUTE STRUCTURE (Chair)
        REMOVE NAMES FROM SET ({Chair})
        ADD NAMES TO SET({FileCabinet})
            SET TRANSFORMATION (t3)
            EXECUTE STRUCTURE (File Cabinet)
        REMOVE NAMES FROM SET ({FileCabinet})
        ADD NAMES TO SET({Table})
            SET TRANSFORMATION (t4)
            EXECUTE STRUCTURE (Table)
        REMOVE NAMES FROM SET ({Table})
    CLOSE STRUCTURE
```

Now create the work area Work surrounded by a rectangle is created. We will later be inserting objects selected from the icon menu into this structure. In order to be able to control detectability of these objects, we insert a name MyObjects into the structure:

```
    OPEN STRUCTURE (Work)
     RECTANGLE (point5,point6)
     ADD NAMES TO SET({ MyObjects})
    CLOSE STRUCTURE
```

The PHIGS structure built up so far is shown in Fig. 9.2..

9.1.2 Interaction

We have now built up the structure hierarchy. The two sub-menus are filled with appropriate contents; the work area is still empty. Somewhat differently than in the PHIGS book cited above, we wish to follow the principle of point-and-act here. So a graphics object is first picked and then subject to one of the functions of the text menu. To reach a sensible dialog design, we must guarantee that only the add-symbol operation can be applied to a selected pattern in the icon menu. In the same way, only delete, rotate and move operations make sense when an object is picked in the work area.

To commence interaction all icons are made detectable. Since the default value for detectable is false (i.e., non-detectable), we can put all menu icons into the inclusion set given to the filter as first parameter. We set the second parameter, the exclusion set, to empty because nothing must be filtered out of what was defined by the inclusion set.

```
    SET PICK FILTER ({MyIcons},empty) .
```

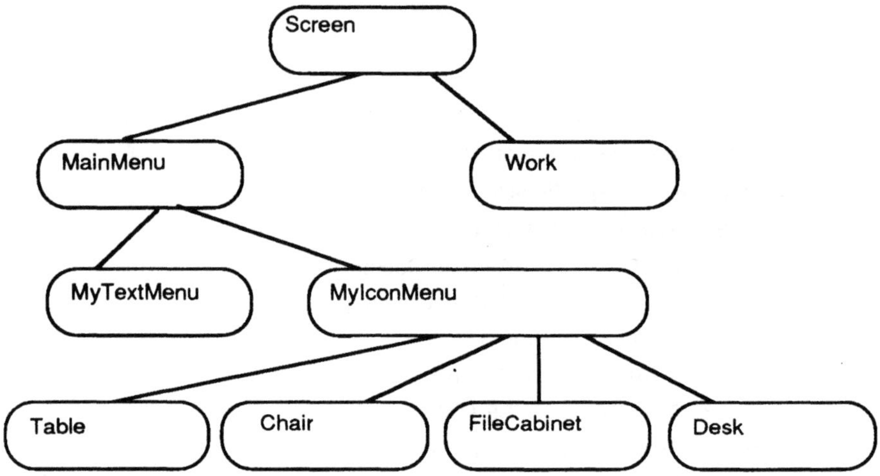

Fig. 9.2. PHIGS structure for office layout before starting the editing process.

9.1.2.1 Picking

Currently, only the objects in icon menu may be picked. Querying the pick device will return the pick path of the picked icon. For each level of the hierarchy traversed, the path comprises three components: structure identifier, pick identifier and the element sequence number (esn). If no pick identifier is defined in a certain level, the default 0 is delivered, so that the triples are defined as:

(1)	(Screen,	0		2)
(2)	(MainMenu,	Two		5)
(3)	(MyIconMenu,	Two,	3)	
(4)	(Desk,	Two,	esn)	

The information in (1) about the pick identifier defined in preparation, allows us to determine immediately whether picking occurred in the correct menu. The sequence of structure identifiers delivers the right information about the picked object. In this special case it is therefore not necessary to evaluate the sequence of element pointers.

By inserting into the highlighting filter, we can ensure that precisely the picked icon is highlighted. Because of our trick of using identical names in the structure and the name set, we can use s4 from the pick path directly for the filter.

```
SET HIGHLIGHTING FILTER ({Desk},empty)
```

We now have to program the editing operations. We proceed with the add operation.

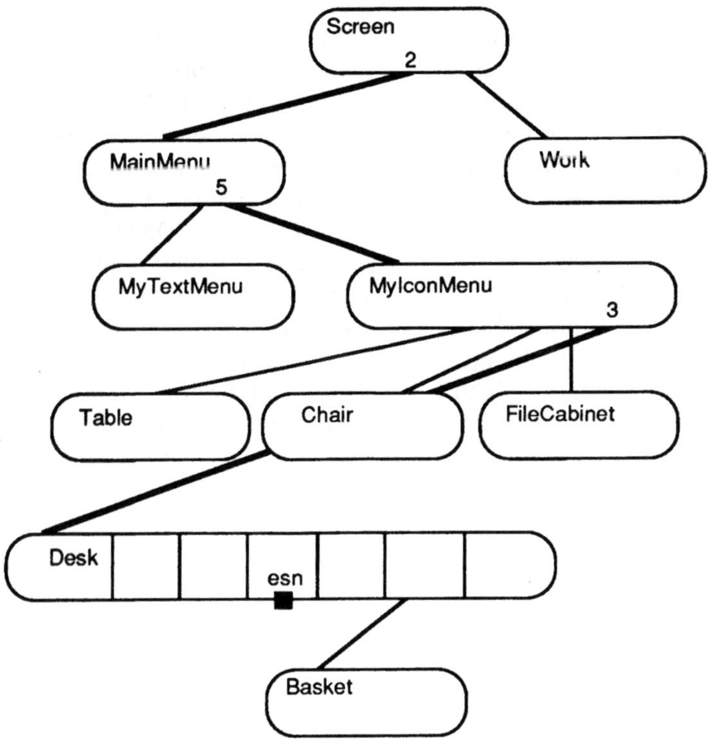

Fig. 9.3. Pick path. The sequence of the triples returned by pick will stop after four levels if the picked primitive lies directly in the highest structure of the Desk. If a primitive lying in a lower level of the structure would be picked, say the basket on top of the desk, then the sequences would be even longer. The reason is simple: PHIGS only supports picking of individual primitives.

9.1.2.2 Add Symbol

Because we have picked in the icon menu (and not in the work area), the only possible operation is add. So only the string 'Add Symbol' is set to detectable; this is done by adding MyText and inserting DeleteTransform into the exclusion set. The objects in the icon menu are automatically set to non-detectable because MyIcons does not appear in the new filter:

SET PICK FILTER ({MyText},{DeleteTransform})

Now a pick occurs, the locator is activated and everything is set to non-detectable:

SET PICK FILTER (empty,empty) .

After activation of the locator and its use by the user, a translation causing transformation of the picked object can be computed. This is then placed in the work area together with a reference to the picked object. To highlight we must insert names again. The trick we used above—using the name of the substructure—no longer works here, unfortunately: continued inserting uses the same icons repeatedly. So we need a mechanism that supplies us with a new name aName (of type integer) for every insertion. We call this function NEW NAME; it gives us a new name with every add operation and saves it in the variable aName.

In order to highlight the object picked in Work later on, we must establish a connection between aName and the information given by the pick path. The pick path returns structure names that are of no use to us. This is because the same structure may be inserted several times into work. It also returns element pointers, such as the element pointer of the current execute statement. But the values of these pointers are not stable. If a delete operation is executed, the value of the higher element pointer changes, which greatly complicates programming. The simplest solution therefore is to establish a pick identifier for every new icon on Work, and assign it the same name we use for highlighting. This again constitutes something of a trick. As a result of all this, we obtain the following construction:

```
NEW NAME (aName)
OPEN STRUCTURE (Work)
  ADD NAMES TO SET ({aName })
  SET PICK IDENTIFIER (aName)
  SET TRANSFORMATION (t2)
  EXECUTE STRUCTURE (s4)
  REMOVE NAMES FROM SET ({aName})
CLOSE STRUCTURE
```

The overall arrangement of our PHIGS structure network is shown in Fig. 9.4.

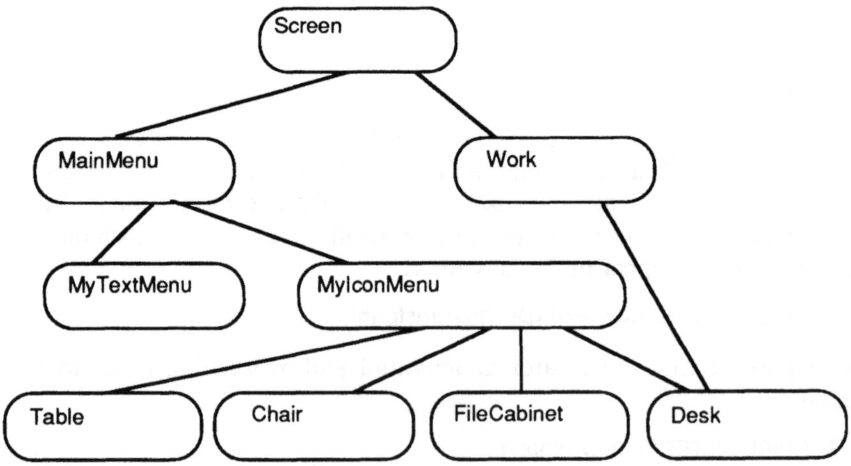

Fig. 9.4. PHIGS structure after insertion of one desk object into the work area, resulting in a directed graph.

After the insertion of the picked object into Work the highlighted icon must be turned off:

SET HIGHLIGHTING FILTER (empty ,empty) .

In case an existing structure is reopened, the element pointer is automatically positioned at the end, so one can insert there directly. So everything we have described here is true not only for the first add operation but for all subsequent add operations too. So we need only concern ourselves with the remaining operations in the following.

For continuing the interaction the following steps remain to be performed by the described mechanisms:

a) Setting all objects in MyIconMenu and in Work to detectable:

SET PICK FILTER ({MyIcons, MyObjects},empty) .

b) Picking an element and analyzing its path. The pick path returns either the integer Work or the integer MainMenu. So it can be determined in which of the two a pick action has occurred.

We then have to turn off detectability:

SET PICK FILTER (empty ,empty) .

If the picked object is from the icon menu, the steps described and programmed above have to be executed.

If picking occurred in Work, then the second triple of the pick path begins with work. The next steps are:

c) The selected object has to be highlighted. The structure work is organized in the way that the second component of the second triple of the pick path, the pick identifier pi, coincides with the name aName—because of our little trick. So the following statement causes the desired action:

SET HIGHLIGHTING FILTER ({ pi }, empty) .

d) Now precisely the three strings with name DeleteTransform must be made detectable:

SET PICK FILTER ({DeleteTransform},empty)

e) Then a string will be picked from the text menu and the returned pick path can be analyzed. The variable i3 now holds the element number 5, 6 or 7 (see definition of the structure MyTextMenu). This allows to determine whether the delete, move or transform operation has to be executed. Alternatively, we could also have used pick identifiers in the definition of MyTextMenu. However, defined as integers, they would have been analyzed in the same way as the element numbers.

We do without highlighting the selected strings in the text menu in our example, although this would be a good style of interaction, else we would have to fill up myTextMenu with even more names!

The selected operation must now be applied to the picked object. For doing this the operations add, delete, rotate and move have to be implemented.

9.1.2.3 Delete Symbol

The following operations delete the proper information in the structure Work. Those parts relevant to an object begin with the element ADD NAMES TO SET. This is situated three positions in front of the execute element. The element REMOVE NAMES FROM SET marks the end of the elements relevant to an object of the work area. It is located one position after the execute element (see 9.1.2.2). The element pointer i2 in the pick path of the selected object gives the position of the execute element. So the area to be deleted from the structure Work can be determined in the following manner:

```
OPEN STRUCTURE (Work)
  DELETE ELEMENT RANGE (i2-3, i2+1)
CLOSE STRUCTURE
```

All object in MyIconMenu and in Work are made detectable so that interaction can continue:

```
SET PICK FILTER ({MyIcons, MyObjects},empty) .
```

9.1.2.4 Move and Rotate

The picked object can be analyzed in the same way as above. Then either move or rotate, which we do not discuss further here, is executed. This results in a new transformation tnew. It is inserted at position i2-1, replacing the structure element that was previously there. This can be done in two ways. One alternative is setting the PHIGS system to replace mode, which causes replacement when the element is inserted:

```
INSERT MODE (Replace)
OPEN STRUCTURE (Work)
  SET ELEMENT POINTER (i2-1)
  SET TRANSFORMATION (tnew)
CLOSE STRUCTURE
INSERT MODE (Insert)
```

One can alternatively activate the wait state, delete the old transformation at position i2-1 and then insert the new one. Simply deleting and then inserting, as is done in "Understanding PHIGS", causes an undesirable intermediate state for the picked objects transformation, so that it jumps to some undetermined spot.

The picked object is still highlighted after its position has been changed. So we have to turn this off:

```
SET HIGHLIGHTING FILTER (empty, empty) .
```

All objects in MyIconMenu and in Work are made detectable so that interaction may continue:

```
SET PICK FILTER ({MyIcons, MyObjects},empty) .
```

9.2 Office Layout Application in GEO++

We now follow through the same example in GEO++. We first construct all necessary building patterns, viz., the menus, rectangles and texts.

9.2.1 Construction of the Screen Layout

We use the class Rect for rectangles in GEO++ because the name Rectangle is already reserved in Smalltalk-80 for a non-graphics, purely geometric class:

```
screen ← Group new .
mainMenu ← Group new .
myIconMenu ← Group new .
work ← Group new .
myIconMenu ← Group new .
myTextMenu ← Group new .

screenBorder ← Rect topLeft: point1 bottomRight: point2 .
menuBorder ← Rect topLeft: point3 bottomRight: point4 .
workBorder ← Rect topLeft: point5 bottomRight: point6 .
addText ← Text string:' Add Symbol' .
delText ← Text string: 'Delete Symbol' .
moveText ← Text string: 'Move Symbol' .
rotText ← Text string: 'Rotate Symbol' .
```

The insert process returns the appropriate indicators as results. The generation and insertion of text primitives is done in a single statement by concatenation:

a) screen:

```
screen insert: screenBorder .
mainInd ← screen insert: mainMenu .
workInd ← screen insert: work .
```

b) mainMenu:

```
mainMenu insert: menuBorder .
textInd ← mainMenu insert: myTextMenu .
iconInd ← mainMenu insert: myIconMenu .
```

c) work:

```
work insert: workBorder
```

d) myTextMenu:

```
addInd ← myTextMenu insert: addText at: x1@y1 .
delInd ← myTextMenu insert: delText at: x2@y2 .
moveInd ← myTextMenu insert: moveText at: x3@y3 .
rotInd ← myTextMenu insert: rotText at: x4@y4 .
```

e) myIconMenu:

```
deskInd ← myIconMenu insert: desk at: x5@y5 .
chairInd ← myIconMenu insert: chair at: x6@y6 .
tableInd ← myIconMenu insert: table at: x7@y7 .
cabInd ← myIconMenu insert: file cabinet at: x8@y8 .
```

9.2.2 Interaction

As in PHIGS, all icons must be made detectable for the beginning of interaction. The simplest way to do this is to use the flexible addressing mechanisms in GEO++. There are several alternatives in this. Since we will be accessing the subparts of icon menu and work area frequently, we first create corresponding parts:

```
myIconPart ← screen part: (mainInd, iconInd) .
myWorkPart ← screen part: workInd .
```

9.2.2.1 Pick in GEO++

With

```
allIcons ← (myIconPart children) detectable: true .
```

the icon menu's children become detectable.

Alternatively, we could of course define allIcons as the set of all three-level parts of Screen whose path has mainInd as first component and iconInd as second. This can be implemented as a wild card search:

```
allIcons ← screen part: (mainInd,iconInd,#* ) .
```

If one of the icons is picked, the pick device delivers the picked part, which we can immediately highlight:

```
pickedPart ← (Pick request) highlighting: true .
```

There are two methods to analyze the picked object:

a) The picked object's path is requested by path and its constituents are analyzed. Such an inquiry operation would look something as:

```
(pickedPart path) at: 3 == deskInd ifTrue:.. . .
```

b) The components of the icon menu are addressed as parts and the parts are compared directly:

```
deskItem ← myIconPart part: deskInd .
pickedPart == deskItem ifTrue: ....
```

The editing process starts with the add operation.

9.2.2.2 *Add Symbol*

To set the 'Add Symbol' text detectable and the menu icons non-detectable, the following operations are used:

```
allIcons detectable: false .
addText detectable: true .
```

We note that the strings are accessed as building patterns, and not handled by part operations. This is unproblematic as the strings are not repeatedly referred. Now a pick action occurs and the locator is activated. The add string is set back to non-detectable:

```
addText detectable: false .
```

After locator input by the user, a position aPoint can be computed. The insert:at: message used above serves to insert the content into the picked object. Then we have to reset the highlighting attribute:

```
work insert: (pickedPart content) at: aPoint .
pickedPart highlighting: false .
```

Here more has to done than in PHIGS: set back the state of a previously assigned attribute, in this case of pickedPart. This is not a substantial difference however, since we could also introduce an operation that globally resets all attributes to their default state.

It should be remarked on the side that we consciously did without the generation of an indicator as result of the insert:at: message above. We don't need it: if the part created by the insertion is picked, then the indicator could be inquired.

Now all objects in work and myIconMenu are defined as detectable and all entries in the text menu as non-detectable, so that interaction may continue.

```
(myWorkPart children) detectable: true .
(myIconPart children) detectable: true .
addText detectable: false .
delText detectable: false .
moveText detectable: false .
rotText detectable: false .
```

Note that instead of the last four operations, the following utility operation could also achieve the same effect:

```
((myTextMenu children) content.) detectable: false .
```

After started the generation of the first object on screen, the following tasks remain to be attended to (just as in PHIGS).

An element is picked and highlighted:

```
pickedPart ← (Pick request) highlighting: true .
```

To determinate whether the picked part is in the work or icon area test the picked part's parent:

```
pickedPart parent == myWorkPart ifTrue: ....
pickedPart parent == myIconPart ifTrue: .....
```

Then setting parts to non-detectable:

```
(myWorkPart children) detectable: false .
(myIconPart children) detectable: false .
```

In case the picked part is in the icon menu, the steps described under add symbol follow.

9.2.2.3 Delete, Move, Rotate

If the picked element is in the work area, the text primitives delText, moveText and rotText are made detectable. Since the three objects are always needed at the same occasion, they should be collected in a set:

```
delTransSet ← GraphicsSet new .
delTransSet add: delText; add: moveText; add: rotText .
(pickedPart parent == myWorkPart ) ifTrue: [delTransSet detectable: true] .
```

As we see here, the set operations replace the filter functions in PHIGS.

An object is now selected from the text menu and could be highlighted with a great deal less effort than in PHIGS. We do not do this, however, to retain the analogy to the PHIGS example and we write:

```
operation ← Pick request .
```

Now the selected operation is applied to the picked object and, in the last two cases, highlighting is turned off. The add symbol case was discussed above; the remaining operations to describe are deletion, rotation, and translation:

```
(operation content) == delText ifTrue: [pickedPart delete] .
(operation content) == rotText ifTrue:
        [pickedPart attribute: aRotation; highlighting: false ] .
(operation content) == moveText ifTrue:
        [pickedPart attribute: aTranslation; highlighting: false ] .
```

All objects in work and myIconMenu are set to detectable, and all entries in the text menu to non-detectable, so that interaction may continue.

```
(myWorkPart children) detectable: true .
(myIconPart children) detectable: true .
((myTextMenu children) content.) detectable: false .
```

9.3 Comparison of the PHIGS and GEO++ Solution

We now point out the main differences between the solution in PHIGS and the one in GEO++.

9.3.1 Filter Handling

In PHIGS, preparation for the construction and modification of a structure includes the definition of filters for visibility/invisibility, detectability/non-detectability, highlighting/non-highlighting. The requirement of assigning names to the definitions of the filters when creating a structure is related to this. Expressions of the form

```
ADD NAMES TO SET (set1) .
REMOVE NAMES FROM SET (set2) .
```

must be inserted into the open structure.

In GEO++, any group, any primitive, or part of the part hierarchy can be addressed. So there is no need to specify special mechanisms for the assignment of visibility, highlighting and detectability. If an attribute, say detectability, is to be changed for a whole set of parts, then the applications programmer simply inserts the names of these parts into sets defined by him, as the above example has shown. The advantage is that an object has exactly one name and keeps it for its lifetime. If only a few parts are to have their attributes changed, then collecting them in a set is not required, since every part and any of its attributes may be addressed individually. In PHIGS, a filter must always be defined. This can be seen in Sect. 9.4, where relatively trivial attribute assignments are performed, but a pick filter must be built every time.

9.3.2 Picking

The example shows that the PHIGS pick path, with its three components, is a quite complicated concept. It is often difficult to coordinate the information returned in the pick path with the desired reaction to the pick—even in simple cases as highlighting the picked object. We used tricks in our example and thereby barely escaped having to administrate lists of information (coordinating pick path information, names from name sets, etc.) on top of PHIGS.

GEO++, on the other hand, simply returns the picked object, which can immediately be subject to the desired operations. The above example showed that the operations delete and transform can be directly applied to the picked part, without having to analyze first what kind of office furniture the part represents. Such analysis can always be avoided if the type of operation to be applied to the picked object is known beforehand.

The situation in PHIGS is more complicated because such operations require that the neighborhood of the picked primitive's element pointer or a reference be analyzed. This environment depends on the picked object's type on screen. In our example, where the graphics objects in Work had been assigned no additional attributes, we had the simple case that the area to be deleted in the delete operation was of constant length. In general, however, this is not the case, and the complexity of programming grows substantially in PHIGS, but not in GEO++.

A further uncomfortable characteristic of the PHIGS pick is that only individual primitives can be picked. In the above example picking inside desk will cause pick paths of different lengths. In GEO++, the same object is always returned when the desk is picked. If we replace the icons in the icon menu with other office furniture taken from the data bank, we obtain different pick paths in PHIGS.

The problems we have mentioned here all have to do with the basic model of PHIGS: the part hierarchy is generated only indirectly by the traversal process; for interaction it must be accessed again indirectly.

9.4 Pick Object and Assign Attribute

The following example may be viewed as a continuation of the first one. We now wish to extend our graphics editor for office layout by introducing the possibility of assigning attributes to the objects in Work. We assume our text menu has been extended by some commands for modifying line thickness and type.

9.4.1 Assigning the Selected Attribute in PHIGS

We can now continue our office layout example and assume a selection designating the assignment of an attribute has been activated in the menu. Analysis of the pick path yields the selected attribute.

9.4.1.1 Alternative 1

We decide to insert the attribute or attributes always directly in front of the execute statement in Work, i.e., the reference to the graphics structure selected by the pick operation. Specifically, line thickness is to be placed directly before the reference, and line type before that. So the following is necessary in PHIGS:

a) Analysis of which attribute is concerned. This can be done quite simply by analyzing the pick path. We assume LINE TYPE (2) is to be assigned.

b) As above, let i2 be the position of the reference to the graphics object picked in work. We now have to determine whether there were already explicitly assigned attributes in front of i2. This can be done with four statements—two to position the element pointers and two to make the inquiries.

c) Depending on the results of the inquiries, we must discern between overwriting old attributes and inserting new ones.

d) Since the effect of the attributes continues on to the other elements in the structure network, we must determine whether the selected attribute type has already been set explicitly for the following reference. If this is not the case, then the effect of the attribute must be neutralized. this can only be done by explicitly re-inserting the attribute that was previously valid for the successor. Now the question arises of how one can determine this attribute.

e) We remember that the first primitive in Work was the surrounding rectangle (see Sect. 9.1.1). So the attributes of this rectangle were transferred to all following elements which have not been explicitly supplied with other attributes. Since this makes little sense, we set (then or at least now) the attributes to their default values after the rectangle, that is in positions 3 and 4 of the structure. If we don't do this, we have to find out somehow which attributes are valid for the rectangle. This would involve a fairly complicated process of picking our way through the hierarchy, or of querying global default values, since PHIGS does not allow asking a primitive about its own attributes (because this would require to ask for the posted tree, which is only defined at posting time). If we follow the first alternative, we must use a copy operation to insert the third or fourth structure element in front of the successor of the picked element. But then it would no longer be possible to change the default of the third or fourth element of Work. In order to support such flexibility, we would have to keep tables of the positions of the values copied into the structure—on top of PHIGS, naturally.

We note that introducing additional attribute types causes another complication: the operations in Sect. 9.1.2.3, where a range of elements was deleted by defining it from i2-3 to i2+1, must also be rethought. This is because the lengths of the areas responsible for an object become longer. Within a structure element, these include the actual reference, i.e., the execute statement, the attributes for line thickness and line type, transformation and the name set elements. So we have to keep a list in a layer above PHIGS that administrates the length of the areas to be deleted for each i2 candidate. Then the delete operation in the example would have to be:

```
DELETE ELEMENT RANGE (i2 - range (i2), i2+ k) .
```

This list must be updated whenever a new element is inserted or an existing one's attributes are changed. An alternative, which also involves additional programming, is to query all structure elements backwards and forwards from position i2, determine their type, and delete the corresponding structure element until one reaches the beginning or end of the current sphere of influence. In the form of organization we have chosen, one would eventually reach the 'ADD NAMES TO SET' element going backwards, and the 'REMOVE NAMES FROM SET' element going forwards.

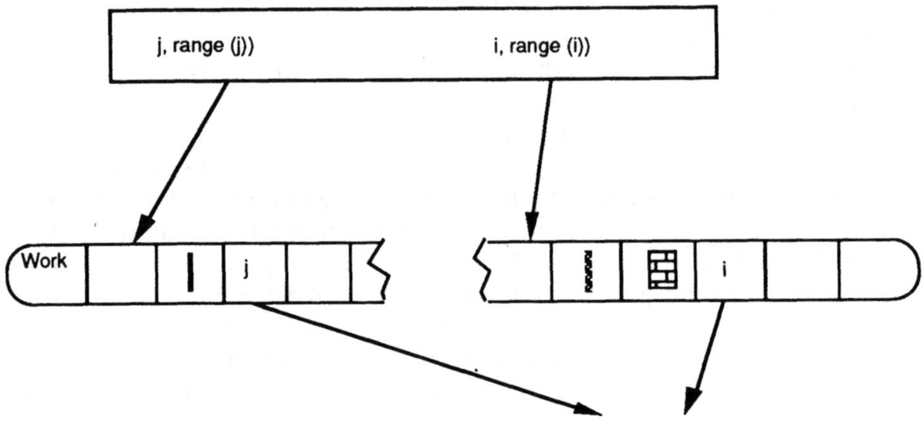

Fig. 9.5. Inserting attributes into Work. If the user has the freedom to assign different attributes to objects of the work area the neighborhood of the execute statement will may grow dynamically and a list has to be built by the programmer for administrating the pointers.

9.4.1.2 Alternative 2

A second alternative that is a little easier to handle consists in changing the organization of the structure network from the very beginning. This is shown in Fig. 9.6. What we do here, instead of putting the object picked from the icon menu directly into the work area, is to establish a reference to a new, intermediate level of "attribute nodes". So instead of

```
EXECUTE STRUCTURE (s4),
```

we create

```
EXECUTE STRUCTURE (aName) .
```

In addition, we generate a new structure for each new object and insert the attributes and a reference to s4 into that. At the same time we transfer down the name for highlighting and transformation; we don't need the pick identifier here. So we obtain the following statements:

```
OPEN STRUCTURE (Work)
  EXECUTE STRUCTURE (AName)
CLOSE STRUCTURE
OPEN STRUCTURE (AName)
  ADD NAMES TO SET ({AName})
  SET TRANSFORMATION (t2)
  EXECUTE STRUCTURE (s4)
CLOSE STRUCTURE .
```

The last structure now allows us to administrate the attributes for line thickness and type. In evaluation of this alternative, we discover that we can do without the pick identifier and the Remove-Names-From-Set identifier. Also, we no longer have to keep the list in a layer above PHIGS to handle the area of influence of an attribute when inserting it into the structure AName. When changing an attribute, however, we still have to search around within the structure AName. And delete has become even more complicated because we must delete a structure and also change the calling structure Work.

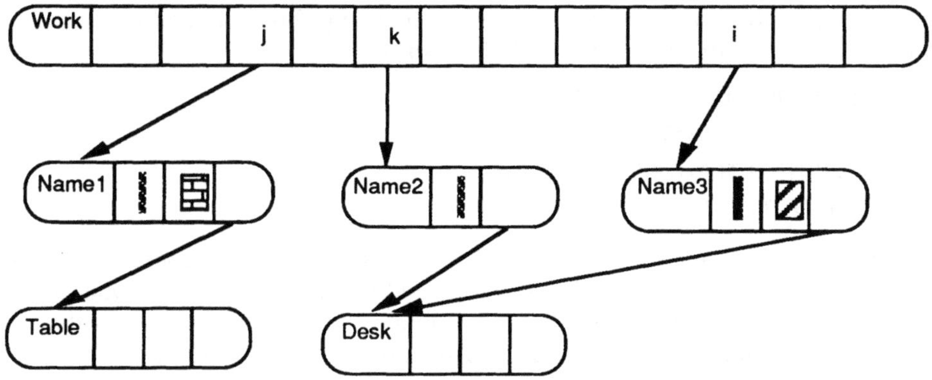

Fig. 9.6. Special structures to store attributes.

9.4.2 Assigning the Selected Attribute in GEO++

We take up the office layout example where we left off in Sect. 9.2.2. A pick action gives us the object pickedOperation. We analyze its path and get the selected attribute myAttribute.

Now we use the following expression to assign this attribute to the picked graphics object:

```
pickedPart attribute: myAttribute .
```

That's all!

9.5 Higher Level Hierarchies

In "Understanding PHIGS", the office layout editor example is followed by a small addendum entitled "Generalizing to Higher Level Hierarchies". It is suggested there to extend the editor by an additional icon combining Desk and Chair to Desk_Chair so that the combination can be placed in Work.

9.5.1 Desk_Chair in PHIGS

We build the new structure Desk_Chair with references to Desk and Chair :

```
OPEN STRUCTURE (Desk_Chair)
  SET TRANSFORMATION (trans1)
  EXECUTE STRUCTURE (Desk)
  SET TRANSFORMATION (trans2)
  EXECUTE STRUCTURE (Chair)
CLOSE STRUCTURE
```

It is now possible to extend the icon menu by using the described mechanisms and to insert the extension at the end of the structure:

```
OPEN STRUCTURE (MyIconMenu)
  SET TRANSFORMATION (t5)
  EXECUTE STRUCTURE (Desk_Chair)
CLOSE STRUCTURE
```

The new icon can be added to the work area, just as the other icons, and can be rotated and moved. If we use this icon repeatedly, execute statements pointing to it are used. It is therefore possible to edit one of the icons. The effect is that all visible objects that refer to the modified icon are changed consistently.

However, the above model has a substantial weak point:

- It is *not* possible to change a part of Desk_Chair for one individual visual representation.
- If, for example, a chair is rotated in the combination without rotating the desk, the transformation trans2 in the above structure has to be changed. As a consequence, *all* of the chairs in *all* displayed Desk_Chair combinations are changed.
- If we modify a transformation in a structure level above the combination, i.e., in the structure executing the combination, this affects only one displayed object, but the *whole* combination, and not only the chair.

For these reasons it is not possible to generate an icon Desk_Chair for the two desk-chair combinations shown in Fig. 9.1, corresponding to the illustration in the "Understanding PHIGS" book.

9.5.2 Desk_Chair in GEO++

We create the new group deskChair:

```
deskChair ← Group new
subDeskInd ← deskChair insert: desk
subChairInd ← deskChair insert: chair .
```

Then we insert it into myIconMenu :

```
deskChairInd ← myIconMenu insert: deskChair at: x9@y9
```

When we have selected this new object from the menu, we insert it into work:

```
work insert: (pickedPart content) at: aPoint
```

Now we can do anything that is possible in PHIGS. But, in addition, GEO++ offers the possibility of rotating the chair in exactly one picked object. To do this we can for example set all the chairs in every deskChair combination in work to detectable:

```
chairs ← screen part: (workInd,#* ,subChairInd )
chairs detectable: true .
```

If a picked chair is returned, then this part can be given a new attribute. So each is handled individually:

```
pickedChair ← Pick request
pickedChair attribute: aRotation .
```

Since attribute setting for parts does not affect geometrical equivalence, i.e., the rotated chair retains its content in GEO++, the building pattern chair may be edited even after an individual rotate or it may be replaced by of a new chair model, loaded from the archive. In this case, all visible chairs change.

9.5.3 Radio Example

We now take up our familiar radio example again and discuss the assignment of attributes to individual objects. First we see the difficulties that arise in PHIGS in this context.

9.5.3.1 FrontPanel as Acyclic Graph in PHIGS

In this example we wish to construct our front panel in the form of an acyclical graph. In other words, we use the way of structuring that PHIGS naturally offers us. We start at the lowest level and work our way up. As in the other examples, we leave out instantiation of the used names (of type integer).

A new, empty structure for Button is created by opening a structure that does not yet exist:

```
Open Structure (Button)
```

Insertion of the primitives for square and circle:

```
POLYLINE (4,x1,x1,....x4,y4)
CIRCLE (cx,cy,radius)
```

We close the structure before beginning construction of the next:

```
Close Structure
```

New structure for switchboard:

```
Open Structure (Switchboard)
```

Insertion of the polylines for horizontal and vertical borders:

```
POLYLINE (2,x11,y11,x12,y12)
POLYLINE (2,x21,y21,x22,y22)
```

Transformations and reference for Button:

```
SET TRANSFORMATION (tr1)
EXECUTE STRUCTURE (Button)
SET TRANSFORMATION (tr2)
EXECUTE STRUCTURE (Button)
SET TRANSFORMATION (tr3)
EXECUTE STRUCTURE (Button)
SET TRANSFORMATION (tr4)
EXECUTE STRUCTURE (Button)
```

Closing the structure:

```
CLOSE STRUCTURE .
```

The structure for the front panel is generated, pseudocode is used to insert a polyline describing the outer borders of the front panel and to describe other parts we won't model explicitly here:

```
OPEN STRUCTURE (FrontPanel)
POLYLINE (coordinates-for-boundary)
• • • other items at top level • • •
```

Transformations and references to switchboard:

```
SET TRANSFORMATION (ltrans)
EXECUTE STRUCTURE (Switchboard)
SET TRANSFORMATION (rtrans)
EXECUTE STRUCTURE (Switchboard)
```

Closing the structure:

```
CLOSE STRUCTURE
```

We now have a structure hierarchy corresponding to the acyclical graph shown in Fig. 9.7.

9.5.3.2 Construction of the Object Structure in GEO++

We repeat here the construction of the hierarchy as described in Chap. 8.

Primitives for circle and square:

```
s ← PolyLine points: sqPoints
circle ← Circle center: cPoint radius: r
```

A new, empty group:

button ← Group new

Insertion into Button:

s ← button insert: sq
c ← button insert: circle.

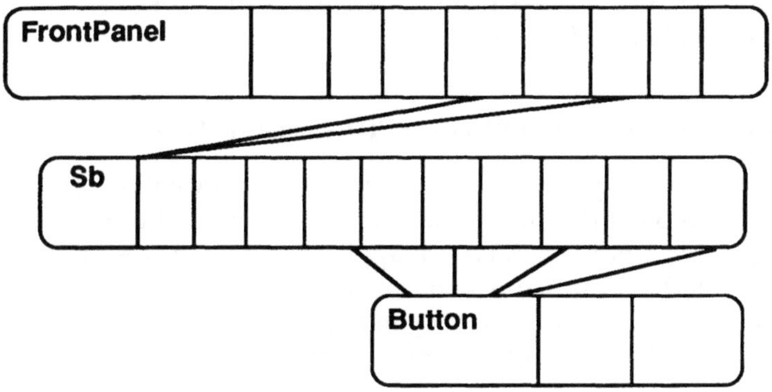

Fig. 9.7 The hierarchy FrontPanel as directed graph in PHIGS.

New group for switchboard:

switchBoard ← Group new

Insertion of polylines for horizontal and vertical borders:

c1 ← switchBoard insert: poly1
c2 ← switchBoard insert: poly2

Multiple use of the button with differing attributes:

tl ← switchBoard insert: button attribute: tr1
tr ← switchBoard insert: button attribute: tr2
bl ← switchBoard insert: button attribute: tr3
br ← switchBoard insert: button attribute: tr4

Insertion of Switchboard with two different attributes:

left ← frontPanel insert: switchBoard transform: ltrans
right ← frontPanel insert: switchBoard transform: rtrans

9.5.4 On the Analogy Between PHIGS and GEO++

We constructed the radio in PHIGS and GEO++ in such a way as to retain as much analogy as possible. We defined geometrically equivalent building blocks such as the button by multiple insertions of button in both PHIGS and GEO++. While GEO++ allows the use of the radio structure for different application problems quite easily, careful thought beforehand is necessary in PHIGS. In PHIGS, several methods of constructing the graphics object structure compete with each other; each of these has both advantages and disadvantages. An optimal construction as in GEO++ is not possible in PHIGS. We look into this problem in more detail in the following.

9.5.5 Redesigning the Building Blocks in PHIGS and GEO++

The acyclical directed graph is well suited to store information compactly and to support global modeling in the sense that the whole graphic changes when construction data are modified. A typical application that makes full use of the advantages of the PHIGS structure above is the consistent modification of all eight buttons. To do this, one has only to open the PHIGS structure button and edit it. The same is possible in GEO++ by applying group operations to button.

9.5.6 Controlling the Radio

In this example, we wish to use our model of the radio in PHIGS and GEO++ to connect the graphics representation of the front panel with an application process lying behind it. In other words, we wish to control an application process interactively. We assume the application is controlled depending on the selection of one of the eight radio buttons. We call the whole system, i.e., the complete interactive application, *Controlling the Radio*. In GEO++ the application could use the request pick operation and decide in the application object what to perform (see Sect. 9.5.6.2); for reacting to selected buttons by highlighting it could assign an attribute a selected button. We give a more elegant alternative solution, by using inheritance and call-back messages, in Chap. 10.

9.5.6.1 PHIGS Solution

The solution we suggest here for PHIGS uses the model of the front panel as a directed acyclical graph, as described above. Once started, the application program sets all eight buttons detectable and evaluates the returned pick path. On the basis of this path, control is forked to the appropriate application module, in this case a sub-program.

To set all eight buttons detectable in PHIGS, an ADD NAMES TO SET element is inserted at the beginning of the structure with identifier button. We designate the positions of the element pointers, which refer to the substructures with the execute elements, with left, right, tl, tr, bl, br. If a button is now picked, the sequence of element pointers returned in the pick path can be compared, from top to bottom, with left, right or tl, tr, bl, br. From this we can determine which of the eight cases, designated caseLeftTl,..., caseRightBr, we have at hand. Depending on this case, the appropriate subprogram can be called. We will not discuss this in any more detail as the principle of analyzing a pick path has already been explained. Figure 9.8 shows how the pick path is evaluated in a multi level acyclical graph.

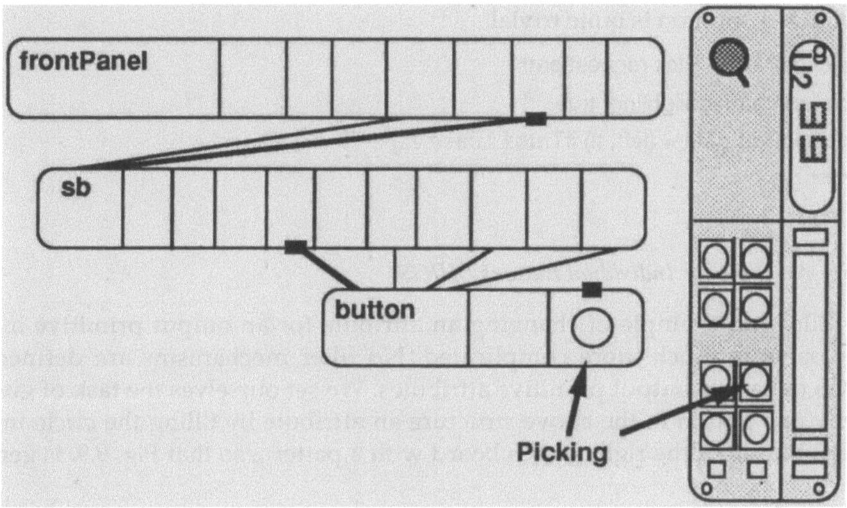

Fig. 9.8. Pick path in a multi-level acyclical graph. Pick path analysis gives us the right button and allows control, for example, of an application that reacts depending on which button was picked. The circle within the button is used for control. So in a certain sense, the pick operation is part-oriented. It is also the only operation in PHIGS that refers to an individual node of the posted tree.

Programming gets a little more complicated In order to highlight the object that was picked. In our example this is just barely possible without having to restructure the directed acyclical graph. We insert ADD NAMES TO SET elements in front of the references, i.e., the execute elements. Behind them we insert REMOVE NAMES FROM SET elements, using the names of the integer variables defined above (that correspond to the positions of the execute elements). By clever using the filter we can then cause the picked object to be highlighted. In this way, for example,

```
SET HIGHLIGHTING FILTER ({tl},{left})
```

causes exactly the top left button of the right switchboard to be highlighted. The inclusion set contains the two top-left buttons in the right and left switchboard, the exclusion set subtracts everything in the left switchboard.

The following should be noted:

- it is not possible to highlight an arbitrary subset of buttons in this way. For being more flexible, we have mentioned in 7.3.6 how the PHIGS definition could be modified.

9.5.6.2 GEO++ Solution

The GEO++ solution is quite trivial:

```
pickedPart ← Pick request path
pickedPart highlighting: true
pickedPart path = (left, tl) ifTrue:[...case 1..]
...
```

9.5.6.3 Attribute for Individual Buttons PHIGS

The following example of changing an attribute for an output primitive in the front panel is much more complicated. No filter mechanisms are defined in PHIGS to handle output primitive attributes. We set ourselves the task of giving exactly one button in the above structure an attribute by filling the circle in the top left button of the right switch board with a pattern, so that Fig. 9.9. is generated.

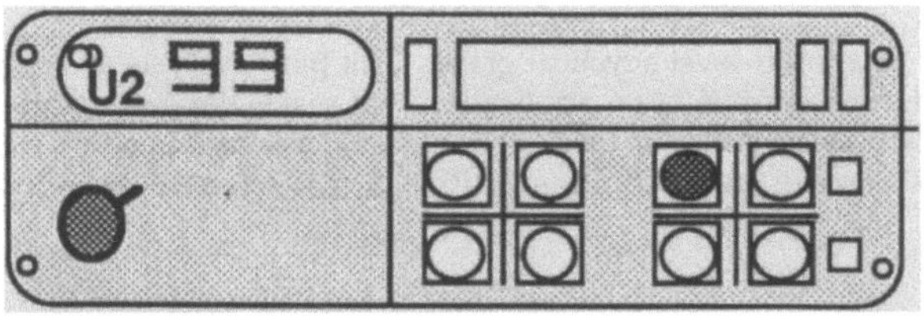

Fig. 9.9. Intended result of the attribute assignment.

This operation can be implemented as a series of copy operations resulting in the structure network depicted in Fig. 9.10. The following operations are necessary:

- Copy operations to insert the old contents into the new structures. This can be used to create Switchboard1, Button1 and to copy the content of Switchboard and Button into them.
- Changing the second reference in Frontpanel and the first reference in Button1.
- Insertion of the attribute into Button1.

Unfortunately, these already complicated operations do not suffice! Since we have also inserted names for the definitions of the filters into Switchboard, we must still change these elements.

This example shows that continued assignment of attributes to individual buttons eventually requires that the graph be rebuilt as a tree. Beyond its complexity, this rebuilding has another very negative effect: geometric equivalence is lost. In order to change all eight buttons in the same way later on, say add another primitive to button, we have to do this eight times. In addition, the knowledge that there are eight buttons with eight different structures must be managed by the applications programmer in a level on top of PHIGS. This means additional programming effort.

We call the process described above *individualization*. This is necessary in PHIGS whenever an attribute is to be changed in a non-trivial graph. In contrast, GEO++ requires it only when a part is to be edited. It is then offered as an atomic action.

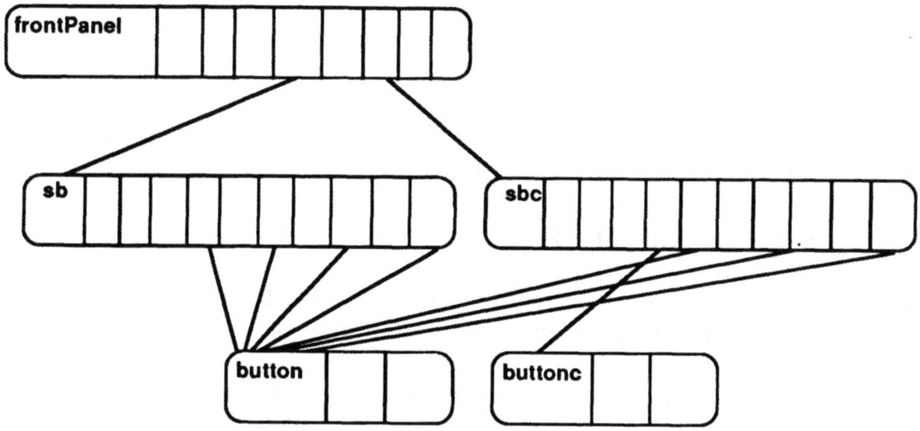

Fig. 9.10 Restructuring actions for the individualization of an object. If the data structure is modeled as a true acyclical graph in PHIGS, then assigning an individual attribute to exactly one button is only possible by reorganizing the graph towards a tree.

We should mention that one can take the tree resulting from individual attribute assignment and reconstruct it again as a directed acyclical graph. Jointly used primitives are then repeatedly referenced and thereby stored compactly. In final consequence the PHIGS concept is then reduced to a world of attribute trees pointing to repeatedly referenced structures that only contain output primitives. The attribute nodes are then similar to part attributes in PHIGS.

At a first glance such a structure looks as an implementation of GEO++. This is not true, however, because we cannot define group attributes: any insertion of an attribute in a multiply referenced structure would overwrite the "part" attribute in the attribute node, because the inserted "group" attribute is traversed later and would override the individual attribute of the "part" node.

9.5.6.4 The Solution in GEO++

As we have already shown, a part in GEO++ is addressed by its path and can so be given an appropriate attribute. Here the circle in the top left button of the right switchboard is addressable by the path (right, tl, circle).

It is important that the geometrical equivalence is retained. If we change button, this still affects all eight buttons.

9.5.6.5 Editing a Part

As we have mentioned already, the situation is different when we edit a part. When an individual part is edited, for example with

```
myButton ← frontPanel part: (right ,tl ,circle)
myButton insert: aBuildingPattern
```

then myButton is individualized, i.e., it gets a new content. This affects the entire ancestor chain, since their contents change along automatically. If the group button is changed now, this affects all parts that have button as content, in this case only *seven* of the buttons. We should note that the entire individualization is defined by the last expression. No new parts are created, the paths remain the same. Only the content is changed, which is what we wanted.

9.6 Interactive Editing of a PolyLine

In Sect. 4.5 the example of interactive generation of a linear fit has shown the advantages of editable output primitives. The same principle is supported by GEO++.

We will show here, how difficult this elementary process is when solved by PHIGS (and how much more difficult by GKS). The following steps are required:

(a) Create a new empty structure as container for the polyline.
(b) Define an array for storing the coordinates.
(c) Define a loop for the input process.
(d) Request input device (locator).
(e) Change array (add point).
(f) Insert polyline into structure (insert mode: replace).

The main difference to GEO++ and Smalltalk-80 consists of (e) and (f). Because primitives are not objects and may not be edited, this must be done for their arrays provided for storing the coordinates. These coordinates are unknown to PHIGS so that a replacement of a primitive is required at any time.

The whole replacement is also very inconvenient if we look to the performance aspects. GEO++ and Smalltalk-80 add a new coordinate and therefore only a line segment must be added to the previous primitive. PHIGS replacement requires a deletion, an expensive operation, and a completely new generation (unless a very clever implementation can avoid it).

9.6.1 Further Examples

Further comparisons (not involving inheritance) between GEO++ and PHIGS where they differ considerable are grouping and ungrouping and complex filter operations. The analysis of these is left to the reader.

9.7 Examination and Comments

9.7.1 Overall Structure of PHIGS and GEO++

Most of the problems with PHIGS have to do with very inhomogeneous structures and the fact that this inhomogeneous information is coordinated at a late point, during traversal. The applications programmer in PHIGS cannot think in terms of the objects he wants to manipulate on the output device or offer the end user for interactive manipulation. So programming has to be performed at an intermediate level—the linearly organized structures with inhomogeneously interspersed elements. He must continuously imagine the effect of posting these structures. The complex and awkward coordinated name concept in PHIGS, which comprehends element pointers, labels, pick identifiers and name set assignments, does not support him in this. This is already apparent in a simple example as assigning an attribute to a part picked on the screen!

In order to ensure consistent update and compact storing of repeatedly referenced structures, PHIGS does without addressing individual components of the displayed information. This means that PHIGS describes its operations in terms of an intermediate structure that is not visible on screen and cannot be appreciated by the end user. This is the directed acyclical graph, whose information becomes visible on a display medium only after the traversal process. In somewhat extreme terms, then, PHIGS describes a concrete implementation, or an abstract device that lies somewhere between graphics programming and display.

Only when the structure network in PHIGS is degenerated to a tree does the representation of structures correspond to the visible objects of the hierarchy. Unfortunately, to do this it becomes necessary to multiply store objects with the same geometrical information. One then also loses the knowledge about equivalent building patterns.

The concept used in GEO++ represents a synthesis of these approaches: a tree with individual parts that carry their own attributes and have building patterns (possibly used jointly by several parts) as content. Such an object structure and its corresponding operations are easily formulated in an object-oriented world, since multiple reference to the same object (which may be very complex) is an elementary principle there.

9.7.2 Dynamics

Comfortable handling of graphics part hierarchies was the central point in the design of GEO++. This led to the goal of supporting the requirements articulated in Sect. 6 in the most natural and simple way possible. GEO++ strives to offer what is generally accepted as an elementary operation for the construction and modification of a part hierarchy in the form of a single, atomic function. Conversely, every function in GEO++ should be easily interpreted as an operation on a part hierarchy, so that a seamless translation into the semantics of part hierarchies is possible. The problems that arise when programming in PHIGS are to be avoided in this manner.

In PHIGS, many important elementary operations on a part hierarchy can only be implemented as a whole series of individual PHIGS operations. The composition of individual operations to the desired effect demands careful planning by the applications programmer. An illustration for this is given in the example, where an attribute of a picked object is to be changed, i.e., where an operation that occurs very frequently in the processing of graphics structures is to be executed.

This process is the same in result to one requiring several operations in PHIGS, where a posted node must be surgically removed with the help of copy functions to be edited, as shown in assigning an attribute to a single button or when editing a part. Only one elementary operation is needed for this in GEO++. So no explicit copy processes involving the generation of new structures, as in the case of PHIGS, are necessary.

9.7.3 Type Checking

In GEO++ a group "knows", for example, what kind of information it can receive. The object-oriented concept and the orientation towards visible graphics object structures automatically results in more error tolerance. Every class is restricted to operations that make sense in its context. This results in more stringent typifying. A group, for example, is either empty or exclusively contains visible graphics primitives. This causes the system to be more sensitive to erroneous programming. Conversely, in PHIGS, it is possible to construct a structure consisting only of attributes and no output primitives without any error message. This would be recognized as an error in GEO++, because every object knows its own methods and watches over their correct use.

9.7.3.1 Efficient Implementation

The GEO++ model of a tree-like part hierarchy would, if implemented one-to-one, require a large amount of memory. For this reason it is important that GEO++ allows a hidden implementation that is completely different from the tree model as seen from the outside by the applications programmer. In Chap. 12 we present an implementation that internally manages an acyclical directed graph of building patterns. An additional subtree of the hierarchy is built up by part attributes. Therefor an internal tree model can be avoided. The implementation is at least as compact as a PHIGS implementation.

9.7.3.2 Naming

In GEO++, every visible primitive, every group of primitives or building patterns, and every attribute can be referenced by name as an instance of a class. In contrast to PHIGS, then, every visible object or group of objects in the part hierarchy has a distinct and well defined name. So there are no different names for the same visible object in different contexts as is possible in PHIGS with name sets, pick identifiers or labels. If several different groupings of the visible information are to be made, this is done by inserting objects into sets using their definite name—an easily understood, natural concept often used in Smalltalk-80 programming. Higher operations that apply to all elements of such a set can then easily be defined by operations on the set.

9.7.3.3 Reducing the Difference Between Aggregates and Primitives

Next to higher functionality, programming is made easier in GEO++ by a simpler conceptual model for primitives, groups and attributes.

Modern graphics user interfaces such as MacDraw allow editing and assignment of attributes both for primitives and for aggregates (segments, structures, groups). The difference in use between groups and primitives is thereby becoming continuously smaller. GEO++ meets this requirement by allowing primitives to be edited, too, as is the case in Smalltalk-80. Beyond this, multiple references to the same primitive are possible, are in fact the usual case.

GEO++ allows, for example, the querying and change of the third coordinate of a polyline, which causes all representations that use this primitive to be changed consistently. In this regard, then, all building patterns show the same behavior. Should this consistency not be wanted, one employs a suitable copy of the object.

GKS strictly distinguishes between attributes for output primitives and those for segments (visibility, highlighting, detectability). This distinction is still present in PHIGS, because name sets and filters are restricted to the traditional segment attributes.

GEO++ makes no distinction between attributes used for aggregates (groups, parts) and those for primitives. Also, the concept of graphics sets allows filtering for arbitrary attributes, i.e., any attribute can be applied to any set of graphics objects of the classes Group, Primitive or Part.

10 Using Inheritance

In the programming examples discussed up to this point, no special concepts as they exist in object-oriented systems have been used. The development of the GEO++ functionality was stimulated by a few simple rules which we already formulated in the introduction, such as: "Call every visible graphics object by its name". It was shown that, as far as the functionality used in the examples is concerned, GEO++ may be easily formulated in traditional languages such as Fortran or Pascal (Wisskirchen, 1989). In this chapter we go a step further and discuss farther-reaching concepts, such as the use of call-backs and inheritance. As mentioned in Chap. 1, we require that subclassing can be performed for all transparent classes whose methods ar part of the functional specification of the the applications programmer's interface. With this in mind, we allow, for example, the creation of subclasses of Group, Primitive, Attribute, Part.

On this premise, we can use the functionality offered by GEO++ to program new characteristics for the subclasses of the external GEO++ classes, and to modify or restrict GEO++ functionality by overwriting.

10.1 Inheritance in GEO++

Before going into the possibilities of inheritance with the help of examples, some additional remarks are needed.

The creation of subclasses of the transparent classes makes it possible to inherit or override all of GEO++'s functionality. Two classes used internally in GEO++ require some extra attention, however. The insert operation generates an indicator that is used in the construction of paths. The class GEOPath used for this is internal; it is not transparent to the outside. So no subclasses can be created for it. But in practice this is not necessary.

The class Part has not been used so far as receiver for class messages. In the examples so far parts were returned as results of messages. In practice it is very is very worthwhile to allow to define sublasses of Part as will be illustrated by the following examples. It would be useful if our tree could have specific kind-of parts as nodes, that is instances of a subclass of Part. For this reason GEO++ supports a second way of generating parts, namely a class method to Part that is inherited by its subclass and can be overridden by methods of these subclasses. We introduce it by some examples. Let root be an instance of Group or subclass of Group; let aPart be an instance of Part or one of its subclasses; let SubPart be a subclass of Part. We define methods for Group and Part with selector for:part: in the following way:

a) aPart 1 ← SubPart for: root part: aPath

b) aSubPart ← SubPart for: aPart part: anIncremPath .

These class methods differ from the methods

c) root part: aPath

d) aPart part: anIncremPath

only in that a) and b) cause an instance of SubPart to be created. These instances, however, have the same attributes and contents as the parts generated by c) and d). But the following must also be noted. If we first apply operations like a) and b), and then use operations as c) or d) and such inquiry methods as

aSet ← aPart children

then these methods are only creating parts which were not created before by the more specific methods a) and b). So for existing parts, the methods sent to an *instance* of Group or Part are merely inquiry operations.

10.2 Alternative Naming

For a variety of reasons we decided to use the assignment of names as it in Smalltalk-80 in GEO++: groups, parts, primitives, indicators are returned as results of messages sent to the kernel. So the applications programmer uses symbolic identifiers which are instantiated by the system, i.e., that the system delivers a references to new objects.

There are also cases where it makes sense to assign name to graphics objects names that are already existing, as is done in GKS and PHIGS. In object-oriented terminology one would say that the created graphics objects are associated with already existing name objects, for example of class Integer. As we have shown in Chap. 5, an exact analogy to GKS or PHIGS would result in a situation where almost all messages are sent to one class of type GKS, PHIGS or GEO++. The drawbacks of this would be that the actual graphics objects would be invisible to the outside and could not, consequently, be specialized in the sense of subclassing. A further disadvantage would be that the applications programmer would be responsible for avoiding name conflicts.

We now show how a slight modification of the naming concept may be reached by specializing Group and Part, which could be programmed very easily. This modification consists of modifying the indicator and path concept towards a model where names for them are instantiated by the application programmer. We use this example for showing how a very small portion of additional code could modify the kernels functionality very seriously.

10.2.1 Index and Route

Group1 is created as subclass of Group and Part1 as subclass of Part.

The inherited insert methods are overridden and new methods of the following kind are added:

```
switchBoard ← Group1 new
switchBoard at: 1 insert: aGroup .
aGroup at: 17 insert: poly attribute: tr1 .
aPart ← Part1 for: switchBoard withRoute: (2, 17) .
```

It is of course possible to instantiate variables and use them as arguments in the following manner:

```
aGroup at: index insert: someThing.
aPart ← Part1 for: aGroup withRoute: aRoute.
```

Just as GEOPath, Route is a subclass of OrderedCollection if we define the comma-selector correctly.

10.2.1.1 Methods for Group1

class name	**Group1**
instance variable names	bridge
superclass	Group
class methods	

new "initialize dictionary"

↑ (super new) initialize

instance methods

private

initialize "initializes dictionary"

bridge ← Dictionary new .

bridge "return bridge"

↑ bridge

insertion

at: anInteger insert: aBuildingPattern

"insert a building pattern"

anIndicator ← super insert: aBuildingPattern .
bridge at: anInteger put: anIndicator .

at: anInteger insert: aBuildingPattern attribute: anAttribute

"insert and assign attribute"

```
    anIndicator ← super insert: aBuildingPattern attribute: anAttribute .
    bridge at: anInteger put: anIndicator
```

mapping

```
translate1: aRoute                "tranlate route to path"
                                  "find indicator for the top element of the route"

    indicator1 ← (self bridge) keyAtValue: (aRoute first)
    aPath ← GEOPath new.
    aRoute size = 1
            ifTrue: [ aPath addFirst: indicator1]
            ifTFalse: [ aRoute removeFirst.

                                  "translate rest by using sub-content"
     aPath ← ((self part: indicator1) content) translate1: aRoute .

                                  "add indicator for top element"
     aPath addFirst: indicator1] .

↑ aPath

translate2: aPath                 "translate path into route"
                                  "find route for the top element of the route"

    route1 ← (self bridge) valueAtIndex: (aPath first)

    aRoute ← Route new.
    aRoute size = 1
     ifTrue: [ aRoute addFirst: route1]
     ifFalse: [ aPath removeFirst.

                                  "translate rest by using sub-content"
     aRoute ← ((self part: indicator1) content) translate2: aPath .

                                  "add indicator for highest element"
     aPath addFirst: route1] .

↑ aRoute
```

10.2.1.2 The Methods for Part1

class name	**Part1**
superclass	Part
class methods	

creation of parts

for: root withRoute: aRoute "aPart via a route"

```
aPath ← root translate1: aRoute
↑ self for: root part: aPath
```

for: aPart withRoute: aRoute "aSubPart via a route"

```
aPath ← (aPart content) translate1: aRoute)
↑ self for: aPart part: aPath
```

instance methods

inquiry

route "my root will translate my path"

```
↑ (self root) translate2: (self path)
```

10.2.2 Advantages of Inheritance

Compared to the traditional layer model, inheritance saves a lot of code. This has three reasons:

a) methods are inherited from Part and Group. For a subclass Part1 of Part, for example, a part, defined as

   aPart ← Part1 for: switchBoard withRoute: (2, 17)

   inherits a method for assigning attributes:

   aPart attribute: myColor .

b) GEO++ is defined so that in all cases where groups or parts are delivered as results of messages, for example, inquiring the content of a part or inquiring a pick device, the system automatically delivers the instances of the subclass. So, for example, Pick may deliver an instance of Part1 and the new method route may be directly applied to it:

   (Pick request) route = (1 20 4) ifTrue: [*...statements...*]

c) GEO++ also accepts as message arguments instances of subclasses of the predefined GEO++ classes created by the application programmer. For example, an instance (or a kind-of) Group1 may be used as argument of the following message:

   aPart replaceContentBy: aGroup .

In traditional systems a modification of the naming concept—for instance changing names from input parameters to output parameters—would require dozens of trivial "bridging" routines. These have to be programmed wherever identifiers for names are used as parameters in the application programmer's interface.

10.3 Construction of a Part Hierarchy with Predefined Slots

If we analyze the functionality of GEO++, we find Group especially to be a class that may accept arbitrarily many building patterns by applying the insert: method. This flexibility is necessary to make possible support for applications as the construction of a graphics editor. In applications of this kind, one does not know beforehand how many graphics objects the user will generate interactively. So constructs such as the segments in GKS, structures in PHIGS or the class Group on GEO++ are required. These are able to take up any number of graphics objects. In our example the Office Layout Application, the group work specifically had to meet such requirements.

In other applications of computer graphics however, it makes sense to offer other, more specialized classes. As an example that has broad application potential, we now discuss the realization of a part hierarchy with a given number of predefined slots. By this we mean a system of special subclasses of Group and Part in GEO++. These classes are defined and implemented in such a way that they know how many parts they are allowed to have and of what type these parts may be. Descriptions structured in this way have two essential advantages. First, faulty programming is much easier to detect since it is impossible to insert to many parts or parts of the wrong type. Second, such classes can be prefabricated for special application areas, and then tailored to the needs of a specific application by subclassing. We now use our familiar radio example to show the basic principles.

10.3.1 Organization and Protocol

In the construction of the radio in the context of the explanation of GEO++ all basic operations for the construction of the part hierarchy were fully transparent, in the sense that all parts of the part hierarchy were visible and accessible from the same level. In the following example, we construct the radio in a more modularized manner. A stronger structure will be reached by defining the number of subparts in the hierarchy beforehand. Parts may only be accessed by predefined access methods. A stronger modularization is given by hiding the graphics code for generation of the part hierarchy, that is, the building patterns are hidden in the methods of predefined objects. The consequences of this are discussed in the following description.

10.3.1.1 The Groups

We define groups FrontPanel, Switchboard, Button as subclasses of Group. Each of these groups owns its special class method new, which generates an instantiated object that can be posted. Instantiation is done in such a way as to allow the following equalities:

```
FrontPanel new = frontPanel
SwitchBoard new = switchBoard
Button new = button .
```

In this, frontPanel, switchBoard, button are as the groups of our earlier example as fare as the output primitives are concerned. The difference is that the internal implementation is invisible from outside, i.e., from the location of the system where the message new is sent.

Next to the groups, there are subclasses of Part, SwitchBoardPart and ButtonPart. Parts of these classes are generated by accessing the root by slot names as shown:

```
a) aFrontPanel ← FrontPanel new
b) leftSwitchboard ← aFrontPanel left
c) topLeftButton ← aFrontPanel left tl
d) topLeftButton ← leftSwitchboard tl
e) topLeftButton attribute: anAttribute
f) topLeftButton newContent: aBuildingPattern
```

Expression a) generates the instantiated part hierarchy i.e., the complete radio. Then b) delivers a part as instance of SwitchBoardPart. A second-level part is then created by c) concatenating two slot accesses or by d) navigating from the one part to a deeper part by using the part-slot tl. An attribute of this part is modified in e). The last expression causes the content of a part to be replaced with a new building pattern. It should be noted that the last two methods are inherited, so they don't have to be coded.

If a new class FrontPanelPart for FrontPanel is defined in the same manner (see Sect. 10.3.3.1), the hierarchy can be extended in an upward direction.

This means that an object of the class FrontPanel can be used in the instantiation message new for a higher root. As can be seen in the code described below, this is possible without having to change the definition of the existing classes. So if aRoot is a group that contains parts with content aFrontPanel, then these parts of the new root can be accessed by:

```
newPart ← aRoot slot1 left tl .
```

In this, aRoot slot1 returns an object of class FrontPanelPart, for which the method left now shows the way down. Next to strict a good structuring, an advantage of this is that one can now use part descriptions to put together arbitrary hierarchies.

A closer look at the code for our slot-oriented part hierarchy shows the main idea behind it:

- The hierarchy is constructed using new:, just as in our earlier GEO++ example.

- A part is able to deliver its subpart by asking its own content for the path (of length one) required for navigation.

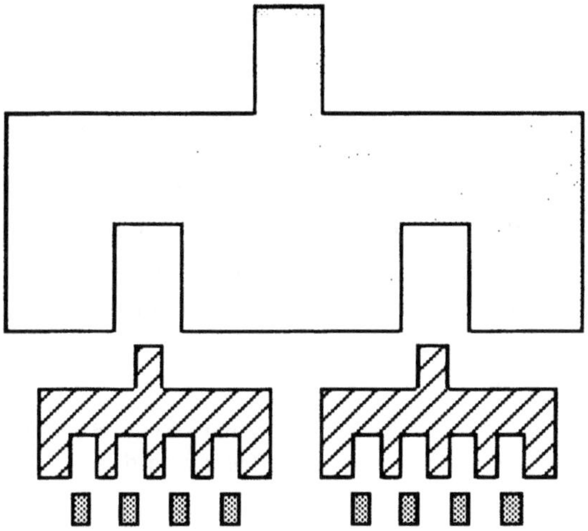

Fig. 10.1. Schematic view of the part hierarchy with predefined slots.

10.3.2 The Subclasses FrontPanel, Switchboard, Button

We begin with a description of the methods for Group's subclasses. Every subclass has a special method new, which returns an instantiated object that can be posted. Since new generates a displayable object with a standard size, we say it returns a *sample*.

10.3.2.1 Methods for FrontPanel

---

class name	**FrontPanel**
superclass	Group
instance variable names	leftPart rightlPart

class methods

new "generation of an instance of class FrontPanel as a sample"

```
aSample ← super new .
↑ aSample initialize
```

instance methods

private

initialize "Initializes the sample"

"Display of the radio's borders and other primitives that aren't modeled in lower levels of the part hierarchy"

```
super insert: myPrimitives .
...
```

"Generation of direct parts:"

```
leftInd ← super insert: (Switchboard new) attribute: leftTransformation
rightInd ← super insert: (Switchboard new) attribute: rightTransformation
leftPart ← SwitchboardPart for: self withPath: leftInd
rightPart ← SwitchboardPart for: self withPath: rightInd
```

inquiries

left "Answers the direct part as a-kind-of SwitchboardPart"

```
↑ leftPart
```

right

```
↑ rightPart
```

10.3.2.2 Methods for Switchboard

class name	**Switchboard**
superclass	Group
instance variable names	tlPart trPart blPart brPart

class methods

new "Generation of an instance of class Switchboard as a sample"

```
aSample ← super new .
↑ aSample initialize
```

instance methods

private

initialize "Initializes the sample"

"Display of the cross in SwitchBoard, i.e., the primitives that aren't modeled in lower levels of the part hierarchy"

```
super insert: poly1 .
super insert: poly2
```

"Generation of direct parts:"

```
tlInd ← super insert: (Button new) attribute: tlTrans .
trInd ← super insert: (Button new) attribute: trTrans .
blnd ← super insert: (Button new) attribute: blTrans .
brInd ← super insert: (Button new) attribute: brTrans .
tlPart ← ButtonPart for self withPath: tlInd .
trPart ← ButtonPart for: self withPath: trInd .
blPart ← ButtonPart for: self withPath: blnd .
brPart ← ButtonPart for: self withPath: brInd
```

inquiries

tl "Answers the direct part as a-kind-of ButtonPart"

```
↑ tlPart
```

tr

```
↑ trPart
```

bl

```
↑ blPart
```

br

```
↑ brPart
```

10.3.2.3 Methods for Button

class name **Button**
superclass Group
class methods

new "Generation of an instance of class Button as a sample"

```
aSample ← super new .
↑ aSample initialize
```

instance variable names squarePart circlePart

instance methods

private

initialize "Initializes the sample"

```
square ← PolyLine points: sqPoints .
circle ← Circle center: cPoint radius: r.
```

"Generation of direct parts"

```
super insert: square
super insert. circle
squarePart ← Part for: self withPath: sq
circlePart ← Part for: self withPath: cl
```

sq "Answers the direct part as a-kind-of Part"

```
↑ squarePart
```

c

```
↑ circlePart
```

10.3.3 Methods for the Parts

The methods for groups described so far guarantee that

```
frontPanel new
```

creates the picture for the radio when posted. For defining the part, subclasses FrontPanelPart, SwitchboardPart, ButtonPart of the Part are defined.

10.3.3.1 Methods for FrontPanelPart

class name **FrontPanelPart**
superclass Part
instance methods

delivery of new part

left "Returns a direct subpart of self"

"Returns a path of length 1 for the component left"

incremPath ← ((self content) left) path

"Generates the subpart of self"

↑ leftLongPart ← SwitchboardPart for: self part: incremPath

right

incremPath ← ((self content) right) path

↑ rightLongPart ← SwitchboardPart for: self part: incremPath

10.3.3.2 Methods for SwitchboardPart

class name **SwitchboardPart**
superclass Part
instance methods

delivery of new part

tl

"Returns the direct subpart of self"

"Returns the path of length 1 for the component tl"

incremPath ← ((self content) tl) path

"Generates the subpart of self"

↑ tlLongPart ← ButtonPart for: self part: incremPath

tr

"Returns a direct subpart of self"

in the same way as for tl

bl

"Returns a direct subpart of self"

in the same way as for tl

br

"Returns a direct subpart of self"

in the same way as for tl

10.3.3.3 Methods for ButtonPart

class name **ButtonPart**
superclass Part
instance methods

delivery of new part

sq "Returns a direct subpart of self"

"Returns a path of length 1 for the component left"

```
incremPath ← ((self content ) sq) path
```

"Generates the subpart of self"

```
↑ sqLongPart ← Part for: self part: incremPath
```

c "Returns a direct subpart of self"

"Returns a path of length 1 for the component left"

```
incremPath ← ((self content ) c) path
```

"Generates the subpart of self"

```
↑ cLongPart ← Part for: self part: incremPath
```

10.4 Using Call-Backs

The part hierarchy is a good example for a sensible integration of call-backs. To demonstrate this call-back, we define for each button a messages which will be triggered when a button is "pressed", i.e., as reaction to a pick action.

First we assign to the four buttons on the left switchboard the message "station". The statement

```
leftButtons ← (aFrontPanel left ) children
```

returns the set of the four buttons on the left hand side, to which we apply

```
leftButtons do: [:aButton | aButton defineCallBack: #station.
```

With

```
(aFrontPanel right tl ) defineCallBack: #am-selection
(aFrontPanel right bl) defineCallBack: #fm-selection
```

the messages are installed at the root aFrontPanel.

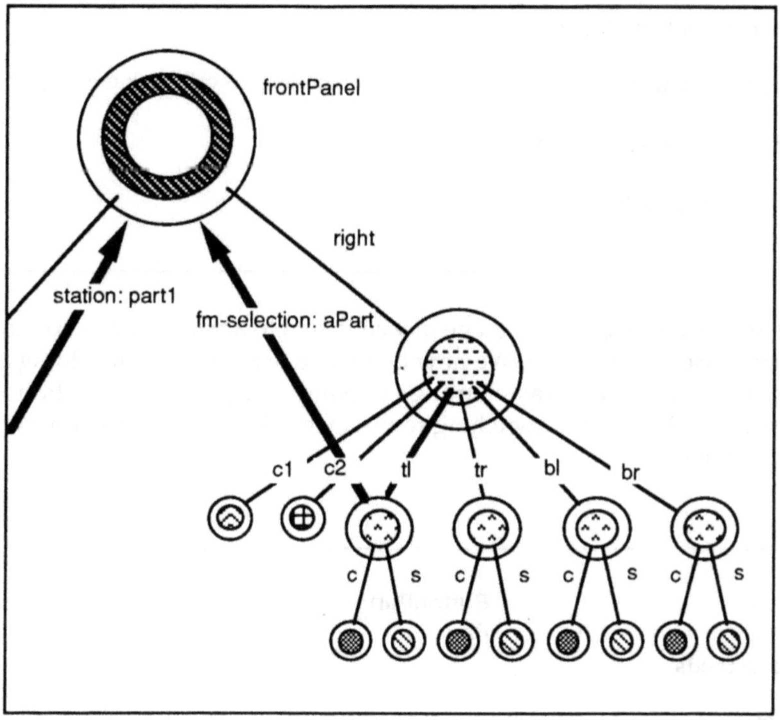

Fig. 10.2. Call-back messages. Call-back messages are sent to the root which is now a subclass of Group, providing application dependent methods for evaluating them.

In order that the root may receive these messages, appropriate methods must be defined for the class FrontPanel:

---

class name	**FrontPanel**
superclass	Group
instance variable names	leftPart rightlPart

call back messages

station: forButton "Processing of call-back messages"

forButton detectable: 'false'

store selected station

fm-selection: forButton "Processing of call-back messages"

forButton detectable: 'false'

realize the right selection

am-selection: forButton "Processing of call-back messages"

forButton detectable: 'false'

realize right selection

As we have mentioned, the message picked is sent to a part as a reaction to a pick operation caused by the user. We now overwrite this message by adding a highlighting message. In this way a strong coupling of highlighted and button pick can be reached. Moreover, switching to undetectable should automatically turns off highlighting.

---

class name **ButtonPart**
superclass Part
instance methods

overriding

picked

"Integrate highlighting"

self highlighting: 'true'
super picked

detectable: status

"combine with highlighting"

status ifFalse: [self highlighting: 'false'] .

super detectable: status

In order to design our system so that the insert: operation causes an error message, we must take up this method, too, in the protocol for the classes described here.

An analysis of the advantages for using inheritance shows that the conclusions described in 10.2.2 are also valid for this example. Moreover, in this example, prototypic samples of part hierarchies were generated by overriding new for subclasses of Group—"enriching" the functionality of a predefined kernel.

10.5 Accessing Parts

If we analyze the access to parts in the previous example, reaching a part lying farther down in the hierarchy is implemented though step-by-step accessing of intermediate parts. In other words we navigate from part to part. In comparison with the usual GEO++ method, the following difference becomes clear. GEO++ allows addressing of a part by a path of arbitrary length. In this mode of access, it is left to the hidden implementation to decide how to reach a part. To make this clear by an example,

a) part3 ← root part: (i1, i2, i3)

delivers the same as

b) ((root part: i1) part: i2) part: i3

but it is left completely to the implementation of GEO++ to proceed internally as b) or to perform a) in a more efficient way.

10.5.1 Censored Messages

In work by Blake and Cook, a concept is introduced for implementing access to parts in a slot-oriented part hierarchy without injuring the principle of information hiding (Blake & Cook, 1987). This implementation does, however, require a slight modification of the Smalltalk-80 procedure of searching for messages.

Blake and Cook introduce a new type of message, the *censored* message. This kind of message allows chaining of the message patterns used to access parts, i.e., of the slot names. The result is a new message pattern. As an alternative to the concatenation

myButton ← (aFrontPanel left) tl

we can now access any part with a single message with message selector left.tl:

myButton ← aFrontPanel left.tl

The following is important in this context. A message with the pattern left.tl can be implemented by a special method, but need not be. If a message with the pattern s1.s2.s3.s4... is sent to an object, the internal search process is controlled in the following way: it searches for a method, written by the application programmer, and evaluates it, if it really exists. Otherwise the reduced pattern is sent to the result of s1 internally, i.e.

(self s1) s2.s3.s4....

is evaluated. We now discuss and illustrate the advantages of this principle.

10.5.1.1 Direct Access as an Alternative?

Why is it required to resort to the censored message method? Can't one reach the parts in lower levels of the part hierarchy with direct access? In our example this would mean programming a method leftTl for the button. For our radio the would mean that the subclass FrontPanel of Group would have the complete knowledge of all eight buttons at class definition time.

The drawback of this method is that one gives up the idea of a hierarchy. One loses the advantage of being able to put together arbitrary hierarchies without changing the parts' methods. One actually ends up with a flat, non-modular system.

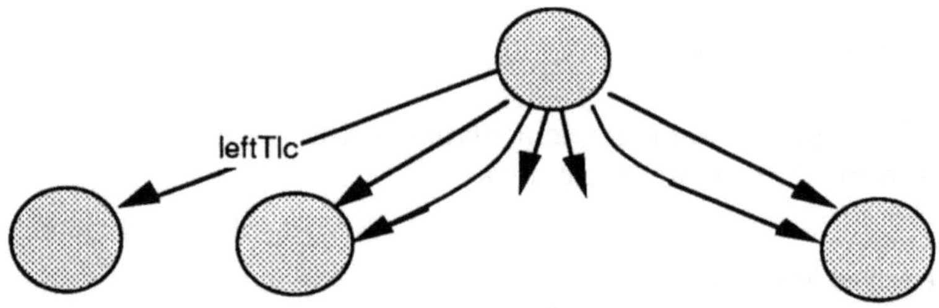

Fig. 10.3. Direct access to all parts would flattening the hierarchy.

10.5.1.2 Access By Censored Messages

The idea and applicability of censored messages will be illustrated with the help of our radio example. We Assume that access to the top left button is required very frequently and should therefore by optimized. To do this, we install an instance tlButton in the highest level of of the hierarchy, i.e., in FrontPanel. We assign the button to this variable after the first access. All this is to remain invisible to the outside, of course. With the first access to the button, using the censored message

```
myButton ← aFrontPanel left.tl
```

the method reaches the button by successively navigating over intermediate parts of the class SwitchBoardPart. In all subsequent accesses, the button is immediately available, as can be seen in the following method.

---

class name	**FrontPanel**
superclass	Group
instance variable names	tlButton

left.tl

```
tlButton isNil ifTrue: [ ↑ tlButton ← (self left) tl]
↑ tlButton
```

With this, we reach the situation shown in the following figure.

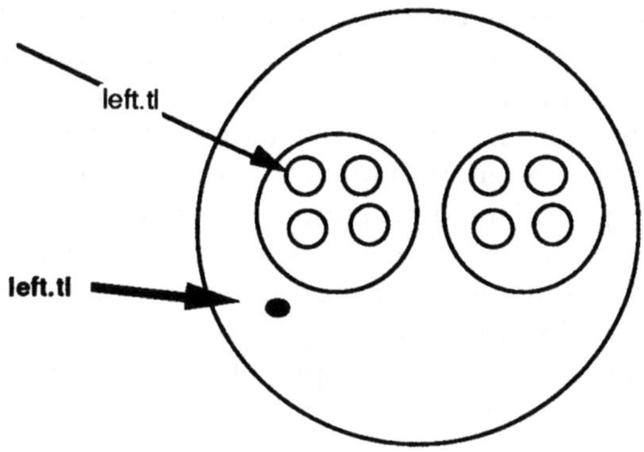

Fig. 10.4. Information hiding and access of parts. Censored messages can be used to optimize the access of parts. This is can be done without violating the principle of information hiding. In the example a second attempt to access the part will deliver it already by an instance variable in the first layer.

11 Prototypes and Delegation

The model for object-oriented programming has so far relied mainly on that supported in Smalltalk-80 classes, methods, instances and (hierarchical) inheritance. Every object is an instance of a class. The class manages methods and variables for its instances. Classes form a hierarchy that determines how methods are inherited. New instances are generated by the message new sent to the class. An instance can be copied; this returns a duplicate belonging to the same class.

This model of object-oriented programming, which we call the *class-instance model*, has an alternative, called the *prototype model*. We explain and discuss this in the following. It is not intended, however, to expand on the myriad models for object-oriented programming individually in this book. The prototype model is an exception in so far as it seems to be especially suited to the needs of computer graphics, as it was especially stressed by Borning (Borning, 1986).

11.1 What are Prototypes?

Let us consider the flexibilities and stabilities of our class model. Programming in a typical environment such as Smalltalk-80 usually proceeds in the following manner. A class is defined by specifying a name and putting it into context in the inheritance hierarchy by specifying a direct superclass. Then the methods new to this class are encoded. Next to the usual programming language constructs (which can be interpreted as message passing in Smalltalk-80), this involves references to existing classes and methods. Encoding as an editing process is terminated by compilation or some other form of passing on to the system (in Smalltalk-80, the menu option "accept"). After a method has been accepted, it is valid until it is edited again at some later point. All objects generated dynamically during execution of a program are therefore stable types, i.e., their message protocol and methods do not change. The class model is especially appropriate if the application calls for relatively few classes with rather many instances. It also seems very natural for providing often-used basic classes, such as the class Integer or the various collection classes. But it does have some disadvantages that call for alternative concepts.

Such an alternative may be seen in the *prototype* model, which is a kind of extension of the class model. Its main feature is that an instance's protocol may change during the execution of a program. Both instance variables and methods may be added or deleted. An instance may benefit from the functionality of another instance, i.e., use a method defined there. It can itself offer its own methods for use by other instances. If an instance does not understand a message sent to it, then it passes it onto another object. As a rule, the initial receiver knows this object will serve its needs. For this reason, this type of passing on is called *delegation*. A new instance is created in this model either by copying an existing prototype or by a descendant operation. A copy may accept the same messages as its prototype but has a fixed protocol as the traditional instance in Smalltalk-80. A *descendant* generated by a prototype has the same protocol after generation but this may be modified later on.

11.2 Relevance for Computer Graphics

In computer graphics objects are created very dynamically by interactive editing procedures. Should these objects be used to inherit their behavior to other objects, it seems very unnatural to define a new class every time. But as descendants these objects would be able both to inherit behavior and change dynamically.

11.2.1 Why Does GEO++ Work?

After putting the rigid class-instance model in contrast to the requirements of interactive graphics as far as flexible typing is concerned, we may ask whether GEO++ works at all. GEO++ has neither prototypes nor delegation. What saved us was the concept of indexed instance variables in Smalltalk-80 and the collection classes based on them. These latter can store a dynamically growing number of components. It was only this that made it possible to dynamically insert graphics information into an empty group and access it with the help of indicators and paths. In this sense, an instance of a collection class can be seen as being midway between a rigid object and a prototype. The number of its values, stored by indexed instance variables, can grow. This is not possible with objects that have the usual fixed number of (named) instances. A collection class is less than a prototype, however, since no new methods may be added.

11.3 A Prototype Model for GEO++

We based GEO++ on the class model because it is in wider use and has been more strongly standardized. We would like, nevertheless, to briefly describe what an alternative to GEO++ based on the prototype model might look as.

11.3.1 Prototype, Descendant, Copy

We now present a simplified prototype model. This is no rounded-off proposal; it merely serves in explaining the alternative graphics system. Borning develops a more realistic model in and shows how it can be implemented in Smalltalk-80 (Borning, 1986).

Our model assumes there are two different kinds of objects *prototypes* and *copies*. Every object has instance variables and methods. A prototype can be used to generate an object based on it, called its *descendant*, which is then also a prototype:

```
b ← a descendant .
```

The object b inherits all methods and instance variables from a. An instance variable may be added to b with addInstVar:

```
b addInstVar: ' v1 v2 v3 ' .
```

A method can be added in the same way. The method is specified as a string, consisting of a message pattern and the statements. Bold type designates the pattern.

b addMethod: ' ***pattern***
statements ' .

In contrast to a prototype, a *copy* has a fixed methods protocol. For example,

```
c ← a copy
```

would inherit the behavior of a, but no further methods or variables could be added. An prototype together with its copies could therefore be considered as a concept similar to a class together with its instances.

11.3.1.1 Construction of a Part Hierarchy

In Sect. 10.3, we showed how GEO++ can be used to construct a part hierarchy with static access methods called slots. Since we extended the functionality of Group and Part in this example, we were forced to build new classes. Furthermore, for every different group and part with different access methods, the new *classes* FrontPanel, Switchboard, Button and FrontPanelPart, SwitchboardPart, ButtonPart had to be created. So we had to define six classes. We now wish to demonstrate how this problem could be formulated in our hypothetical prototype model.

We assume we have the central prototype group whose functionality corresponds to that of an empty group in GEO++. Another central object is part, the predefined prototype supporting the protocol for parts. Graphics primitives are also predefined as a set of prototypes, one for each different *type* of primitive. Each of these prototypes may generate a descendant of itself upon receipt of an initialization message. This descendant initialized with coordinates specified in the message:

```
square ← polyLine points: sqPoints
circle ← circle center: cPoint radius: r .
```

We create a new, empty group:

```
button ← group descendant .
```

Now we add the access methods for button. Since we don't need the indicators, we use the auxiliary methods makePart: and makePart:attribute: within the method (see Sect. 8.3.2.2). Here, in the modified GEO++ model, makePart: has to deliver a descendant of part, the prototype for all parts, provided by the GEO++. The primitives are inserted into these.

```
button addMethod: ' sq
  ↑ self makePart: sq '
button addMethod: ' c
  ↑ self makePart: circle '
```

The other descendants of group are constructed in the same manner. As an example, we show how the access to switchBoard by tr is implemented:

```
switchBoard ← group descendant
switchBoard makePart: poly1
switchBoard makePart: poly2
switchBoard addMethod: ' tr
  ↑ self makePart: button attribute: tr1
```

To support access to subparts, we must derive corresponding methods for parts. We give one example for this. First, create

```
leftSwitchBoard ← frontPanel left .
```

Then we extend this part by the access tr. To do this we use the navigation method defined in Sect. 8.3.3, which descends the hierarchy from a given part.

```
lefttSwitchBoard addMethod: ' tr
  incremPath ← ((self content) tr ) path
  ↑ self part: incremPath '
```

If we compare the prototype frontPanel constructed in this way with the example in Sect. 10.3, then we see that the entire procedure is simpler and more natural to program. All creation of classes and instantiation is avoided. One uses the inherited GEO++ functionality and modifies or extends it directly, with the visible object always at hand.

It should be noted that we can also do without the special message defineCallBack: aSymbol to initialize parts with call-back messages. In the prototype model, the reaction to pick, i.e., the method for picked (see Sect. 8.3.8.2) sent from the pick device may be defined for each part *individually*.

The prototype model is also of advantage when generation of additional methods is to be made dependent on conditions. That is, the decision, which of a set of conditionally preprogrammed methods is to be added to a prototype, is made late, at run time. So the following is possible:

```
condition1 ifTrue: [ myPrototype addMethod: ' method1 ' ]
        ifFalse: [ myPrototype addMethod: ' method2 ' ] .
```

These examples show that the prototype model is well suited to computer graphics problems, even in connection with a preprogrammed kernel as GEO++. Coming developments will show whether the prototype model as a whole—and the related idea of actor languages—will become as widely accepted as the class model. We should not fail to note, however, that the greater flexibility also causes new problems, such as inferior system transparency.

12 GEO++ in Smalltalk-80

In this chapter, aspects for implementing GEO++ in Smalltalk-80 are discussed. In this, we concentrate on the problem of how a group with its parts may be represented compactly. It should be noted that GEO++ is not completely implemented as of this writing.

12.1 Internal Representation of a Group

As previously mentioned, GEO++ supports a tree model. The main reason for this is that a tree best represents the part hierarchy the applications programmer wants to model. PHIGS supports a graph model.

If one compares GEO++ with PHIGS, the fear might arise that GEO++ must also be a tree in its internal implementation. This would indeed be fatal. If one thinks of applications in which the same building patterns are used very often in a drawing and belong to a multi-level hierarchy, then a tree representation results in an explosively growing number of objects. Such applications exist, for example, in the CAD field, especially in the design of electrical circuits.

The implementation of a graph is always more compact than that of a tree. A graph avoids generating separate nodes for multiple references to the same substructure. So some serious thought as to how we reach a compact representation in GEO++ must be given. In this section we concentrate on the representation of a group with its parts. This concerns the non-posted state. When a root is posted, visible objects are created on an output medium in addition to the tree. Here GEO++ as well as PHIGS must manage the same amount of information, i.e., the *visible* information. We won't be going into this.

12.1.1 The Acyclic Graph of Contents

In Sect. 8.3.1 , we constructed the radio in the following manner:

```
s ← PolyLine points: sqPoints
circle ← Circle center: cPoint radius: r
button ← Group new
s ← button insert: sq
c ← button insert: circle
switchBoard ← Group new
c1 ← switchBoard insert: poly1
c2 ← switchBoard insert: poly2
tl      ← switchBoard insert: button attribute: tr1
```

```
tr      ← switchBoard insert: button attribute: tr2
bl      ← switchBoard insert: button attribute: tr3
br      ← switchBoard insert: button attribute: tr4
left    ← frontPanel insert: switchBoard transform: ltrans
right   ← frontPanel insert: switchBoard transform: rtrans
```

In the use of the insert: and insert:attribute: messages, objects (such as the button for example) are used repeatedly. If we analyze the parts created so far, i.e., the actually generated objects, we see that no true tree has been generated. In fact we have a conglomerate that can be represented as an acyclical directed graph. This is also illustrated by the tree in Fig. 8.2, in that there are many repetitions of the same shadings and indicators. For this reason a group with contents—in this case frontPanel—is internally represented as a graph. The attributes and indicators used in the insert operations—in our example these were transformations—are stored together with the receiver object. This organization is described in more detail below.

Figure 12.1 serves to illustrate the basic concept of the graph. We must note however, that this is already an expanded graph. It shows all references, including these provided by the referencing concept of Smalltalk-80 itself. The current state of frontPanel includes, strictly spoken, only two attributes, the transformations lt and tr, and two *references* to the object switchBoard. This is true correspondingly for the other groups switchboard and button.

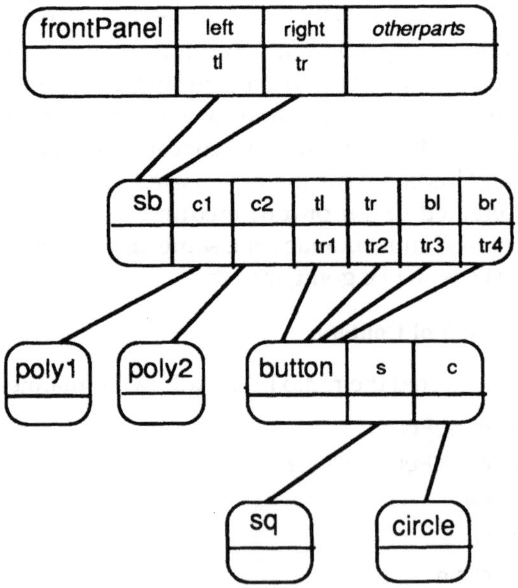

Fig. 12.1. The internal organization of the radio's part hierarchy, schematically illustrated, after the insert operations. The only part attributes of frontPanel at this state are the transformations tr and tl.

Group attributes, e.g., the color gray for frontPanel, are stored in an instance variable groupAttributes of the group as shown in Fig. 12.2. This form of organization makes clear how a group is edited and how attributes are assigned to a group or building pattern—insertion is the establishment of a reference to an already existing object, group attributes are assigned directly to a group.

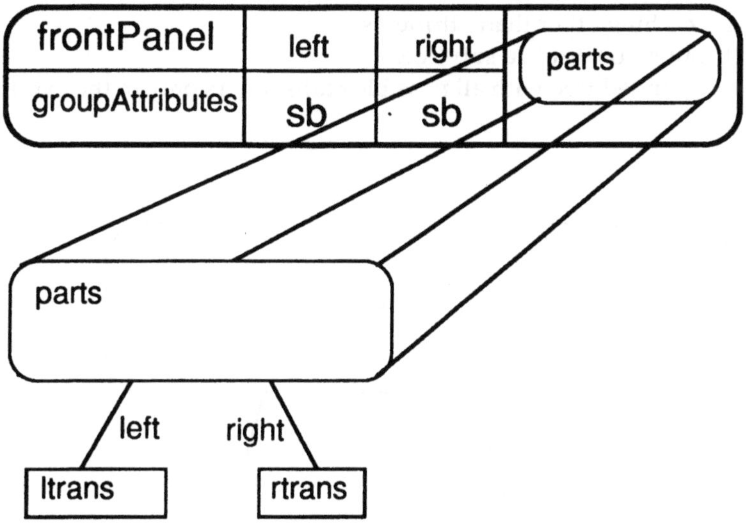

Fig. 12.2. Internal organization of a part hierarchy. The graph of the contents for all parts is modeled by a set of pairs, each consisting of an indicator and a building pattern. The information owned by parts is modeled by an object parts. The object parts is modeled by a tree whose nodes contain part attributes; the part tree is a subtree of the GEO++ tree containing only leaves for parts which were explicitly created as objects.

12.2 Implementation of Parts

Real nodes in the tree (with path longer than one) are created only when parts are explicitly constructed. We create the following part and assign it an attribute:

```
tlRightButton ← frontPanel part: (right, tl)
tlRightButton color: 'red'
```

Since this part has the group frontPanel as root, it must be represented in frontPanel. Its content, however, is already represented by the group button. This is (indirectly) accessible from frontPanel by switchBoard. So we need only save the path (right, tl) and associate the attribute types (color) and value ('red') with it. This gives us the following Fig. 12.3. The part attributes constitute a fully expanded tree, isomorphic to the GEO++ tree, only in the extreme case. It makes sense to ask when this extreme case occurs. The building patterns used for the radio (switchBoard, button, poly, etc.) already have their own attributes. If we now build the radio, we essentially have to set one transformation for every insert operation, i.e., as often as there are edges in the graph. This results in the drawing of the radio we see so often in this book. *Parts occur only when we are not satisfied with the attributes of the "prefabricated" building patterns.* So the extreme case of the full tree occurs only if we are dissatisfied with every visible node!

As a whole, a group is represented in the following manner:

- The building patterns constitute an acyclical directed graph.
- Parts are nothing other than attributes.
- The attributes constitute a sub-tree.
- A fully expanded tree with all possible paths occurs only in the extreme case.

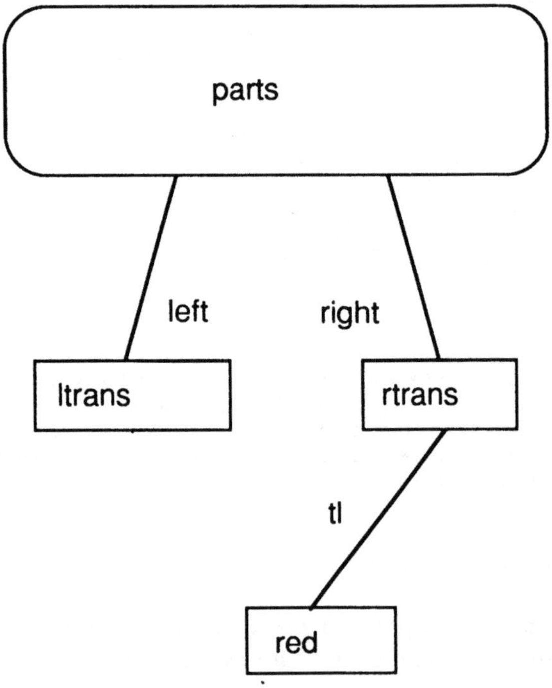

Fig. 12.3. Tree spanned by the part attributes. Only attributes for the parts with frontPanel as root are to store in the part tree.

12.2.1 Comparison with PHIGS

If there are no part attributes, GEO++ can be compared to PHIGS as far as storage costs are concerned. If there are part attributes, GEO++ is actually more economic that PHIGS, as the example 9.6.5 shows. This is because PHIGS requires that the intermediate structures lying between a part and its root be copied. In GEO++, we simply get a new part attribute. Furthermore consistency checks must be programmed on top of PHIGS to monitor individualization caused by the copy processes.

In part *editing*, GEO++ employs an internal copy procedure similar to that of PHIGS. Here PHIGS and GEO++ do not differ considerably.

12.2.2 Realization of the Internal Representation

The class Group is implemented as subclass of the built-in Smalltalk-80 class Dictionary. Because of this, a group inherits from Dictionary the ability to manage a set (not a series as in PHIGS!) of key-value pairs. The operation

```
anIndicator ← aGroup insert: aBuildingPattern
```

internally corresponds to:

```
super at: aKey put: aBuildingPattern
↑ aKey
```

As result, the insert process returns the key aKey. In insert:attribute:, the same happens, and in addition a part is defined for storing the attribute. For this, the internal state of Group's instance variable parts is modified for aGroup. We now take a closer look at the definition of parts.

The instance variable parts refers to an instance of class Part. Part is also a subclass of Dictionary. The set of keys of the part dictionary is always a subset of the set of indicators of its root. The value of a key is also an instance of Part. Attributes valid for a part are stored in its own instance variable, attributes.

Since parts is a dictionary with parts as values, subtrees can be built up accordingly so that the edges of the part tree are corresponding to the keys. Because every node contains the instance variable attributes, there is room for the attributes.

Experience with our implementation, realized so far, has shown that the dynamics of editing and attribute assignment can be supported quite aptly with this organization.

There were also some surprises with the class Dictionary during implementation. The copy method inherited from the Smalltalk-80 system, for instance, was not prepared to copy along the newly generated instance variables (parts, attributes) with subclasses of Dictionary. Similar surprises were encountered with the grow method used internally, which is activated when dictionaries and their subclasses grow in size. It was therefore required to implement some extensions to take into account newly generated instance variables!

It should be noted that the use (in the sense of inheritance) of predefined methods of Dictionary makes many functions defined for GEO++ directly available. Next to the access methods, the predefined enumeration messages (see Sect. 2.5.2.3) were especially useful.

12.2.3 GEO++ Allows Parallel Posting

Another implementation aspect not relevant for our environment, but for future multiprocessor systems, is the following: With its object-oriented assignment of attributes and other important data directly to the objects that "own" this information, the GEO++ model offers possibilities of parallel processing. All artificial forms of traversing sequentially ordered structures are avoided in GEO++. As a consequence, the posting process can be implemented in parallel, because all the parts on one level can be processed concurrently. This is also true for the implementation of the GraphicsSets, where a set of groups, primitives or parts is assigned an attribute.

13 Additional Concepts and Tools

In this chapter we will discuss how a graphics system can be enriched with additional semantic support alongside the part hierarchy. After an introductory look into this field, farther-reaching concepts, *constraints*, are discussed. At the end of the chapter we ask about relations between hybrid knowledge representation concepts and computer graphics.

13.1 Additional Semantical Concepts

So far we have concentrated on semantic support of part hierarchies in graphics systems. The integration of object-oriented ideas automatically, so to speak, provided us with a second semantic concept. This was the direct result of the class-instance and class-subclass relations. For instance, an object-oriented programming environment makes the inherited methods available to the programmer free of charge. He need not re-implement these for a subclass, nor bring them down into his new subclass by copying the code of the superclass methods. The semantics of part hierarchies in GKS, PHIGS, GEO++ offers the programmer support for attribute assignment, consistent modification of a building pattern, identification of a part with a pick operation, and so on.

There are of course other semantics within the different fields of application of computer graphics. These will be discussed with the help of a few examples. We consider these new semantic concepts as additions and not as replacing part hierarchies—in *addition* because we are convinced that part hierarchies, where primitives have to be composed to higher aggregates, are relevant for every important field of computer graphics applications.

Before we go into some examples of semantic concepts, some preliminary remarks should be made. As a rule, support of additional semantics to be given by a graphics system is in general application specific. So a general purpose kernel as GKS, PHIGS, or GEO++ cannot support these aspects directly. For this reason, we proceed in the following manner:

- Another semantical concept, *connectivity*, is introduced, and it shown how it can be supported by the subclassing of GEO++.
- Tools for the realization of graphics semantics (outside a kernel) are described.
- Prerequisites for a graphics system to be friendly to the integration of these tools are discussed.

13.2 Connectivity

By connectivity we mean a semantic concept that models and supports the connection of parts in space. Connectivity is seen here as a directed (unsymmetrical) relation of type connect(a,b) between graphics objects. This relation should express that b is connected with a (in the sense of attached, fixed to).

The difference between connectivity and the part hierarchy is that, in a part hierarchy, we collect objects in (unordered) sets and structure these hierarchically. In connectivity, n objects are attached to each other, so that we get a *sequence* of objects on the same hierarchical level.

13.2.1 PHIGS Connectivity Model

Let us first discuss the difference between these two concepts in the context of PHIGS. The following example of a robot arm comes from "Understanding PHIGS", although sadly it is not discussed thoroughly there.

For modeling the same drawing, PHIGS supports two alternative ways of structuring: PHIGS allows, as already mentioned, the construction of "deep" hierarchies by extensive using references to substructures (using execute statements). Besides this, PHIGS may also be used in a more "horizontal" sense, by putting graphics information side by side to generate a rather long but not deep structure.

Also these alternatives may result in the same visual representation, the semantics of the two structures are quiet different: the vertical model corresponds, as we show, more with the part-of concept, the horizontal with connectivity.

If the robot arm, shown in Fig. 13.1, is seen as an example of connecting objects together, then the parts Upper Arm, Elbow, Lower Arm, Wrist, Hand are a sequence of parts attached to each other. They are connected by concatenating modeling transformations.

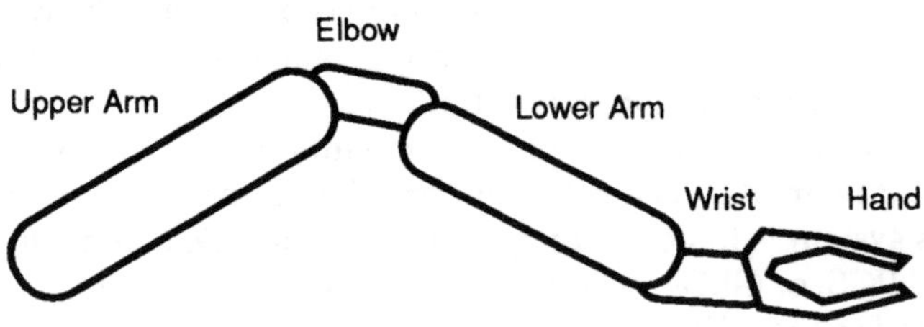

Fig. 13.1. Robot arm as a typical connectivity structure.

If we try to model the robot arm by the horizontal alternative, the following structure, shown in Fig. 13.2 could be defined as:

a) robot_armh (upperarmh, t1, elbowh, t2, lowerarmh, t3, wristh, t4, handh)

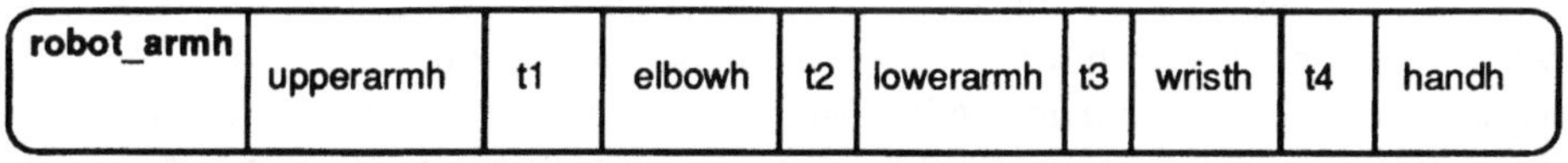

Fig. 13.2. Horizontal structuring of the robot arm. The elements 1, 3, 5, 7, 9 stand for the primitives of the respective components or they can also be interpreted as a reference to a respective substructure.

The horizontal structure reflects the connectivity aspects in a convenient way. Upperarm, elbow, lowerarm, wrist, hand each represent a structure that consists entirely of its own primitives. This means that in the vertical direction a robot part knows only its own graphics components, and the complete knowledge about the different components holding the robot arm together is modeled by robot_arm, knowing its sequentially connected components.

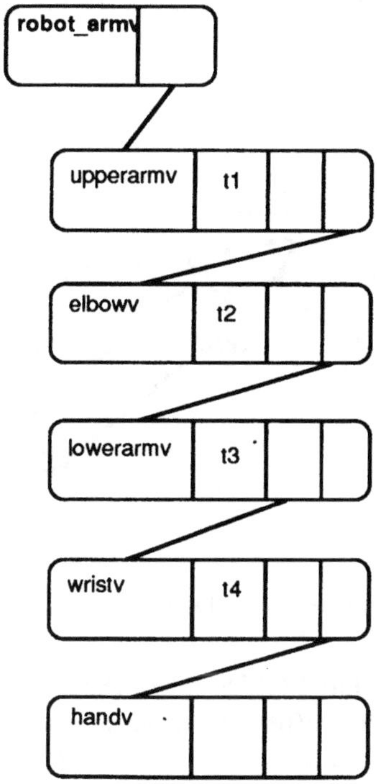

Fig. 13.3. Vertical structuring of the robot arm. The second structure elements of the substructures stand for the primitives of the respective components.

A vertical alternative could be expressed by the PHIGS structure, illustrated in Fig. 13.3:

b) robot_armv(upperarmv(t1, elbowv(t2, lowerarmv(t3,wristv(t4,hand)))))

PHIGS uses the same rule for transferring attributes, in this case transformations, for both forms of traversal. So there are no visible differences in display, i.e., when the structure is posted. And yet the two structures have very divergent semantics even in PHIGS. All structures differ in content and number of structure elements. This becomes especially clear when they are used in other contexts. Substantial differences result also when they are edited. An example for this is the re-outfitting of the robot arm where a different grasping tool is to be appended, i.e., where a different hand is to be used. This is unproblematic in the horizontal model. We only have to replace the last structure in a). The other objects are unaffected by this. In the vertical model, on the other hand, a replace operation for the hand affects all other objects—wherever they are used. This is definitely not what we wish in this application and it could be prevented in this alternative only by a series of copy operations.

Next to the connection of individual parts, the purpose of connectivity is that when a transformation is changed, all following parts transform along, e.g. rotate. If we change transformation t2 to t2new (a rotation), then everything below the elbow rotates together. This can also be done in PHIGS by replacing the element at position 4.

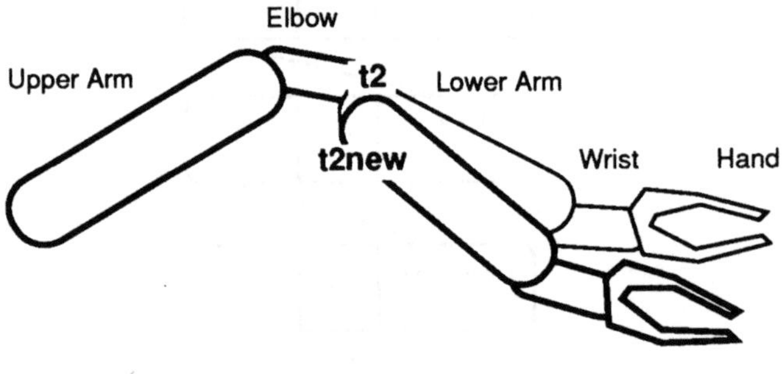

Fig. 13.4. Rotation of the parts connected to Elbow.

The example has shown that PHIGS support with its two alternative ways of creating structures caters to different semantic aspects—the vertical alternative models a part hierarchy more conveniently, the horizontal structure models connectivity aspects more conveniently.

13.2.1.1 Connectivity and GEO++

GEO++ supports part hierarchies quite extensively, but lacks in supporting connectivity. If one tries to proceed in the same way as in case a) i.e., apply a series of insert:transform: operations in a group representing the robot arm, then the transformations are not concatenated. The parts created in GEO++ are intended to constitute a set of independent objects and the order of insert operations is arbitrary.

So to support the semantics of connectivity, GEO++ must be extended. We don't consider this to be a disadvantage: two different semantics should be cleanly separated from each other.

GEO++ could be extended with a connect operation add:transform:. With this, the following correspondence to the horizontal model of PHIGS may be achieved:

```
robotArm ← Connection new .
c1 ← ConnectorPart for: robotArm first: upperArm
c2 ← c1 add: elbow transform: t1
c3 ← c2 add: lowerArm transform: t2
c4 ← c3 add: wrist transform: t3
c5 ← c4 add: hand transform: t4 .
```

Rotation of the arm below the elbow can be caused by the following operation:

```
c3 transform: t2new .
```

There are other methods next to these, by analogy with those of the collection class OrderedCollection. An instance of Connection may be inserted into a group as well as a building pattern. In addition, what is inserted into a connection sequence can itself be an object of class Connection. The objects c1, c2,... are instances of ConnectorPart.

One may ask if the connectivity semantics are general and important enough to become installed in of a general purpose kernel. Connectivity may easily be added to existing GEO++ functionality. The class Connection can be defined as subclass of Group and ConnectorPart can be defined as subclass of Part. In the internal implementation of the method add:transform:, the receiver inquires its own transformation and concatenates this to the transformation received as second argument; this new transformation is then used for the inherited insert:attribute: operation, establishing the new connector.

It should be noted that we have consciously arrived at a semantic slightly different from the one on our PHIGS model. In PHIGS, connection causes all attributes to be transferred to following objects. This is not the case here. All other attributes are set as the rules of GEO++ dictate. If for example, no color is set for c3 and lowerArm, then c3 obtains its color from its parent, robotArm, and not from elbow. This seems more natural to us, since the semantics of connection are confined to sequence and transformation only.

The above example shows how additional semantics in the field of computer graphics can be implemented in terms of programming. Additional semantics tailored to specific applications could be implemented in the same way. This has always been a relevant task in computer graphics. In traditional systems as GKS and PHIGS, such semantic relations must be implemented in an application-oriented layer above the kernel. The example shows how inheritance allows a more elegant integration of semantic aspects into a kernel.

13.3 Graphics Constraints

In the above example for connectivity, a *directed* relation between a connector part and its successor was established. The direction defined by this relation was important because the modification of a transformation in a chain of connected objects should affect the successors and not the predecessors. There are, however, graphics problems where we would like to model symmetrical relations. In the simplest case, we have two objects a and b that are related in such a way that a modification of a transformation ta (assigned to object a) should cause a modification of tb, and vice versa.

Such relations, which can be expanded to more complex ones between n objects, often require a great deal of programming effort. To reduce this it makes sense to look for higher programming concepts and make these available. These would allow the applications programmer to describe relations between objects in a declarative style and save him the trouble of having to evaluate them. The most important concept of this kind is that of the *constraint*. The concept of constraints is independent of the object-oriented programming paradigm and of applications in the special area of computer graphics. But it is of great interest for this area and the design of user interfaces. Most research work on graphics constraints was treated in connection with the realization of object-oriented systems. Constraint-oriented research in is a broad filed, and we cannot go into the detailed problems in this book. Therefore, we focus on how constraints can be defined as an addition to an object-oriented graphics systems by asking for the prerequisites a graphics kernel should fulfill to this end.

13.3.1 What are Constraints?

Constraints will be introduced informally. In our context we understand by it a relation between individual objects. An example is the relation

```
+ (a,b,c)
```

which should state that three values are supposed to be in the relation

```
c = a+b.
```

At first, there is no condition specifying which variable may be instantiated. Therefore, we do not speak of a rule or procedure. We see relations as predicates (as they are used in predicate calculus).

We now add two additional constraints of the form

```
* (d,e,f)
```

and

```
= (a,d).
```

As a consequence, a set of more complex relations is obtained that can be seen as a network, a *constraint network*. If values are assigned to some of the variables, this results in a *partial instantiation* of the network, as illustrated in Fig. 13.5. For initial assignments b=7, c=12, f=25, the solution d=5 is obtained for the constraint network. Such a solution is called a *constraint satisfaction*. If we started from a different partial instantiation in this example, the migration through the network would have been considerably different. Clearly, with unsuitable initial data, the constraint problem cannot be solved. If too few assignments are given to variables, infinitely many solutions may be available. It should be noted that the domain of artificial intelligence is above all concerned with so-called symbolic constraints, i.e., constraints whose values represent symbols. A nice example of a symbolic constraint network is the assignment of the values (green, red, yellow) to the four traffic lights at a crossing.

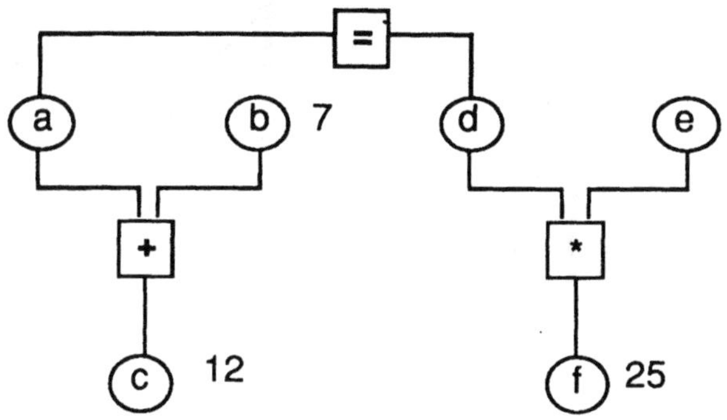

Fig. 13.5. Constraint network. A partially instantiated constraint network is shown. Note that the definition of the constraints that make up the network should be seen independently of the partial instantiation and subsequent evaluation.

If a system has a constraint mechanism at its disposal, complex relations may be formulated without speaking about the method for evaluating them. Therefore, one can speak of a declarative programming style (or some kind of knowledge representation).

Where in computer graphics may constraints be used? As far as the basic idea behind constraints is concerned, this question may be answered very simply. They may be used everywhere for formulating interrelations of graphics objects or relations between non-graphics objects and graphics ones.

13.3.2 Geometrical Relations Between Visual Objects

Constraints may be used for expressing symmetrical relations between graphics objects. One very specific example is that of merge constraints between points of different graphics objects. Borning presents a nice example from the domain of geometry in order to illustrate a theorem by graphics. In this demonstration, midpoints are added to the sides of a quadrilateral. The next step is to add four lines connecting the midpoints, resulting in a parallelogram, as is generally known from geometry. Interactively modifying one part of the parallelogram or the square will cause other parts to move as well to keep the constraints satisfied.

The constraint network may be specified very simply by formulating a midpoint constraint for each side of the quadrilateral and by merging the midpoints with the endpoints of the four lines. Fig. 13.6 shows some examples. It should be mentioned that this example can only very be programmed very laboriously by using traditional procedural programming.

Another example of a semantic structure that can be described by constraints is a network with nodes and with edges connecting these nodes (see Fig. 13.7).

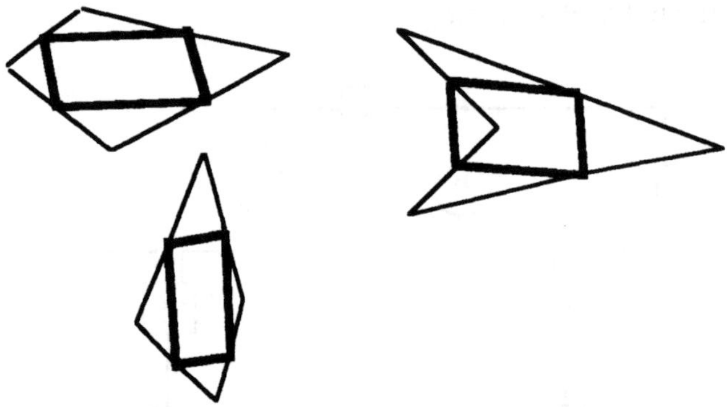

Fig. 13.6. Example of a graphics constraint network. This example stems from Borning, who implemented a graphics constraint editor in the context of the ThingLab development. It allows interactive input of constraints and automatically satisfies them when a modification occurs.

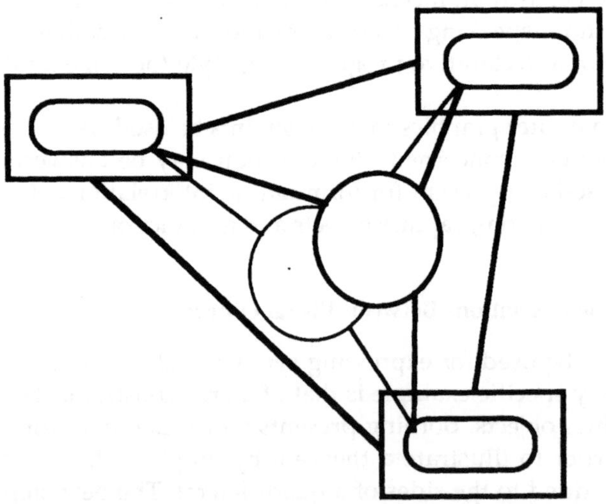

Fig. 13.7. Net with nodes modeled by part hierarchies and edges, connecting the nodes, described by constraints.

When a node is moved, the edges should move along. The edges endpoints may merge with parts far down in the part hierarchy of the nodes. So one should be able to formulate relations between parts of different nodes orthogonal to the hierarchy and evaluate them.

In addition to inter-object relations between graphics objects, constraints have also be applied for defining relations between application objects and display objects. The approach of the filter paradigm, described by Ege et al., establishes the types of constraints for formulating interaction of the model and its view in the MVC model (Ege et al., 1987). Depending on the source of modification, the other partner is automatically kept consistent within the constraint definition. Interaction between a changing representation and a changing model can be formulated in a declarative style, and automatic constraint satisfaction avoids separate programming of mutual dependencies between changing objects.

13.4 Adding Semantics to a Graphics Kernel

What characteristics must an object-oriented graphics kernel provide to simplify the incorporation of additional semantics? We believe the following characteristics to be sensible, both for extension by constraint mechanisms and for conventional programming techniques:

1. To integrate new semantic concepts elegantly and to allow use of existing functionality inheritance must be supported, i.e., a real object-oriented environment is required.
2. All graphics information for describing additional semantics should be easily addressable by a powerful naming mechanism.
3. The formulation of geometrical/graphics relations orthogonal to the part hierarchy has to be supported.
4. Output primitives have to be editable.
5. Different objects may refer to identical information.
6. The graphics system should be able to manage partially instantiated hierarchies as well as completely instantiated ones..

Some of these demands are self-evident, or they have been already discussed. The second and third items are related to the fact that programming additional semantics requires access to practically all imaginable information contained in a graphics object hierarchy. In GEO++ terms, this is any information about parts, contents, attributes, paths, output primitives, individual geometric coordinates, and so on. The net example shows that one must reach far down into the part hierarchy to define the connections with the edges. The fifth demand makes it easy to define merges or consistent updates of building patterns.

Point 6 is the most important one as far as constraints are concerned. Its fulfillment allows construction of a an incomplete hierarchy, which will become completely defined by adding constraints in a separate step. Constraint satisfaction can then be retained until a group is posted on a display medium. This could be implemented in GEO++ by defining a subgroup of Group with an overridden posting method, augmented by constraint satisfaction.

If a graphics structure is already posted on a screen, constraint evaluation could be triggered by a call-back message of a part, informing the evaluator about its own change. The evaluator will use this information for recalculating the old set of solutions leading to a modified state of the part hierarchy.

Note that a system as PHIGS does not allow partially instantiated structures and does not provide object-oriented access methods. This makes it practically impossible for the applications to formulate constraints. Borning showed, already in 1979, how well an object-oriented approach is suited for the formulation of parts in connection with constraints (Borning, 1979).

13.5 Graphics and Hybrid Knowledge Representation

In the area of artificial intelligence, especially for the development of expert systems, *hybrid knowledge representation* is of great importance (Tichy, 1987). Tools for representing different types of knowledge may be seen as a special framework for programming. What distinguishes them from a conventional programming environment is that they offer mechanisms of substantially different types simultaneously and in an integrated form. These always include the mechanisms for object-oriented programming such as classes and inheritance or prototypes and delegation. Compared to Smalltalk-80, classes are more stringently. structures (one speaks of *frames* in this context), mainly for accepting or delivering values by named slots. Compared to Smalltalk-80, where methods are programmed by the "general purpose" language Smalltalk-80 itself, methods are coded differently. They will be formulated by rules, constraints, or logic-oriented mechanisms. Methods are directly associated with the slots, and they are executed when a slot value is accessed or changed. All in all, there is a great variety of different mechanisms, so that our general statements about these systems are only valid with restrictions.

The conception and realization of new mechanisms for knowledge representation is motivated by the objective to map phenomena of the real world as "naturally" as possible onto computer systems. This is the central research topic for those active in this field. Of course, it is arguable to what extent research so far has been successful in this sense.

The attempt in this book has been borne along to model the requirements of graphics programming in as natural a way as possible—as far as they can be fulfilled by a general purpose graphics kernel. Our efforts were carried by the facilities of object-oriented systems and by the motivation they are based on: "See the world as a system of classes, instances and assigned methods." In this light there are connections between the goal of modeling the functionality of computer graphics systems, and that segment of artificial intelligence concerned with knowledge representation. In the remainder of this chapter we would like to look at computer graphics from another perspective, to make suggestions for further research, but not to present complete solutions.

13.5.1 Semantic Networks

One of the basic concepts for modeling knowledge is that of *semantic networks* (Winston, 1984). Semantic networks may be seen as modeling aid for describing knowledge of the real world. A semantic net is a directed graph with nodes describing entities of the real world and arcs describing relations between them. Definition and description of the semantic net can be accomplished in various ways (informally, strictly formally, say with a logical calculus, or with a program language implementation on the computer), as described by Winston.

An object-oriented system may be interpreted as a special kind of semantic network. Here we have the important relation types *"is instance of"* (the so-called *isa* type) and *"is subclass of"* (the so-called *ako, a-kind-of,* type).

The following figure, adopted from Charniak & McDermott, shows a semantic network (Charniak & McDermott, 1985). This example is taken from a book on artificial intelligence and has been left almost unchanged. It shows that an object-oriented graphics system offers semantic support for many of the node and arc types that occur here. Of course, this support is restricted to the goals of computer graphics.

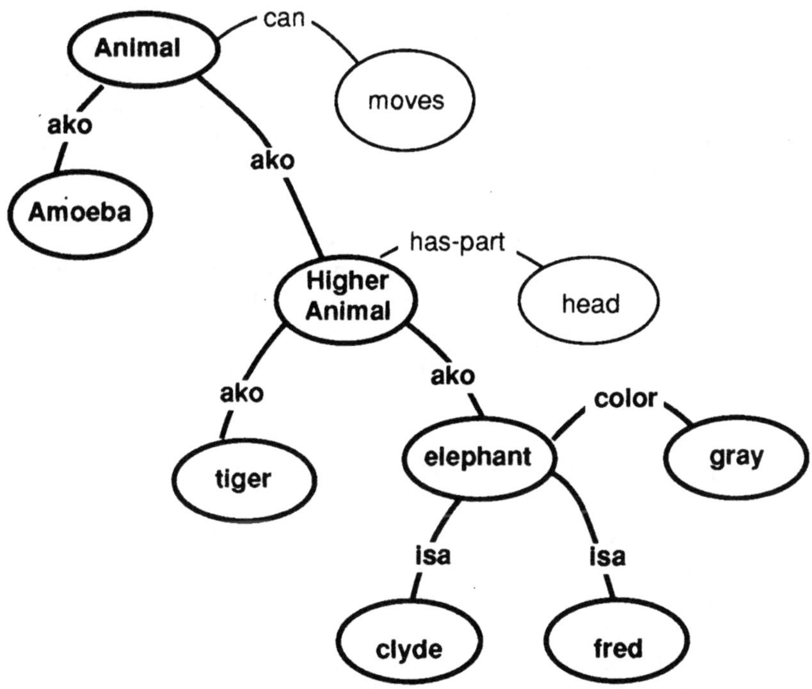

Fig. 13.8. Semantic network. The semantic network, taken from an AI book, shows semantic support offered by an object-oriented graphics system in bold type. Support of the has-part and color relations, restricted to the aims of graphics modeling , is offered by graphics systems as GEO++. Aspects of the network that are not semantically supported by a programming system must be implemented by the applications programmer—as far as this is possible.

For expressing the dynamic aspects of a system, methods may be formulated by alternative mechanisms, that may be triggered by access to or change of slot-values :

- Rule packages are mainly used for modeling procedural aspects. The if-component of a rule may express requirements for slot values, which have to be valid for causing firing of the rule. The then-component performs the action part of the rule, for example changing slot values.
- Constraints may be preferred for formulating relations between objects (frame instances) that must hold.
- Besides these, many hybrid systems allow the application programmer to assign ordinary procedures to slot values (*attached procedures*), that must be formulated by traditional programming in the basic language of the system, e.g., Lisp or C.

13.6 Computer Graphics and Hybrid Systems

As far as we know, there is no description of a complete graphics kernel system by means of a hybrid knowledge-representation system. Systems with hybrid representation mechanisms do often employ support for graphics display and interaction, but the graphics functionality itself is not fully represented using these mechanisms. Typically, all graphics components are defined by attached procedures with access to a low-level graphics kernel. This does not mean however that all attempts at a more elegant integration of graphics must fail. Systems for knowledge representation are relatively young and are primarily used in the AI community. Therefore there are good chances to overcome current drawbacks of hybrid systems and to extent them mainly in the direction of more flexibility as required by interactive computer graphics with its highly dynamic structures. This may be seen as bearing a certain analogy to research activities extending classical database systems towards geometric database systems.

13.6.1 Is Computer Graphics an Appropriate Candidate?

Computer graphics is only a promising candidate for hybrid systems if the main mechanisms provided by these systems are convenient for describing various aspects of graphics modeling and interaction. Tradition has modeled interactive computer graphics systems essentially as an abstract machine editing a graphics data structure. In GKS, this structure is described as a sequentially ordered display file, in PHIGS it is defined as a multi-layer traversal graph—both structures are very device-oriented in principle. There are several (historical) reasons for describing the functionality of graphics systems in this way. First, the concept of classical programming languages influenced the description, although the description of GKS and PHIGS was intended to be defined in a language-independent way. Another reason is that definitions of these systems were influenced by the characteristics and limitations of available hardware, especially hardware with internal display files to be traversed sequentially. In our opinion, essential aspects of interactive computer graphics are not optimally modeled in this way.

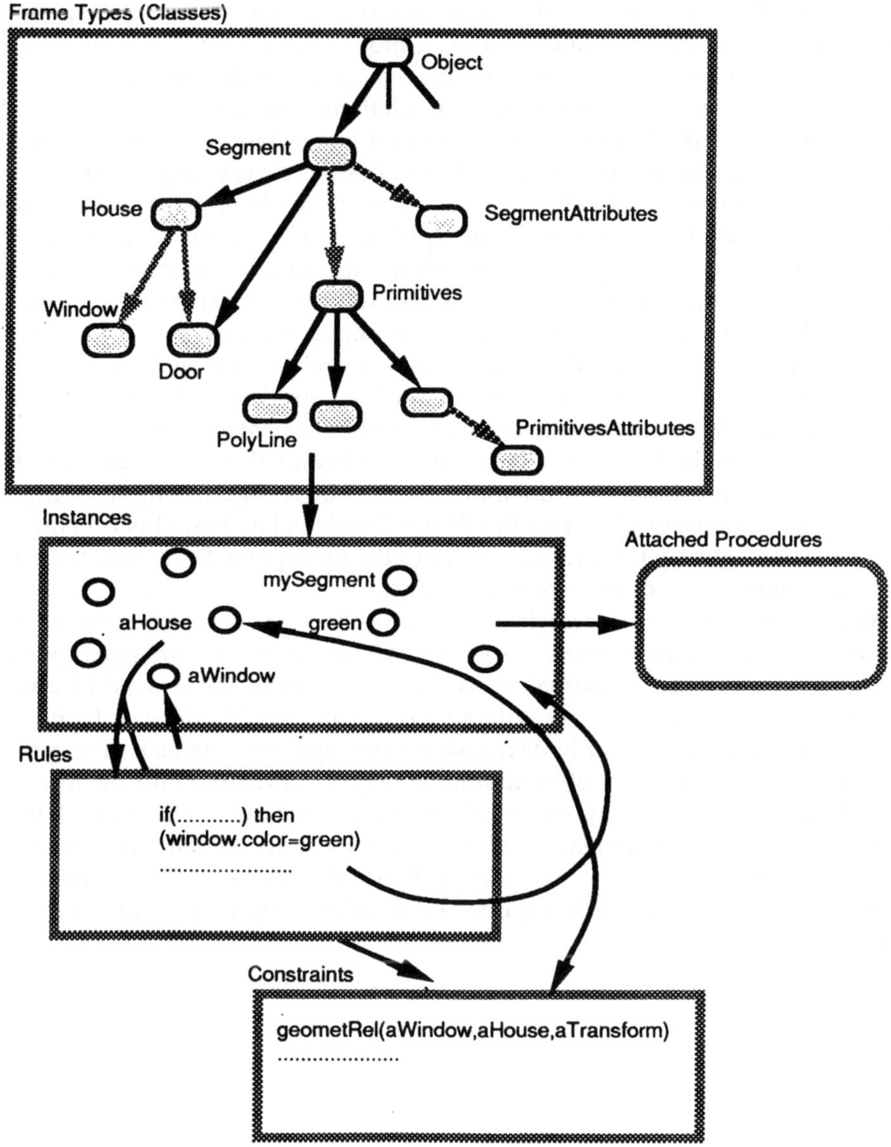

Fig. 13.9. Hybrid knowledge representation. A feeling for the interplay of different representation mechanisms in applications of computer graphics. The most important mechanisms, currently employed mainly in the field of expert systems, is shown to have relevance for computer graphics.

If we analyze graphics applications from the viewpoint of a knowledge engineer we come to a much better interpretation of computer graphics when we mirror it against mechanisms provided by hybrid systems. Part hierarchies may be implemented by frames, with slots for subparts when using hybrid systems. Also attributes should be handled by defining specific slots. Class hierarchies (or frame hierarchies) which inherit predefined functionality are also convenient, especially for extending the functionality of hidden kernels as shown by various examples. This makes it clear that the frame component of hybrid systems is unquestionably useful. Complex geometrical relations between visual graphics objects—going beyond relations modeled by part hierarchies anyway—can be expressed declaratively by rules or constraints. Besides a very elegant description of these relations, the application programmer will be freed from mixing these descriptions with his own complex and application-dependent code for solving these relations. In hybrid systems, rule interpreters or constraint solvers are offered as existing built-in functionality. These solvers will carry out all relevant changes if a given constellation has been changed, e.g., by user interactions. Therefore, our working hypothesis for future research is that the domain of computer graphics is a very promising candidate for hybrid knowledge representation, which may be seen as an extension of the object-oriented approach.

Figure 13.9 reflects a feeling for the interplay of these mechanisms. The combination of mechanisms, illustrated in the above figure, might be implemented as an extension of a predefined kernel such as GEO++. This is because a frame mechanism may be realized similar to the example in Sect. 10.3, and rules and constraint can be added to part hierarchies.

We do not yet have a conclusive concept for the support of the complete representation of a graphics system in keeping with the hybrid knowledge representation paradigm. The alternative, prototypes and delegation instead of classes and inheritance, would end up with a substantially modified formulation of a system. The great variety of hybrid systems concepts and the lack of standardization of these approaches offer additional degrees of freedom for the formulation of graphics systems by using hybrid representation mechanisms. Hybrid systems are usually implemented in Lisp. The object-oriented language extension of Lisp, CLOS, is currently being standardized (Keene, 1989). But, as far as we know, no work is presently being done on standardizing hybrid representation mechanisms.

14 Towards an Object-Oriented Standard?

In this chapter we discuss some requirements for an object-oriented graphics standard. We discuss briefly the political aspects of standardization and then continue with open questions to be decided by a standardization committee.

The political situation for the definition of an object-oriented standard is quite good at the time of this writing. Work towards the second generation graphics standard under the heading *New Application Programmer's Interface* (New API) has just started. This work is being tackled by the standardization committee ISO/IEC JTC 1 SC 24 WG 1. In contrast to the standardization committees, who are concerned with maintenance and extension of existing standards such as GKS and PHIGS, the New API is not limited by the existence of current standards.

Standardization requires much more than the specification and implementation of a useful kernel for a given object-oriented environment. The definition of its functionality must be language independent; different aspects of portability have to be assured. In this context, questions arise concerning an object-oriented approach, to be discussed in this chapter as a first step for further discussions.

14.1 Chances for an Object-Oriented New API

We hope to have shown in this book what new possibilities the object-oriented programming paradigm offers for computer graphics. These results are in sharp contrast to the present specifications in graphics standardization. Systems such as GKS or PHIGS are not affected by the object-oriented paradigm and philosophy.

14.1.1 Historical Remarks

The first graphics standard, the Graphics Kernel System GKS (Enderle, Kansy, Pfaff, 1987), was developed around 1980 and completed in 1985. It was aimed at the applications programmer and described a programming language for the definition and manipulation of graphics. However, the hope of covering the needs of a majority of graphics programmers with one standard graphics language was not fulfilled. Since GKS, the development of more standards has continued. The need for three dimensional graphics was covered by GKS-3D (Enderle, Kansy, Pfaff, 1987), an editable hierarchical graphics structure was provided by PHIGS, and advanced surface primitives and rendering techniques are currently defined under the label of PHIGS PLUS.

These continuing efforts do not compromise the existing standards but reflect the complexity of graphics and the vast diversity of differing requirements which can hardly be fulfilled by one standard. For example, cartographers need specific line primitives (for highways), signatures (characterizing land use), elaborated text (along rivers), specific transformations, etc. For realistic images, complex surface primitives with reflectance attribute, lighting models, etc., are needed. CAD applications require different data structures than geographical applications. In addition, technological progress (increased capabilities and potential of graphics workstations, new user communities due to plummeting prices) and developments in related areas (windowing, document architecture, print technology) led to new demands.

The major areas requiring further development—as articulated by members of different committees and users of existing standards—include:

- new output primitives and attributes,
- picture structuring and access,
- attribute setting and binding to primitives,
- flexible input techniques correlated with output,
- interfacing to text and document standards,
- refined data types.

It is not desirable to provide a separate standard for each constituency. This would be too expensive for developers of graphics system, too difficult for educating graphics programmers, and it would destroy the benefit of portability of programs. Therefore, with a New API, an effort has been started to generate a second generation graphics standard, which comprises the capabilities of existing standards while avoiding errors and pitfalls of the first generation standards. Such a standard should be sufficiently flexible to be adaptable to the needs of a variety of applications, and to provide all these capabilities in a well structured way.

14.1.2 Why do we Need an Object-Oriented Standard?

The deficiencies of existing graphics standards are primarily limitations in functionality, in picture structure and in flexibility. We believe to have illustrated in this book that the object-oriented philosophy could provide appropriate solutions to cover the requirements reasonably.

14.1.2.1 Characteristics of Existing Graphics Standards

We will briefly review the main characteristics the existing graphics systems GKS and PHIGS.

Graphics systems provide a language to describe a drawing and the operations on drawings. Traditional graphics systems, as we have shown, have focussed on providing sufficient functionality but have missed the target of specifying a language which is elegant and appropriate for the description of graphics items and their features. They either restrict, as GKS does, the functionality to a level which is unacceptable today, or they provide elementary graphics operations on pictures only by complicated constructs of the programming language, as we have seen by analyzing PHIGS.

For example, we have shown that PHIGS does not deal directly with the interactive graphics interface but allows the definition of a picture as an hierarchical acyclic structure which is the basis for the interaction. This structure allows efficient modeling of pictures where specific items are reused several times, but individual parts can only be identified by a pick path yet not be addressed to assign attributes to them (see 9.5).

GKS, on the other hand, does not have these problems. But its restricted functionality does not support multi-level picture structure and editing.

The advantage of existing graphics standards is based on the well defined functionality which meets the needs of significant constituencies. A model is provided for defining and structuring application objects by means of graphics primitives. A set of manipulation functions is provided in the terms of this model. Therefore, the overall model yields more benefits than just the sum of the single functions.

Graphics primitives cannot be employed in an arbitrary way; their use within the given model is restricted, e.g., in PHIGS primitives are used only within a structure where control of the display, the transformation, and the attribute setting is exercised by the structure mechanism. The model forces the user to obey certain rules when writing a graphics program. This discipline is rewarded by additional services provided by the graphics kernel: device independence, a well formed attribute and transformation concept, inquiry facilities, predefined matching of input and output (pick operation). A traditional graphics kernel, therefore, provides more than a mere graphics toolbox.

14.1.2.2 Characteristics of Existing Object-Oriented Graphics Kernels

There are several reasons why graphics standardization cannot be directly based on any of the graphics kernels incorporated in existing object-oriented programming environments, e.g., the Smalltalk-80 graphics kernel. As we have mentioned, the Smalltalk-80 kernel (and other existing kernels) does not provide the range of functionality that has proved useful and necessary for traditional graphics kernels and that, therefore, is expected by the graphics community from a graphics standard.

Existing object-oriented graphics kernels offer many concepts and methods which can be used to an advantage as a good starting point for future graphics standards. Relevant concepts include inheritance, flexibility and elegance of input models, and graphics constraints.

14.1.3 General Advances – Short Summary

Let us summarize the general advances for an object-oriented standard. Interactive graphics, in an intuitive way, has been object-oriented since its very beginnings: the presentation and manipulation of graphics objects on a display was the central objective. Thinking in objects as guided by the object-oriented paradigm leads to a model

- with direct naming of visual items,
- with attributes directly assigned to visual objects as part of their own inherent information,
- with concurrently existing and instantiated graphics objects which may be freely selected and edited by the user,
- where different object with the same behavior can be regarded as instances of one class.

In an object-oriented system, application and kernel objects may call each other mutually:

- By this mechanism, the reaction to user input can be programmed in a more natural way than in traditional systems.
- Inheritance can be used by an object-oriented graphics systems in many different situations.
- By using inheritance, new types of primitives (composed primitives, special purpose primitives for cartography, etc.) may be integrated into an existing standard by defining additional classes using the functionality of the predefined kernel.

14.2 Requirements and Problems

In the following, we will list some requirements and open question for an object-oriented graphics standard. Most of these requirements were motivated before and discussed previously.

(a) The standard should fulfill the general goals of a graphics standard: *application independence, language independence, device independence,* and *information hiding*. Information hiding means that the internal implementation is completely hidden such as discussed in the GEO++ context.

(b) For an object-oriented language binding, *inheritance* should be supported for all methods defined in the standard.

(c) The standard should provide a *multi-level part hierarchy* with a well defined semantics. This means that a precise definition for all aspects of creating and editing graphics hierarchies must be worked out for all components of the hierarchy.

(d) The standard should support a *dynamic model for part editing*. The number of subparts should be allowed to change dynamically during run time. This point is in accordance to the GKS and PHIGS model.

(f) *Rule* interpreters and *constraint* solvers become more and more important for supporting new declarative (and less imperative) styles of graphics programming. Therefore, at least the prerequisites for adding rules and constraints should be provided.

(g) Besides portability of graphics applications, a *graphics archive* for storage and transfer of pictures should be supported. Different applications should be able to access the content of a common archive. This is a traditional requirement, which has to be solved again in this context.

14.3 Guidelines

Our discussion is based on some guidelines which have to be observed. They reflect general rules which have proved useful with traditional standards and which should be obeyed as far as possible for new developments. These guidelines include:

- In the functional standard, a set of classes and methods (visible to the outside) should be provided for the applications programmer in a language independent way (*language independence*). In a set of language-binding documents (worked out for object-oriented languages and language extensions) the same classes and methods should be specified as a concrete application programmer's interface.
- The applications programmer must have available an implementation which conforms to the standard. Such an implementation consists of a library of classes and methods, in accordance with the standardized language binding. One way of using this implementation is creation of instances of the delivered classes and message passing to these instances. This is a certain analogy to the traditional procedural binding of predefined functionality.
- In addition to this, subclassing should be allowed for all transparent classes.
- Changing methods of standardized classes is prohibited. Access to internal methods should be impossible or is at least not allowed.
- Graphics applications should be portable between the same types of environment.
- Graphics presentations should be portable, facilitated by a language independent picture format.
- It should be possible to store and retrieve graphics objects by using an archive.

Under these preconditions we will discuss some of the open problems not mentioned before in the previous chapters.

14.3.1 Language Independence

If we try to formulate an object-oriented system, the first problem that arises has to do with the great variety of object-oriented models.

First one has to decide on what object-oriented model the language independent description should be based on. Which of the different alternatives, for example, the class-instance model or the prototype-delegation model should be preferred?

There is a good argument for delegation: "Delegation permits more flexibility, since communication patterns can be determined at message reception time rather than at compile time or object creation time." (Liebermann, 1986a). We have shown in Chap. 11 how delegation can be favorably used by a graphics application.

The pro-argument for inheritance is that the actual candidates for an object-oriented standard are based on inheritance (Smalltalk-80, C++, CLOS). If we use inheritance which is based on a description of predefined classes and methods, we must think about a convenient functionality for providing all the aspects of flexibility in computer graphics programming. Our analysis of existing kernels has shown that the dynamics of graphics systems are (only) required when graphics object hierarchies have to be edited at runtime. This becomes obvious when graphics editing has to be implemented by using the applications programmer's interface, where new objects are created by copying and editing, and where part hierarchies are continuously changing. To solve this problem, however, a compromise can be achieved. This means that the graphics hierarchy can be modeled by collection classes, as we have shown with GEO++.

14.3.2 Different Types of Inheritance in the Extended Layer Model

If the class-instance model should be selected for the specification of an object-oriented standard, because it is supported by so many environments, then we have to deal with the different inheritance mechanisms.

If we describe the functionality of a kernel, different organizational principles are possible, depending on the different concepts of inheritance (hierarchical inheritance, different mechanisms of multiple inheritance up to a more method centered model as supported by CLOS). Rather than describing the class and its associated methods, CLOS describes, for a given method, the set of classes for which it is valid (Bobrow et al., 1988). This diversity led us ask whether and to what extend this has to be taken into consideration as well. Even in the case of the extended layer model defining a kernel with a hidden implementation different types of subclassing are possible depending on the type of inheritance. Therefore, an analysis has to be done how to define the functionality of the standards; in particular, how to organize the transparent classes which can be used for specialization.

14.3.3 Part Hierarchies and Constraints

We have shown that constraints can put additional semantics on part hierarchies to allow for an "intelligent" graphics system. The background for this development is the fact that there are additional semantics beside the part semantic which have to be taken into account.

This discussion leads to the question whether a new graphics standard should posses a constraint mechanism or whether it should only allow the addition of constraints as articulated in Sect. 13.4, which can be seen as a minimal requirement for a modern standard. If constraints should be included in a standard then the question arises what class of constraints would be convenient.

14.3.4 How can Portability be Achieved?

One of the major objectives of standardization is portability. What should be portable within a computer graphics system? There are different requirements and options.

Portability of application programs can be achieved if all application-specific methods that use the graphics kernel as well as subclasses defined by the application as extensions are transferred. This should pose no major problems.

For storage and transfer of pictures, a metafile standard (Computer Graphics Metafile CGM (ISO, 1987) has been defined that allows sequential storage of graphics data structures. This does not cover the storage of a part hierarchy.

Object-oriented systems with part hierarchies generate two additional problems when storing graphics data:

- A part hierarchy allows the mixture of graphics and application data if subclassing was use. The GEO++ subclasses, defined in Chap. 10 contain pure graphics information together with user-defined code. How can the graphics portions be extracted? A first solution could be to store a pure graphics part hierarchy, analogous to that which will be produced when a root (as subclass of Group) is posted. In this case the "algorithmic information" represented by the methods of the subclasses of Group and Part is lost.
- At present, an archive for graphics object hierarchies including application-dependent methods could only be exchanged between the same types of environment, i.e., not in a language independent manner.

14.3.5 Resume

We have discussed the benefits future graphics system could have by the use of object-oriented philosophy and principles. However, there is a gap which has to be bridged between the definition of a single powerful object-oriented graphics system such as GEO++ for *one* programming environment and a general object-oriented graphics standard.

But nevertheless, the definition of an object-oriented graphics standard seems to be a realistic goal at the current state. To achieve this standard the help and active cooperation of experts from the field of object-oriented programming in the respective standards committees within ISO/IEC JTC 1 SC24 is necessary as there are still open problems, which must be resolved. With an object-oriented graphics systems the discipline of object-oriented graphics could leave the status of research and experimentation and could find widespread acceptance.

References

Adobe Systems (1985): PostScript Language Reference Manual. Addison-Wesley, Reading, Mass.

Agha, G. (1986): An overview of actor languages. ACM SIGPLAN Notices 21 (10) 58-67

Agha, G. and Hewitt, C. (1987): Actors: A conceptual foundation for concurrent object-oriented programming. In: Shriver, B. and Wegner, P. (eds.): Research Directions in Object-Oriented Programming. The MIT Press, Cambridge, Massachusetts, pp. 49-74

André Weinand, Erich Gamma, Rudolf Marty (1988): ET++—An object-oriented application framework in C++, OOPSLA '88 Proceedings, ACM, pp. 46-57

Arnold, D.B., Bono, P.R. (1988): CGM und CGI. Metafile and Interface Standards for Computer Graphics. Springer, Berlin, Heidelberg

Badler, N.I. (1987): Articulated figure animation: Guest editor's introduction. IEEE Computer Graphics and Applications 7 (6) 10-11

Barth,P.S. (1986): An object-oriented approach to graphical interfaces, ACM Transactions on Graphics 5 (2) 142-172

Berlage, Th. (1990): Understanding OSF-Motif. Addison-Wesley, Reading, Mass.

Blake, E. H. Cook, S. (1987): On including part hierarchies in object-oriented languages, with an implementation in Smalltalk. In: Proceedings of the European Conference on Object-Oriented Programming, pp. 45-54

Blake, E.H. (1989): Introduction to Aspects of Object-Oriented Graphics. Report CS-R 9009, Centre for Mathematics and Computer Science, Dept. Interactive Systems, Amsterdam

Blake, E.H., Wisskirchen, P. (1989): Object-oriented graphics. In Puttgarthofer, W., Schönhut, J. (eds.): Advances in Computer Graphics V, Springer, Berlin, Heidelberg, pp. 109-154

Bobrow, D.G., DeMichiel, L.G., Gabriel, R.P., Keene, S.E., Kiczales, G., Moon, D.A. (1988): Common Lisp Object System Specification. X3J13 Document 88-002R

Bobrow, D.G., Mittal, S., Stefik, M.J. (1986): Expert systems: perils and promise. Comm. ACM (1986) 880-894

Borning, A., Ingalls, D. (1982): Multiple inheritance in Smalltalk-80. In: Proceedings AAAI, pp. 234-237

Borning, A.H. (1979): ThingLab: A Constraint-Oriented Simulation Laboratory. Xerox Palo Alto Research Center Report SSL-79-3 (a revised version of: Stanford University PhD. thesis, Stanford Computer Science Department Report STAN-CS-79-746)

Borning, A.H. (1981): The programming language aspects of ThingLab, a constraint-oriented simulation laboratory. ACM Trans. Programming Languages and Systems 3 (4) 353-387

Borning, A.H. (1986): Classes versus prototypes in object-oriented languages. IEEE/ACM Fall Joint Computer Conf. Dallas, Texas, Nov 1986, pp. 36-40

Borning, A.H., Duisberg, R. (1986): Constraint-based tools for building user interfaces. In: ACM Transactions on Graphics 5 (4) 345-374

Borning, A.H., Duisberg, R.A., Freeman-Benson, B., Kramer, A., Woolf, M. (1987): Constraint hierarchies. SIGPLAN Notices 22 (12) 48-60

Breen, D.E., Getto, P.H., Apodaca, A.A., Schmidt, D.G., Sarachan, B.D. (1987): The Clockworks: An object-oriented computer animation system. Eurographics'87. Elsevier, Amsterdam, pp. 275-282

Brodlie, K, Duce, D., Hopgood, F.R.A (1989): GKS-N Initial Draft. Document. ISO/IEC JTC1 SC24 WG1 N79

Brown, M. D. (1985): Understanding PHIGS. Megatek Corporation, San Diego, Ca.lif.

Cardelli, L., Wegner, P. (1985): On understanding types, data abstraction, and polymorphism. Computing Surveys 17 (4) 471-522

Charniak, E., McDermott, D. (1985): Introduction to Artificial Intelligence. Addison-Wesley, Reading, Mass.

Coutaz, J. (1987): The construction of user interfaces and the object paradigm. Proceedings of the European Conference on Object-Oriented Programming 1987, pp. 135-144

Cox, B.J. (1984): Message/object programming: An evolutionary change in programming technology. IEEE Software 1 (1) 50-61

Cox, B.J. (1986): Object-Oriented Programming: An Evolutionary Approach. Addison-Wesley., Reading, Mass.

Dahl, O.-J., Hoare, C.A.R. (1973): Hierarchical program structures. In: Dahl, O.-J., Dijkstra, E.W., Hoare, C.A.R. (eds.) Structured Programming. Academic Press, London, pp. 175-220

Densmore, O.M., Rosenthal, D.S.H. (1987): A user-interface toolkit in object-oriented PostScript. Computer Graphics Forum 6

(3) 171-180

Duisberg, R.A. (1986): Animated graphical interfaces using temporal constraints. ACM CHI'86 Proceedings, pp. 131-136

Ege, R.K., Maier, D., Borning, A. (1987): The filter browser: defining interfaces graphically. In: Proceedings of the European Conference on Object-Oriented Programming, pp. 155-165

Enderle, G., Kansy, K., Pfaff, G. (1987): Computer Graphics Programming. GKS—The Graphics Standard, 2nd edn. Springer, Berlin, Heidelberg

Fischer, G. (1987): Cognitive view of reuse and redesign. IEEE Software, July 1987, pp. 60-72

Fiume, E., Tsichritzis, D., Dami, L. (1987): A temporal scripting language for object-oriented animation. Eurographics'87. Elsevier, Amsterdam, pp. 283-294

Foley, J.D., van Dam, A. (1982): Fundamental of Interactive Computer Graphics. Addison-Wesley, Reading, Mass.

Goldberg, A. (1984): Smalltalk-80: The Interactive Programming Environment. Addison-Wesley, Reading, Mass.

Goldberg, A., Robson, D. (1983): Smalltalk-80: The Language and its Implementation. Addison-Wesley, Reading, Mass.

Ingalls, D.H.H. (1986): A simple technique for handling multiple polymorphism. SIGPLAN Notices 21 (11) 347-349

ISO (1985): International Standard 7942, Information Processing Systems: Computer Graphics—Graphical Kernel System (GKS), Functional Description

ISO (1987): Metafile for the Storage and Transfer of Picture Information. International Standard ISO 8632

ISO (1989a): Programmer's Hierarchical Interactive Graphics System (PHIGS). International Standard ISO/IEC 9592

Kahn, K.M. (1976): An actor-based computer animation language. In: User-Oriented Design of Interactive Graphics Gystems (ACM/SIGGRAPH Workshop Proceedings), pp. 37-43

Kay, A.C. (1977): Microelectronics and the personal computer. Scientific American 237 (1977) 230-244

Krasner, G. E., Pope, S. T. (1988): A cookbook for using the model-view-controller user interface paradigm in Smalltalk-80. Journ. Object-Oriented Programming 1 (3) 26-48

Leler Wm (1988): Constraint Programming Languages: Their Specification and Generation. Addison-Wesley, Reading, Mass.

Liebermann, H. (1986a): Delegation and inheritance: Two mechanisms for sharing knowledge in object-oriented systems. In: Bezivin, J., Cointe, P. (eds.) 3eme Journées d' Etudes Languages Orientés Objet, pp. 79-89

Liebermann, H. (1986b): Using prototypical objects to implement shared behavior in object-oriented systems. SIGPLAN Notices 21 (11) 214-223

Magnenat-Thalmann, N., Thalmann, D. (1985): Computer Animation: Theory and Practice. Springer, Berlin, Heidelberg

Meyer, B. (1988): Object-Oriented Software Construction. Prentice-Hall, London

Myers, B.A. (1987): Creating interaction techniques by demonstration, IEEE Computer Graphics and Applications (1987) 51-60

Myers, B.A. (1989): User-interface tools: Introduction and survey. IEEE Software, January 1989, pp. 8-23

NeWS (1987): NeWS Technical Overview. Part No: 800-1498-05. Sun Microsystems, Inc, Mountain View, Calif.

Olsen, D.R.Jr. et al. (1987): Results of the ACM SIGGRAPH Workshop on Software Tools for User Interface Management (several reports). In: Computer Graphics 21 (2) (1987) 73-147

Pineda, L.A. (1988): A compositional semantic for graphics. In: Duce, D., Jancence, P. (eds.) Eurographics '88, Conference Proceedings. Elsevier Science Publishers B. V., North-Holland

Rentsch, T. (1982): Object-oriented programming. SIGPLAN Notices 17 (1982) 51-57

Reynolds, C.W. (1982): Computer animation with scripts and actors. Computer Graphics 16 (3) 289-296

Rome, E., Wisskirchen P. (1988): Object-Oriented Graphics. SIGGRAPH '88 Tutorial Notes

Schmucker, K.J. (1986): Object-Oriented Programming for the Macintosh. Hayden Book Company, Hasbrouck Heights, New Jersey

Sibert, J.L. et al. (1986): An object-oriented user interface management system. Computer Graphics 20 (4) 259-267

Sonya E. Keene (1989): Object-Oriented Programming in Common Lisp—A Programmer's Guide to CLOS, Addison-Wesley, Reading, Mass.

Stefik, M., Bobrow, D.G. (1985): Object-oriented programming: Themes and variations. The AI Magazine VI (4) 40-62

Stroustrup, B. (1986): An Overview of C++. SIGPLAN Notices 21 (10) 7-18

Sutherland, I. (1963): A man-machine graphical communication system. In: Proc. of the Spring Joint Computer Conference (IFIPS 1963), pp. 329-345

Szekely A.P., Myers B.A. (1988): A User Interface Toolkit Based on Graphical Objects and Constraints, OOPSLA '88 Proceedings, ACM, pp. 36-45

Szekely, P. (1987): Modular implementation of presentations. Proc. CHI+GI (Toronto, April 5-9), ACM, New York, pp. 235-240

Tichy, W.F. (1987): What can software engineers learn from Artificial Intelligence? IEEE Computer, November 1987, pp. 43-54

Wegner, P. (1987): Dimensions of object-based language design. OOPSLA'87: SIGPLAN Notices 22 (12) 168-182

Weinreb, D., Moon, D. (1980): Flavors: Message Passing in the Lisp Machine. MIT AI Laboratory Memo No. 602

Winston, P.H. (1984): Artificial Intelligence (2nd ed.). Addison Wesley, Reading, Mass.

Wisskirchen, P. (1986a): Towards object-oriented graphics standards. Computers & Graphics 10 (2) 183-187

Wisskirchen, P. (1986b): GEO—Graphics system with editable objects. In: T. L. Kunii (ed.): Advanced Computer Graphics. Springer Verlag, Tokyo, 172-179

Wisskirchen, P. (1989): GEO++—A system for both modelling and display. Eurographics '89 Conference Proceedings, Hamburg, September 4-9, 1989. Elsevier Publ. , Amsterdam, pp. 403-414

Zeltzer, D. (1985): Towards an integrated view of 3-D computer animation. The Visual Computer 1 (1985) 249-259

Subject Index

FSC
www.fsc.org
MIX
Papier aus verantwortungsvollen Quellen
Paper from responsible sources
FSC® C105338

If you have any concerns about our products,
you can contact us on
ProductSafety@springernature.com

In case Publisher is established outside the EU,
the EU authorized representative is:
Springer Nature Customer Service Center GmbH
Europaplatz 3, 69115 Heidelberg, Germany

Printed by Libri Plureos GmbH
in Hamburg, Germany